Growing Up Degrassi

Growing Up Degrassi

Television, Identity and Youth Cultures

EDITED BY
MICHELE BYERS

SUMACH PRESS

WOMEN'S ISSUES PUBLISHING PROGRAM

SERIES EDITOR: BETH MCAULEY

LIBRARY AND ARCHIVES CANADA CATALOGUING IN PUBLICATION
Growing Up Degrassi : television, identity and youth
cultures / editor, Michele Byers.

Includes bibliographical references.
ISBN 1-894549-48-1

1. Degrassi junior high (Television program). 2. Degrassi high
(Television program). 3. Degrassi the next generation (Television
program). 4. Television and youth — Canada. I. Byers, Michele, 1971-

PN1992.77.D43G76 2005   791.45'72   C2005-904729-1

The *Degrassi* photo on the cover and the photos accompanying
the section openers of this book are used with
the kind permission of Epitome Pictures Inc.

*Sumach Press acknowledges the support of the Canada Council
for the Arts and the Ontario Arts Council for our publishing program.
We acknowledge the financial support of the Government of Canada through
the Book Publishing Industry Development Program (BPIDP).*

ONTARIO ARTS COUNCIL
CONSEIL DES ARTS DE L'ONTARIO

Printed and bound in Canada

Published by
SUMACH PRESS
1415 Bathurst Street #202
Toronto Ontario Canada
M5R 3H8
www.sumachpress.com

Contents

Acknowledgements

THIS WORK would not have been possible without funding from the Social Sciences and Humanities Research Council of Canada (SSHRC). I am indebted to all the people who work so hard to make the funding of research projects like this one a reality. Early funding from the Saint Mary's University Faculty of Graduate Studies and Research also helped make this research possible.

Television Studies is a relatively new field and one of its obstacles is the distance between those who produce television and those who study it. For that reason, it is so important for me to acknowledge the people involved with Epitome Pictures Inc. who made themselves, their offices, their studios and their photo archives available to me as I worked on this project. I would especially like to acknowledge the unparalleled generosity of Linda Schuyler, Stephen Stohn, Yan Moore, Shelley Scarrow, Aaron Martin and Dolly Shanthakumar. Relatedly, it is only right to acknowledge Kit Hood and Playing With Time who, along with Epitome, have brought *Degrassi* to life for the last twenty-five years.

Beth McAuley came to listen to a very early version of one of the chapters included in this volume that I presented at the Canadian Women's Studies Association Conference in Halifax in 2003. It was her enthusiasm for this project right from the start, and throughout what turned into a very long process, that made this book possible. Thank you Beth and Sumach Press for believing in this work.

My colleagues at Saint Mary's, particularly Val Johnson and Diane Crocker, have listened to me chatter at length about *Degrassi*. Mary Jane Miller, the pre-eminent scholar of Canadian drama, has been a wonderful mentor. David Lavery, the father of the television anthology, has been a true believer and a great inspiration as well as a groundbreaker. I would like to acknowledge other mentors, so crucial to a junior scholar like myself: Randi Warne, Richard Wassersug, Imre Szeman, Kari Dehli, Robert Morgan, Sandra Acker, Graham Knight and Sherrie Inness. I am also grateful for the growing community of scholars working in the area of Canadian media, television and cultural studies — including the contributors to this volume — for the truly inspired and inspiring work they are producing.

Life without friends is empty, and I have been very blessed with friends old and new, near and far ... it is impossible to name you all. And certainly I cannot forget my family in Montreal, and my growing family right here on Chebucto Road; you have my heart.

★

PREFACE

Geoff Pevere

THE MOST VITAL FAN PHENOMENA spring from a Frankenstein clause. What this means is that it does not matter who planted the seeds of the phenomenon or for what purpose. At a certain point it takes on a life of its own. What sustains it in this independent existence is the enthusiasm it generates. The deeper and more intense the enthusiasm, the stronger and more unstoppable the monster it feeds.

The *Degrassi* phenomenon is some kind of monster. Now spanning to include twenty-five years, two generations, four series, several countries, countless academic investigations and a drastically rearranged media technology landscape, the program that once began as a low-budget, no-frills, socially conscious Canadian public broadcasting project about urban teen life has become one of the most passionately watched and discussed artifacts of teenage culture television has ever produced.

This book is testimony not only to the scale of the *Degrassi* universe, but also to the life forms within the life forms within that universe. For this is another precondition of fan-based pop cultural vitality: the artifact must be sufficiently versatile in its potential uses to accommodate a host of interpretations and modes of engagement. Your *Star Trek* may well chart final frontiers other than mine, and my *Buffy* might slay differently than yours. To thrive as an enduring object of fan appropriation, the artifact must be public in production but personal in consumption.

Obviously, it must be able to speak to a lot of people. But more importantly, it must speak differently to each one. Indeed, if pop cultural fan groups can be called communities of sorts, the sense of community only plants stakes around the artifact itself. Where it builds and thrives is in the sharing of personal meanings the artifact generates.

A recurring experience recounted throughout these essays involves someone getting hooked, usually despite themselves, on one of the *Degrassi* series because they encountered something — a story, a character, a situation — that echoed from personal experience. A moment when the screen caught the reflection of the viewer.

Herein, you will encounter discussions of the *Degrassi* phenomenon from a number of perspectives: as an experiment in TV narrative; as a challenge to predominant pop cultural representations of adolescence; as a Canadian cultural artifact; as a Frankensteinian monster up and running around all on its own, propelled by those who love it.

But underlying all the various interpretations, readings, arguments and tributes is a shared conviction that the *Degrassi* phenomenon is both a distinct and a distinguished one. A conviction that it offers a representation of teenage life that stands in stark contrast to the vast majority of such representations in the media mainstream, and that that contrast is valuable and positive. And that's another necessary condition of enduring fan-based enthusiasm. The object not only creates a universe that can be entered, inhabited and richly explored, but a universe that makes it worthwhile doing so. It beckons with the promise of a better way.

Geoff Pevere has been writing, teaching and broadcasting about popular culture for over twenty-five years. He is the co-author of the best-selling *Mondo Canuck: A Canadian Pop Culture Odyssey* and a movie critic with the *Toronto Star*.

CREATING A CLASSIC IN TELEVISION HISTORY

Mary Jane Miller

Growing Up Degrassi IS SOMETHING A WHOLE GENERATION of kids and teens managed to accomplish. In this book, *Degrassi Junior High* (1987–89) and *Degrassi High* (1989–91) — the sequels to *The Kids of Degrassi Street* (1979– 85) — are known as *Degrassi Classic*. These shows spanned the height of the Cold War, the fall of the USSR, the first Quebec referendum, the repatriation of the British North America Act, "stagflation," the first Gulf War and saw the women in Canada rising in their wrath when the Constitution of Rights and Freedoms "forgot" to include them. It was an age of disruption and major transition — a macrocosm of the world of the average teen. Broadcasting was changing too. Television began to fragment into more choices and was directed at more clearly defined demographics; for the first time teenagers, with their disposable income, became the target of programming directed specifically at them. Many of the writers in this book first saw the shows of *Degrassi Classic* as children and teens themselves. They grew up with television sets in more than one room, with colour and cable and the early days of the VCR.

Unlike them, I was not one of those *Growing Up Degrassi* and had no access to any other programs directed specifically at teenagers. I am a child of the radio, and my generation is likely to be nostalgic for the radio serials. Who can forget "On King! On you Huskies!" the weekly cry which opened *Sergeant Preston of the Yukon* (1938–55) and his wonder dog King in the American depiction of a Canadian Mountie? Or the 1940s adaptations of Maggie Muggins from the *Just Mary* books of our childhood written by

Mary Grannan. Every episode ended with Maggie reciting a rhyme and then saying, "I don't know what will happen tomorrow!"[1] But we teens were too old for the television versions of *Sergeant Preston* (1955–58) or *Maggie Muggins* (1954/55–62) or the other children's TV shows of the 1950s. I was eleven when the CBC began broadcasting television in September of 1952, years before CTV was granted a licence. It was a time when television antennae in Canada were turned to receive the U.S. border stations. Television sets, black and white of course, were not common for another few years — ours arrived in 1955 and colour transmission on the CBC waited until the Centennial in 1967. In the early years simultaneous transmission across the country was impossible, which meant that, although most dramatic series and anthologies were live, they were recorded on poor quality "kinescope" from the master monitor which were then sent by train and bus across the country. Whoever owned the first TV set on the block was likely to have two dozen kids show up for NBC's *Howdy Doody* (and his friend Buffalo Bill) and eventually for CBC's Canadian version with a Canadian replacement named Timber Tom. CBC also created *Mr. Dressup* and *The Friendly Giant,* whose viewing times overlapped throughout their run from 1958 to 1996. These were the most successful shows of many featuring a mix of adult actors and puppets and were aimed squarely at children. *Mr. Dressup* is still in reruns.

Although older children and teens were not targeted as a demographic, they had much to choose from with family friendly programs ranging from the earliest *Sunshine Sketches* and *Jake and the Kid* to variety shows, hit parades, quiz shows and sports, all genres with their own Canadian variants. Even adult cop shows like *Dragnet* and *Perry Mason* were suitable for older children and teens. When *Hopalong Cassidy* and *Roy Rogers* were replaced by adult westerns, which dominated television during the early to mid-1960s, only a few, memorably *Have Gun Will Travel,* had adult themes. Some occasionally ventured into adult territory like *Gunsmoke* (but how many kids at that time thought to ask themselves about the relationship between Matt and Miss Kitty?), but most were family oriented westerns like *Bonanza.*

In 1957 *Radisson,* the biggest investment in CBC / Radio-Canada history to that date and for years after, was broadcast. Intended to interest families as well as children, *Radisson* was the CBC's very self-conscious answer to the 1955 *Davy Crockett* craze. Although I do remember it, the first episode did not capture my attention as a fifteen year old. Unlike many

Canadians, my family could tune into two or three American channels that offered more interesting shows. For many others, though, it was the CBC or nothing. *Radisson* was the first Canadian filmed series and, as one of the first "national" projects, it was filmed twice, once in English and again in French. The scripts were written by John Lucarotti from England; most of the production crew, producers and directors were from Radio-Canada or the Montreal film company hired to help out. All of the leads and most of the other roles were played by francophone actors, which was appropriate given the period and the focus on the two pioneering voyageurs Radisson and Des Grosseilliers. Authentic locations were constructed or found, authentic props were built and costumes sewn. However, there was not one First Nations actor in the whole series (or in any other fictional portrayal on the CBC in the 1950s as far as I can determine).[2]

Radisson had a reasonably successful run in some American markets under the series name of *Tomahawk*. However, as far as I can find out all thirty-nine English episodes have since disappeared.[3] *Radisson* met with mixed reviews in newspapers but large audiences did come back for the next episode of a series that sometimes used the serial format, and there was a report that teenagers had besieged the handsome star. It was also the subject of some very early audience research among grades five and six students in a pair of English schools and a pair of French schools. Nevertheless, it had no immediate Canadian made successors although, as I point out in the next section, two other historical series for children were made years later.

THE FORERUNNERS TO DEGRASSI

A quick overview of children's programming in the 1960s and 1970s, before *The Kids of Degrassi* aired in 1979 and opened up the world of *Degrassi*, demonstrates the argument often made in this book that, in the United States, television specifically made for teens was not made until the 1990s and, therefore, the airing of *Degrassi Junior High* starting in 1987 and then *Degrassi High* was quite revolutionary.

One of the most successful shows specifically for kids in the 1960s was *Razzle Dazzle*. Blaine Allen, on his invaluable Web site documenting CBC programs up to 1982, describes it this way:

> A high-powered, fast-moving half-hour, *Razzle Dazzle* (1961–66) is still fondly remembered as required after-school viewing for children of the baby

boom. Its title sequence was a rapid montage of images cut to a raucous version of *Tiger Rag*, and the action took place in Razzle Dazzle Alley, which was populated each day by a gallery of children bused in daily from Toronto area elementary schools. The most esteemed inhabitant of the alley was Howard the Turtle. Sometimes wide-eyed and childlike, sometimes clownish, sometimes irreverent, often Buddha-like in his serenity, Howard the Turtle was an icon of Canadian television in the first half of the l960s.[4]

Razzle Dazzle also featured the short clips which were the forerunner of the children's action adventure series *The Forest Rangers*.

Six years after *Radisson* ended, *The Forest Rangers* (1963–65) was produced in colour, on film and with quite high production values. The directors of the series were some of the best working for the CBC: Ron Weyman, Eric Till, George McGowan and Paul Almond. *The Forest Rangers* was set near a Metis community which provided a recurring character called Joe Two Rivers as a Metis guide, played by a white actor. But five years later, teens were being recognized as a demographic by program heads. The two seasons of *Adventures in Rainbow Country* (1970–71) focused much more clearly on teenagers than the earlier shows.

The place of *The Forest Rangers* in Canadian popular culture is summarized in the irreverent *Mondo Canuck* by Geoff Pevere and Greg Dymond, who remember watching this series when they were kids: "To kick back after an invigorating game of road hockey by watching *The Forest Rangers* while eating packaged butter tarts off the back of the first Guess Who LP cover was to just know that you were up to something culturally distinctive … We knew that *The Forest Rangers*, an 'adventure' show with a polite emphasis on collective problem-solving, was different from *Lost in Space*."[5] In their assessment of *Adventures in Rainbow Country*, they quote Leslie Millin of the *Globe and Mail*: "[Billy] leads the life of the true North strong and free in that he goes fishing for brook trout, puts down his sister and accepts his buddy as damn nearly an equal."[6] I note, as Millin does not, that Bucky Petawabano, who plays his friend, the older teen Pete Gawa, is Anishnabe.

Peter Kentner in *TV North* calls *Adventures in Rainbow Country* "*The Forest Rangers* in bell bottoms" and points out that it was a Canadian/Australian/British co-production.[7] I saw a few episodes on the Aboriginal Peoples Television Network (APTN) in 2000. Billy (Stephen Cottier), the series' lead, was a blond, blue-eyed teen heartthrob. Pete, who was

Aboriginal, made wry comments about his own heritage and his interrelationship with white culture. There were no multicultural or multiracial characters on these shows, but *Forest Rangers* did have a francophone character as well as the Aboriginal character Joe Two Rivers. Fred Rainsberry, in *A History of Children's Television in English Canada 1952–1986*, writes in his brief outline of the series that "the stories ranged from scenes of actual forest firefighting to gold prospecting to slapstick comedy."[8] Both series were set in the near "north" of Ontario. In each episode problems arose, some of them highly improbable. No matter. The problems were quickly solved. As for girls, *Forest Rangers* did have one female cast member; a junior forest ranger who was usually the one in peril. *Rainbow Country* had none.

In the 1980s, historical subjects reappeared and two successful historical series were produced. Broadcast in 1981, *Matt and Jenny on the Wilderness Trail*[9] was co-produced by Société Radio-Canada (not the English CBC so it would not need to be dubbed into French) and the Global TV network. For teenaged viewers there was Kit, a rugged woodsman in his late teens who was the guide for the younger Matt and Jenny. *The Campbells* (1986–89) was a Canadian-Scottish co-production of 100 episodes, which made the series easy to syndicate around the world. Set in southeastern Ontario in the 1830s, it featured Dr. Campbell's handsome teenaged son, Neil, along with two younger children. The family built a cabin and cleared a farm in the bush against the opposition of Captain Sims, the veteran of the War of 1812 and member of what was then the ruling class. The series lasted four seasons and was nominated for several Gemini Awards.[10] The list of thirty-seven writers includes Bill Gough, Cedric Smith (who played Sims), Charles Israel, Ken Gass (who worked in alternative theatre), Lyal Brown, M. Charles Cohen, Marc Strange (from *The Beachcombers*), Rob Forsythe (who went on to write several of the best episodes of *North of 60*) and Suzette Couture (who also wrote many CBC drama specials). Unlike *Degrassi Classic*, no one writer or set of writers dominated the series. Among the twenty-four directors were the stalwarts of series television: Alan Kroeker, Don Haldane, George Bloomfield, Eleanor Lindo, Peter Rowe and Randy Bradshaw, many of whom went on to direct or had already directed drama specials. John Delmage, the producer, kept it all together.

In many ways, *The Campbells* was the training ground for young television professionals and the bread and butter for more experienced writers and directors. Note that, as in the earlier series in the 1970s and 1980s, the older teen was male. Both series also featured strong, unattached men as the continuing adult characters, and both included younger girls: Jenny was definitely feisty, and Emma, in *The Campbells*, grew into a teenager with ambitions to be a writer. As in *Forest Rangers* and *Rainbow Country*, both were set in the "wilderness." *Matt and Jenny* actually begins when the brother and sister run away from the ship in Halifax to find their uncle. The concepts of wilderness and "the north" shift from time period and location of the viewer, from southeastern Ontario to the near north of *Forest Rangers* and *Adventures*, later to *The Rez*, and finally to the 1990s adult series which is set in the true north, *North of 60*.

I must also mention the excellent but almost unknown 1985–86 series *Spirit Bay*, which appeared during the run of *Degrassi*. The show focused on older children and not adults, was set in the mid-north and named for its fictional setting on a First Nations reserve, Spirit Bay. There was a sharply observed, credible and refreshing quality to some of the episodes. *Spirit Bay* resembled and perhaps was influenced by its contemporary *Degrassi*. The producer used the local community for "authentic" details, invited story ideas (but not full scripts) from a workshop of First Nations writers and focused on an ensemble of mostly inexperienced actors who were, in this case, almost all Aboriginal. APTN resurrected *Spirit Bay* along with *Forest Rangers, Adventures in Rainbow Country* and *The Beachcombers* in 2000–03, presumably because the earlier series each had at least one running character who was First Nations or Metis. *The Rez*, a series for young adults, also appeared on APTN.

The most successful family friendly series by far was the over-300 episode, nineteen-year-long *The Beachcombers* (1972–90). The show featured a male teenager, Jesse, as a major character, as well as the first of the unattached adult males, Nick Adonidas (in this case, not always the most responsible character in an episode), and it had a spectacular wilderness setting bordering the Pacific Ocean and encompassing British Columbia's Rain Forest. Jesse was a sixteen-year-old Coast Salish from the Seahost Band, living away from his family but strongly attached to his culture. Eventually, Jesse married and adopted a son named Tommy. Tommy and Jesse's younger sister, Sarah, who lived at the beach, replaced Hughie and Margaret, Molly's grandchildren, after a few seasons. In mid-run, Pat O'Gorman, a homeless white teen with no family, was added to the show. *Beachcombers'* Margaret was well ahead of *Forest Rangers'* Cathy. She was a strong swimmer, comfortable around boats and more inclined to get into and out of scrapes than her older brother Hughie. Sarah, who was very much part of her Salish culture, was allowed to grow up on the show.

The Beachcombers is the program that most Canadians will think of when they think of television made for the whole family in this period. It spans *Adventures in Rainbow Country* and all of *Degrassi Classic*. It was scheduled in the then child-friendly, prime-time slot of 7 to 8 p.m. on Sundays, until 1989. But it was not intended for one demographic, as the age span of its characters and the layered writing of some of the episodes suggest.[11] It was not focused on the kids and teens, who were featured in some episodes and had little to do in others. Rather, *The Beachcombers* was a mix of comedy, drama and adventure, offering "lessons to be learned" in some episodes and broad farce or ghost stories in others. Ambivalence and ambiguity were regular features of its early years.

In contrast, the 123 episodes of *Danger Bay* (1984–90) featured more of the North West Coast, one more unattached male in the character of Dr. Grant Roberts, a widowed marine specialist at the Vancouver Aquarium, and Jonah and Nicole, the children. It was a family/adventure series with an emphasis on ecology that featured a woman bush pilot as the "love" interest and chauffeur. I wrote that the series suffered from an emphasis on action formulae and was sometimes sentimental.[12] Manon Lamontagne writes that "moral and psychological tensions were also muted and reflected the Disney producers' reluctance to deal with controversial issues such as sex, drugs, or alcohol as did the other contemporary Canadian teenage drama series, *Degrassi Junior High*."[13] (*Degrassi* had censorship problems with its American partners PBS and later The N, but only after the initial uncensored Canadian broadcasts.) In *Danger Bay*, Jonah became the male teen who grew up into a university student by the sixth season. The show also had a wide variety of skilled writers and directors.

All of the *Degrassi* series, including the more recent *Degrassi: The Next Generation,* are focused on kids and teens, not on adults. This is urban drama, not set in a small village close to the wilderness. It includes almost every "ethnic" group to be found in Canada, except, I must note, First Nations children and teens. This omission must have seemed obvious to urban kids and teens from cities like Winnipeg, Regina, Calgary and Vancouver, even in the 1980s and certainly in 2000, after *The Rez* and six seasons of *North of 60* (1991–97). Yet it is an omission so invisible to many in its audience, then and now, that none of those writing in this book have noted it. "Urban Indian" teens had to wait until the two short seasons of *The Rez* ran in 1997 to see themselves on TV. There may well be something to the oft-repeated charges that much of our television is Toronto centric, but that provides no alibi. Toronto has a thriving community of First Nations adults, children and teens. It's where Sadie, one of the four leads in *The Rez*, will go to university on scholarship when she decides to leave the rez for more education. It's where her friend Lucy wants to make her fortune as a singer. It's where Sadie's boyfriend, the series' narrator Silas Crow, and his friend Frank Fencepost had gone to Ryerson for a while and where Silas would publish his first stories.

The Rez was one of a series of programs designed by the CBC to appeal to teens in the mid-1990s. *Liberty Street* (1994–95), with clear *Degrassi* connections,[14] focused on a group of young working people living in an old apartment building; it ran for twenty-seven episodes over two seasons. *Straight Up* (1996–97), from writer Andrew Rai Berzins, was a "six-pack" featuring high-school students which, in its slightly longer second season, used one story arc over the whole season. *Drop the Beat* (2001), the "first interactive broadcast of a Canadian dramatic series ... on CBC,"[15] was connected to *Straight Up* through its executive producers Janis Lundman and Adrienne Mitchell (who made their reputations with *Talk 16*) and one or two of the characters. It featured two Black teens running an alternative radio station specializing in hip-hop music — both shows took place in an urban setting. Two earlier series made in Vancouver offered a handful of episodes focused on First Nations teens, but were otherwise variants on many of the themes of *Degrassi*. *Northwood* was an award-winning and gritty series about teens and young adults, while *Madison* focused on a high school whose episode logs sounded more like a soap opera than a challenging teen series.

In work yet to come, Michele Byers may trace the influence of *Degrassi Classic* on two contemporary series in which "urban Indians" finally appear on a regular basis. The first is *renegadepress.com* (2004), a series made for specialty channels. One of the four or five leading characters, Jack, is a First Nations teen played by Jackson Pelletier; Lorne Cardinal plays his father. It is filmed in Regina for APTN, and broadcast to the educational channels TVO (Ontario), TFO (francophone Ontario), SCN (Saskatchewan), ACCESS (Alberta), the Knowledge Network (BC) and

Book Television (national). The executive story editor and one of the writers is Jordan Wheeler from *North of 60* and *The Rez*. The second series is the first-ever drama series produced and directed by First Nations people, *Moccasin Flats*, which began airing in 2004 on APTN and continued with a second season in 2005. Jennifer Podemski, who has was one of the young stars of *The Rez*, is the executive producer.

GROWING UP DEGRASSI

Although in recent years a second wave of scholars interested in Canadian television series, anthologies, mini-series and specials — that is, television "drama" — has arrived, most of the series outlined above are still waiting for critical voices to tackle them. In contrast to its richer literary cousin the theatre, popular culture seems only to have the occasional paper presented at a conference or an occasional book published on a specific program. The various *Degrassi* series, including the current *Degrassi: The Next Generation,* are more fortunate. This book presents several very different voices about one set of programs, which is indeed a rare occurrence. Moreover, the chapters look at the programs themselves, not just at the contextual issues of economics, politics and audience research. Bringing together a cross-section of scholars in Canada and in the United States (made possible, in part, by the PBS broadcasting *Degrassi Classic* in the 1980s) to look at a major Canadian cultural artifact is a very useful thing to do. Adding the more informal voices of articulate and knowledgeable fans reflects current practice in many collections of work on popular culture.

As has been traditional in critiques in literature and drama since the sixteenth century, some of the writers observe and describe their own first reactions to the series as useful data. Others consider changes in broadcasting technology and other factors relevant to the production process. The progenitor of the long-running *Degrassi* series, *The Kids of Degrassi Street*, with its early, somewhat more didactic twenty-six episodes, is not the focus of these essays. Rather, most of the contributors have chosen to focus on *Degrassi Junior High,* which ran for forty-two episodes over three seasons (1987–88); *Degrassi High*, twenty-eight episodes over two seasons (1989–91); and the more recent *Degrassi: The Next Generation* (2001–), now into its fifth season and still counting.

Michele Byers, who is the founder of this feast, opens the book's first section "*Degrassi* and Youth Cultures." In her essay "Revisiting Teenage Truths" (chapter 1), she outlines the pressures experienced by producers Linda Schuyler and Kit Hood and writer Yan Moore from the CBC's American funding partners and points out how they were determined to use their own narrative strategies despite these pressures. For example, *Degrassi*'s major characters rather than the "guests" experienced unwed pregnancies, abortions, AIDS, interracial dating and living on their own; experiences that ran over several story arcs that took a season or two to develop. She then takes on Simonetti's essentialist arguments of a decade ago regarding whether or not the series is "Canadian," specifically exploring those values which are posited as either "Canadian" or "American," looking at the deeper questions of national identity.

In this section, several writers compare *Degrassi* to the critically acclaimed but short-lived *My So-Called Life* (1994–95) and *Freaks & Geeks* (1999–2000), and others contrast it to the long-lived 1990s teen soap *Beverly Hills 90210* and the not-so-sensational *Saved by the Bell*. Some also find significant differences between *Degrassi Classic* — with its early emphasis on educational value, a deliberately unpolished look, the large number of inexperienced actors who formed a large company of characters and the lack of narrative closure in some episodes — and *Degrassi: The Next Generation* (*TNG*), which has more polished production values, experienced actors forming a smaller cast and less politicized issues. Some explain this in terms of audience expectations, others by the fact that it is produced by CTV, a private network rather than the publicly owned CBC, where the *Degrassi* series first aired.

Tom Panarese, in "Sometimes a Fantasy: *Degrassi* and Teenage Entertainment in America" (chapter 2), sets the series in the context of assumptions and expectations about entertainment for American teenagers; the limitations of The N, the network which is the current home of *TNG* in the U.S. in contrast to PBS (where the series originally aired in the U.S.), which had its own limitations, as he documents; the influence of teen films of the 1990s; and the ways *TNG* is coded as "cool."

In "*Degrassi* Then and Now: Teens, Authenticity and the Media" (chapter 3), Sherri Jean Katz is interested in the series' interaction with fans, as well as issues of authenticity, which are raised by her definition of the "teen condition." She also looks at how the *Degrassi Classic* shows were financed, shot and scheduled in the 1980s, then looks at the more polished *TNG*, comparing its media savvy with its less technological predecessor.

Ravindra N. Mohabeer, in his essay entitled "Changing Faces: What Happened When *Degrassi* Switched to CTV" (chapter 4), felt a real loss when the series resumed as *The Next Generation* on the private network CTV. He describes *Degrassi Classic* as "bumpy, slow, rough around the edges and evolving in contradiction" and laments the smoothing over of texture in the newer incarnation. He argues that the look of the new series is defined by the choice of products and the quality of the commercials run on CTV, and argues that there are too many perfect characters like Emma, "eloquent, poised and flawless," in too many episodes that offer closure, a structure and style preferred by advertisers rather than the viewers. Although *TNG* is "a hot commodity," Mohabeer concludes that it is much less Canadian than its predecessors.

Laura Tropp's essay, "*The Next Generation* Goes Digital: Technology, the Medium and the Message" (chapter 5) explores the way *Degrassi Classic* and *TNG* reflect a major cultural change over their twenty-year span through the uses of technology in the lives of teens. Teens in the earlier series are computer literate but teens in the current series access all kinds of technology from gameboys to cell phones in every episode. She shows how e-mail eases teen interaction, makes it easier for parents to keep track of them and, intertextually, creates material for teachers on the Web.

Michael Strangelove is more concerned with collaboration and resistance in online fan "communities." In his essay "Online Fan Fiction: Is Self-expression Collaboration or Resistance?" (chapter 6), he explores what kinds of material fans appropriate and what they choose to write as fan fiction — which (I wonder why I was surprised) includes erotica and slash fiction.

But how does *Degrassi* influence identity, especially youth identity and especially in Canada? Jennifer MacLennan, who opens the second section "Building Identity on *Degrassi*," uses the trope from a once famous Red Rose Tea advertisement in the title of her chapter — "Only in Canada, You Say? The Dynamics of Identity on *Degrassi Junior High*." She argues that the multicultural nature of the series, as well as subjects like drug use, family violence and the death of a parent whose consequences are played out over many episodes, set it apart from American television's depiction of teens at the time. She situates the "realism" of the series within the strong documentary tradition of Canadian film (and, I would add, radio) and television, which created a style and voice for its characters that young viewers perceived as "looking and sounding like us."

There are other difficult issues that make *Degrassi* more Canadian than American. Race, sexuality, class and feminism are raised in all of the series, but again there are differences between *Degrassi Classic* and *Degrassi: The Next Generation.* Some can be explained in part by the ten-year gap, some reflect the different broadcasting context of publicly funded co-production, in which the CBC and the producers had the guiding vision, a broadcasting mandate and the clout to make the series they wanted to make versus the current CTV production. Even so, CTV is ready to take a few risks on subjects like abortion (the episode involves one of the ensemble cast, not a guest, and the decision is not "punished"). Their American distributor, Noggin (or The N), will not broadcast it.

Also in the second section are Michele Byers and Rebecca J. Haines, who played earnest Kathleen in the *Degrassi Classic* shows and is now, like Byers, a scholar interested in television for youth. Their essay "That White Girl from *That Show*" (chapter 8) is set up as a conversation about the series from an insider's perspective building on their common interests. They discuss the friendship of Yick, a Vietnamese boat person, and Arthur, his white Canadian-born friend whose mother wins a lottery. The subsequent wealth drives apart their friendship. They also look at the mixed-race relationship between Michelle and BLT, from the storyline's inception through parental objections to their eventual drifting apart and contrast it with a similar but more nuanced variation a decade later on *Drop the Beat.* Haines also describes what it was like to go to high school and be identified and even bitched at as her character, not as her real self. The discussion then moves into more general issues raised by working in the field of popular and youth cultures in Canada.

Their discussion segues into Byers's essay "Have Times Changed? Girl Power and Third-Wave Feminism on *Degrassi*" (chapter 9), in which she contrasts *Degrassi Classic* and *TNG*, comparing the second wave of much more explicit and consistent feminist behaviour in *Degrassi Classic* and the more tangential, less explicitly articulated feminist issues of *TNG*. Like others, Byers sees the differences in part as an accurate reflection of the societal changes that occurred in the decade between the shows. "Girl power" is not the same as "feminist" in 2000, which may not be the same as "feminist" in the 1980s. And while definitions may have changed, many of the issues remain the same — eating disorders, girls in sports and cheerleading, boys, looking good, girlfriend abuse, saying no in a sexual situation, alcohol and drugs.

In the final three chapters of this section, the contributors grapple with other identity-shaping experiences: sexuality, drugs and class. The knowledge about and treatment of HIV/AIDS certainly has changed since the mid-1980s, as Kylo-Patrick Hart outlines in his essay "Getting It Wrong and Right: Representing AIDS on *Beverly Hills 90210* and *Degrassi High*" (chapter 10). Ryan Robert Mitchell recalls with wry adult amusement his identification with Arthur K, a teen of the same age, as he grows up and discovers his sexual identity in "Swamp Sex Robots: Narratives of Male Pubescence and Viewer (Mis)Identification" (chapter 11). Bettina Spencer looks at the themes of drugs, sex, and money in *Degrassi High* in her essay "Everybody Wants Something" (chapter 12), arguing that, far from enticing young viewers to experiment, the shows demonstrate that consequences of these behaviours — from all-nighters on caffeine to sex — can be the beginning of something new or the end of something familiar.

In the closing section of this book, "Web Sites, Fan Clubs & Reminiscences," the contributors are long-time fans of *Degrassi* and their essays are much more whimsical. In "Degrassi.ca: Building a Fan Community Online" (chapter 13), Mark Aaron Polger details the history of his discovery of the Internet and his futile search for *anything Degrassi* on the new World Wide Web. Not finding what he wanted, he initiated what became one of the most popular online fan clubs. Mark Janson documents the founding of another fan club in 2002, this one at Queen's University in his essay "The Queen's University *Degrassi* Club" (chapter 14), which was launched by a group of restless classmates accidentally discovering *Degrassi* reruns and becoming passionate about promoting the show across campus. Sean Bilichka's recalls in "I Wasn't Born in the South …" (chapter 15) that his introduction to the series, which he has never seen in sequence, began with a teacher in North Carolina who put on the show for the class every morning at 8:30. Finally, Brian Jones nostalgically remembers how, in "True to My School: An American's Love Affair with *Degrassi*" (chapter 16), he travelled to the streets of Toronto to search out the *Degrassi* locales as a way to re-experience his passion for the series. For him, *Degrassi* is "a niche … a boutique, a trailblazer."

★

Degrassi Classic and *Degrassi: The Next Generation*, programs that were and continue to be directed primarily at a niche market, are a long way from the adventures and fantasies of the 1950s radio programs and from their television descendants of *Razzle Dazzle* and *Fraggle Rock.* Nor does it appear that *Degrassi* was influenced by the historical series of 1957 and then the 1980s, or the modern wilderness adventures of the 1960s and early 1970s, or the family adventure series of the 1970s and 1980s. It could be argued that *Degrassi Classic* influenced *Spirit Bay,* as well as the urban teen high-school series of the 1990s, and even the edgier experiments like *Straight Up* and *Drop the Beat.* But unlike the research and viewing limitations of those decades, academics, scholars and viewers alike have been in rerun heaven from the mid-1990s. The 300 channels available on contemporary television allow viewers to check out nearly fifty years' worth of Canadian television shows for children and teens, most of them successful exports. *TNG* is available on video and DVD. There are *Degrassi* books, fan clubs, Web sites and chat groups (many of which are listed in the Fun Stuff Section at the back of this book). Somewhere in the world, *Degrassi Classic* is playing. It might well be available on your cable or satellite service. If it is, tune in and enjoy.

NOTES

1. And vice versa. See the Canadian and American versions of *New Maggie Muggins Stories: A Recent Selection of the Famous Radio Stories* (Toronto: Thomas Allen, 1947); *Maggie Muggins Stories: A Recent Selection of the Famous Canadian Radio Stories* (Philadelphia: John C. Winston, 1950).

2. The bad wigs for the "Indians" in *Radisson* came in for derisive comment from both critics and young viewers. The producer/directors of *Cariboo Country* (an intermittent anthology from 1960 to 1968) — Frank Goodship who produced and directed the early studio episodes and Phil Keately who produced and directed some of the studio and all of the filmed segments — seem to have been the first to insist on casting "Indians as Indians."

3. No episodes in English survive in the National Archives of Canada. Radio Canada archives may have the French versions.

4. "Directory of Television Series: 1952–1982," by Allen Blaine. *Queen's University*. Retrieved May 11, 2005, from www.film.queensu.ca/CBC/R.html.

5. Geoff Pevere and Greg Dymond, *Mondo Canuck: A Canadian Pop Culture Odyssey* (Toronto: Prentice-Hall Canada, 1996), 156.

6. There is no date for the *Globe and Mail* reference in Pevere and Dymond, *Mondo Canuck*, page 2 of the introduction. The quote at the top of that page is from *Isn't It Ironic* by Alanis Morissette to set the tone.

7. Peter Kentner, *TV North: Everything You Wanted to Know about Canadian Television*, with notes by Martin Levin (Vancouver: Whitecap Books, 2001), 1–2.

8. Fred Rainsberry, *A History of Children's Television in English Canada 1952–1986* (Metuchen, NJ: Scarecrow Press, 1988), 128.

9. The series was first broadcast on January 7, 1981, with money for dubbing from TF1, Antenna 2, Channel J, RTBF and TMC. Twenty-six episodes were translated into French. There is not much to be found about this series anywhere I have looked. Since it is an independently made series (Global with the SRC, which has its own library), there is nothing about it in the CBC library and it has not been deposited in the National Archives of Canada.

10. Retrieved May 12, 2005, from a short article without attribution at www.tvtome.com/Campbells.

11. Mary Jane Miller, *Turn Up the Contrast: CBC Television Drama since 1952* (Vancouver: University of British Columbia Press; Vancouver: BC, 1987) 90–110, a section which defines the family adventure formula to that date but stops before the decline of the series in the late 1980s.

12. Ibid., 92–93.

13. Manon Lamontagne, "Danger Bay," in the online version of the first edition of the *Encyclopedia of Television. The Museum of Broadcast Communication.* Retrieved May 12, 2005, from www.museum.tv/archives/ etv/D/htmlD/dangerbay/dangerbay.htm.

14. Joan Nicks "Degrassi." *The Museum of Broadcast Communication.* Retrieved May 12, 2005, from www.museum.tv/archives/etv/D/htmlD/degrassi/degrassi.htm. *Liberty Street* was created by *Degrassi's* Linda Schuyler. The executive story editor was Yan Moore, and it starred Pat Mastroianni as Frank, still trying to be a wheeler-dealer.

15. "Alliance Atlantis Press Release," February 7, 2000. *The Extend Media Production Company.* Retrieved May 12, 2005, from www.extend.com/news/2000.02.07-press-firstinteractivedrama.html.

PART I

DEGRASSI AND YOUTH CULTURES

Revisiting Teenage Truths:
Simonetti's Questions of National Identity and Culture Ten Years Later

Michele Byers

THERE IS LITTLE DOUBT that *Degrassi* is among the most successful examples of television franchising in Canadian history. The series — which includes *The Kids of Degrassi Street* (1979–85), *Degrassi Junior High* (1987–89), *Degrassi High* (1989–91), *School's Out* (1992), *Degrassi Talks* (1992) and *Degrassi: The Next Generation* (2001–) — has enjoyed both enormous success and critical acclaim throughout the twenty-five years of its run in Canada, the United States and around the world. The last two and a half decades have seen incredible changes in television, both in terms of its technologies and in terms of the type of stories that it can tell. We have seen this ambivalence about representation in a recent debate, widely covered in the Canadian and U.S. news media, about The N's decision — the MTV-owned cable station that airs *Degrassi: The Next Generation* (*TNG*) in the United States — not to air a fall 2004 two-part episode of *TNG* in which a fourteen-year-old unremorsefully decides to have an abortion. *The New York Times* used the event, and the subsequent collection of a 6,000-name petition of young American viewers presented to Viacom in protest of The N's decision, to highlight abortion as "television's most persistent taboo."[1] But, clearly, this taboo is not equally persistent on both sides of the border. According to a Canadian Press article printed in the *Montreal Gazette*, the petition called the cable channel's decision "unjust and asinine."[2] It is not only the series' writers and producers who are to be commended for their firm stand on the issue; CTV, the Canadian TV station that aired the episode, also deserves kudos, as does the audience who raised "nary a blip on the censorship radar" at the time of the original airing.[3] This incident shows that there are certainly differences between Canadian and American television, but this isn't the only example. This chapter addresses the issue of differences through questions about television, representation and national identity raised by the *Degrassi* series over the last twenty-five years.

Degrassi is an unusual cultural artifact; it provides a (by no means complete) historical record of the way Canadian television, youth culture and socio-political issues have changed (or not) since 1980. In this chapter, I briefly explore this long-lived artifact of Canadian television, beginning with a discussion of the goals that the creators of *Degrassi* hoped to accomplish when they conceived of this project and the ways in which it differed from existing programming for youth in both Canada and the United States at that time. I mention some of the other series that were likely influenced by the *Degrassi Classic* (or *DC,* the name often used to refer to the shows in the "classic" series: *Degrassi Junior High* and *Degrassi High),* how the series helped set the stage for their emergence and the way *TNG* fits into and points to further changes and consistencies within Canadian television and the youth market.

But I am also concerned with the question of national identity: Is there such a thing, is *Degrassi* an example of it, and if so, does this "Canadianness" occur at the level of the text or at an extra-textual level, that is, does it point to some essential difference within the Canadian national imaginary? I undertake this analysis in relation to the only published full-length article (prior to my own work) that I have found that deals specifically with *Degrassi*: Marie-Claire Simonetti's 1994 "Teenage Truths and Tribulations Across Cultures: *Degrassi Junior High* and *Beverly Hills 90210.*" Simonetti argues that these two youth texts both "impart" and "shape different cultural perceptions of the world."[4] In the second section of this chapter, I critique Simonetti's article and the issues it raises about television and national identity.

Youth and Canadian Television

In most interviews with some of the original writers and producers of the

Degrassi franchise, someone mentions the fact that their initial goal was to present television for youth that spoke to young people in a voice that was authentically their own. Yan Moore, head writer since the earliest days of *The Kids of Degrassi Street,* relates how right from the start there was conflict over the way these stories should be told: "When it was being put together [in 1980], the American partner wanted a wise old lady living down the street and whatever problems were brought to her, she would fix; this was an anathema."[5] Instead, the series continuously strove to find ways to tell stories that started from the teens' points of view; *DC*'s creators drew on their own experiences as well as those of their young performers. Episodes were even shot, intentionally, at a "kid level" to increase the sense of authenticity of the show and its characters, rather than take the "Disney" route.[6] Moore insists that the *Degrassi* concept, if you can call it that, has always been to resist the tendency, so prevalent in youth programming, to protect kids from the "big bad" rather than acknowledging young people's need for, and ability to, negotiate the complex situations in which they tend to live anyway. Often, this protectionism is linked to ideas about what is appropriate for young people to see — and to be — that often have little connection to the everyday experiences of teens. A great deal of television, particularly American television, creates a context in which both the mundane and tragic experiences of young people are not included. Linda Schuyler argues: "Aaron Spelling ... [is] just doing adult television with young people in it, which is very different from what we are doing."[7]

Schuyler, as *Degrassi*'s creator and top executive, continues to insist that on *Degrassi*, "no subject is taboo."[8] But more than that, Schuyler points to the investment the show has made not only to presenting issues — and their consequences — but to presenting them in relation to the characters that viewers are already invested in, rather than playing it safe by averting consequences or by bringing in a "very special guest star" to deal with the issues that teenagers deal with every day. Audrey Fisch, discussing the way abortion was dealt with in a story arc on Felicity, insists: "Of course it could never happen to Felicity — she's the title character. She can't be written out of the show the way Ruby can. (And, of course, Felicity could never have an abortion)."[9] We can certainly contrast the multitude of spontaneous miscarriages that plague so many television teens to the *Degrassi* teens who make their own choices: a junior-high student becomes pregnant and keeps her baby; a high-school student pushes through protesters outside an abortion clinic; and another teen quietly, and without telling anyone, makes an appointment to have an abortion.

What really distinguishes *Degrassi* from most other teen series — both its contemporaries and those which came after *DC* — is that these things happened to core characters, characters that the show's viewers were deeply connected to and this, undoubtedly, made the narratives more meaningful than they would have been had they been created for special guest stars. Thus, dealing with the subject of interracial relationships and parental racism has a different impact when both partners are regular cast members, as they were on *Degrassi*, than if the non-white character is a guest star who can easily be written out of the series as, for example, occurred on *Beverly Hills 90210*.[10] And this is equally true of the abortion episodes mentioned above; their power is not only in presenting an issue which was (and is still) largely taboo on television, but also in the way that the viewer is allowed to live through the before, during and after of the experience with a character they already know and will continue to know through story arcs beyond this one issue.

While cultural scholar Joan Nicks suggests that *Degrassi* is somewhat formulaic in its problem-solving convention, she does not mention the fact that, in many ways, the formula is *Degrassi*'s own, at least in terms of demonstrating what topics might be worth touching upon in youth programming. As Moore points out, "These were not issues that kids shows touched on traditionally, and we [*Degrassi*] ran them back to back."[11] Nicks is critical of what she sees as *Degrassi*'s co-optation of the youthful imagination by moral (adult) discourse. In comparing *Degrassi* with the 1996–98 CBC series *Straight Up*, which ran during the period of time that *Degrassi* was off the air (except in syndication), she argues that *Straight Up*'s characters are not bound by the types of moral formula or value lessons that she sees subsuming the *Degrassi* series.[12]

Certainly it is true that *Degrassi* is and has always been an issues-oriented show, but issues are central to most television, even to series — like *Seinfeld*, for instance — that purport to be about nothing.[13] Nor is it clear that the issues, and the way they are presented on *Degrassi*, are problematic for the show's audience in the same way that they are for the researcher. Perhaps the ways in which these different teen series present issues serve to meet different "adult needs" for different adult viewers, fans and researchers.[14] Nicks writes that unlike many other Canadian teen series, including *DC*,

Northwood (1991–94) and *Madison* (1993–97), *Straight Up*'s characters "transgress topical boundaries and popular formats" and are "not dumbed-down as popular television fodder."[15] And yet, while Nicks suggests that of all these shows *Straight Up* provides the most (or perhaps the only) authentic vision of adolescence, a teen named Anabela Carneiro responds — not to Nicks but to the series — by arguing that *Straight Up* is not about showing an authentic vision of teen life, at least not one that she can recognize as her own. She writes that *Straight Up*'s creators have managed merely to "create a new 'reality' that many of us [teens] can't ever live up to." She ends her piece by insisting, "I'm tired of having my life as a teenager presented to me on a spoon in such a patronizing manner."[16] This is not to argue that Nicks is wrong and Carneiro is right, or that one TV series provides a better or more authentic depiction of Canadian youth culture than another, but to point out that each viewer (including the author) will have their own investments in, and will make their own assumptions about, teen series and their audiences.

Stephen Stohn, executive vice-president of Epitome Pictures, touches on this in his discussion of *Degrassi*'s history:

> If you try and create something that is iconic, or you are trying to create something that's cool, you are doomed to failure … let's just go out and try and tell the stories we can, and if we are particular and true to the story we may have a universal appeal. And if it has a universal appeal then it may have popularity, both in other countries in the world and also ongoing popularity in your own country, but that's not what the goal is. The goal is just to try and do one episode and what comes will come.[17]

This is not an attempt to argue that *Degrassi* is better than *Straight Up*, or any other teen show for that matter, but to point to the importance we, as adult fans and researchers, place in teen series and their audiences.[18]

During the last twenty-five years, Canada has produced and exported many critically acclaimed series for young people. *Degrassi* was the first teen series to put stories about teen pregnancy, abortion, suicide and girlfriend abuse on prime-time. But it is important to note that at the time that *DC* was being produced, it was not only doing something new in terms of content but also in terms of genre. Prior to the mid-1980s, teens were primarily found in pop music (in the 1950s and 1960s) and family oriented television (1960s to mid-1980s); the teen series as we understand it today did not exist. As Rachel Mosley's entry for "The Teen Series" in *The Television*

Genre Book notes, the contemporary teen sitcom (and drama) only became visible in the 1980s.[19] But the television series she mentions, beginning with her description of *Saved by the Bell* (*SBTB*), all began airing in the 1990s, *SBTB* in 1989. The other teen show usually mentioned as an early forerunner of American teen TV, *Beverly Hills 90210*, began airing in 1990. It is not unusual for *DC* not to be mentioned, despite the fact that the series aired from 1987 to 1991 and was broadcast by the Public Broadcasting Service (PBS) extensively in the U.S. However, it is not merely an urban legend that *90210*, and likely *SBTB* as well, grew from seeds that came from the ideas Schuyler and her partner Kit Hood developed for *Degrassi*. As well as creating the context for the development of American teen TV, *DC*'s popularity "lead to the more gritty *Northwood* and Global's *Madison*, as well as the excellent 'tween' show *Ready or Not*," all popular Canadian teen programs.[20]

There are differences between *DC* and the American series that were produced in the few years after it aired (as well as those that came later), but there are similarities as well. In moving away from a focus on intra-family dynamics and generational conflict that had fuelled series like *The Brady Bunch*, *The Partridge Family*, *Happy Days*, *The Cosby Show*, *Roseanne* and dozens of others, *DC* moved the vision of the televised teen into the more autonomous space of peer culture, whether the action took place at home, school or on the street.[21] The influence this had on programming for young people cannot be underestimated. The shows that had come before, particularly the comedies and dramas — as opposed to the music and quiz shows — went for a broad appeal across the generations. *Degrassi* may have appealed to a broad range of viewers, but it did not do this by creating story arcs that dealt with different age groups: its focus remained firmly on its teen stars.

By the late 1990s, a shift towards a youth focus was working its way across the pop culture landscape, and it began to circulate globally. The topics *Degrassi* had helped introduce to television had become standard, although the way these stories were (and are) told did not. With in-creasing audience segmentation, and not only a surge in programming but also the development of whole channels geared to children and teens, making something "new" became a real challenge. The Canadian series that followed in *Degrassi*'s successful footsteps, including *Northwood*, *Madison*, *Ready or Not*, *Straight Up*, *Drop the Beat*, *Edgemont*, *renegadepress.*

com and *Moccasin Flats,* developed within this expanded youth market. American series like *Party of Five, My So-Called Life, Buffy the Vampire Slayer, Dawson's Creek, Roswell, Clueless, Felicity* and *Popular* did as well. It was out of the old and into the new television environment that *Degrassi: The Next Generation* (*TNG*) emerged. Stohn relates:

> The environment when we looked at producing the original *Degrassi* was so different. There were not a lot of agents who represented kids, there was not a lot of work for kids, there was no YTV, look at all the specialty channels we've got now. So it came out of its time, and this show [*TNG*] is coming out of its time.[22]

TNG also had the specter of *DC*'s successes to contend with. As Yan Moore points out: "The second was so much scarier than the first, but again we were being compared to ourselves ... we were being compared to our own work, along with shows like *My So-Called Life* and all the various things that had come subsequently."[23] In several discussions with key people at *Degrassi*, the idea that there was no new ground to tread was raised; however, time has revealed that there is always something the television audience has not seen before. Moore insists that *TNG* is being produced in a "more conservative time" than *DC*, and that this requires that it be "told with a new sensibility."[24] But this is not as straightforward as it seems.

As a viewer, I find that many of the differences between *DC* and *TNG* are rooted in changing production values. New technology has allowed smaller production companies like Epitome Pictures to produce series that have production values similar to series being produced in the U.S. The first *Degrassi* shows were frequently contrasted with U.S. series in terms of the actors, who were not professionals, not gorgeous, not always thin, did not always have clear skin and often wore rather unstylish outfits. Not so of *TNG* (and many other new Canadian series). Most of its young stars are not new to acting. They are attractive in conventional ways and are usually fashionably dressed in styles that reflect the global nature of much of youth fashion culture. Unlike the original series, shot almost exclusively on location, *TNG* is filmed in a studio with permanent sets depicting the school, shopping malls and homes, with a backlot complete with houses and neighborhood landmarks that include The Dot Grill. This lends *TNG* a different feel from *DC*, and its popularity among U.S. teens suggests that they do not distinguish the series from locally produced shows — many viewers, in fact, think *TNG* is produced in Los Angeles.

TNG has remained committed to presenting "firsts": a teenaged boy getting an erection in class (and actually showing the erection), blood on the skirt of a girl getting her first period, as well as central characters being beaten by parents and experiencing date rape. Further, the way that even familiar narratives are told on *TNG* suggests that although the world may be more conservative, and even though *TNG* is now housed with a private (CTV) rather than a public (CBC) network, *Degrassi* as a franchise is still doing many of the same things it always has. In the late 1980s, PBS recut an episode of *Degrassi High* that dealt with abortion, in order to make it more acceptable to American audiences. As mentioned in the opening paragraph of this chapter, in 2004, The N chose not to air a similar episode of *TNG*. Both episodes aired in their original form on CBC and CTV, respectively. Here is a major difference between American and Canadian television, but does it represent an essential national difference in the way that Marie-Claire Simonetti suggests?

SIMONETTI: NATIONAL IDENTITY AND YOUTH CULTURE

Scholars of Canadian media history locate much of their project within a context in which cultural distinctiveness (from the United States) and the development of a distinctly Canadian national cultural identity are primary. Some scholars, like Aniko Bodroghkozy for example, challenge the idea of an essential Canadianness embedded in Canadian media. She argues that "most of the indigenously produced Canadian cultural texts, which tend to be rooted in the particularities of region, do not provide either the polysemy needed or the 'American' signifier necessary to be broadly useful in pan-Canadian strategies of meaning-making."[25] Rather than pit American and Canadian television against each other in a battle over who will do best by the Canadian viewing public, Bodroghkozy argues that audiences create meaning, including understandings of national identity, through their readings of American as well as Canadian texts. Thus, we might say that viewers may have their national (or regional, or class, or political) identities shored up precisely through their disidentification, as well as identification, with particular series. Simonetti discounts the incredible diversity of the audience, reading national myths onto the television texts she studies. While her assertion that *Degrassi* and *Beverly Hills 90210* are different is valid, she ignores the way these differences emerge from the generic, historical, production and narrative differences between the locations of the texts, choosing instead to root them in essential national differences.

Simonetti's article begins with the idea that *Beverly Hills 90210* and *Degrassi Junior High* share content but differ in terms of their "different cultural perceptions of the world."[26] She argues, based on quotes from both shows' executive producers, that the series share a desire to educate as well as entertain their audiences without offering simple solutions and pat answers. Where the shows diverge, Simonetti continues, is in their culturally distinct backgrounds. Drawing on the work of Seymour Lipset, she states that "Canadians are more traditional, tolerant, law abiding, egalitarian, collectively oriented, and multicultural than Americans. Americans, in contrast, are more entrepreneurial, individualistic, materialistic, and religious."[27] Simonetti then sets out to prove that these essential differences are present in the two texts under her scrutiny. This is a dilemma in Simonetti's article: she argues that Canadians and Americans are essentially different, but then also argues that on many levels the series are the same. I would argue, by contrast, that the two series reflect the contexts of media production in which they were produced; their narrative strategies — if not specific topics — are different, reflecting not only these contexts but also the generic strategies through which they each tell their stories.

A central problem that stands out in Simonetti's article is that she presents the idea of an essential national character uncritically, appearing to assume that these qualities are intrinsic parts of individuals because of their national locations. Although many of the points she raises are valid and well argued, the conclusions she draws rest on the idea that there are monolithic "Canadians" and "Americans" that somehow pre-exist her evocation of them. The way this works is not unlike the way Benedict Anderson theorizes his by now ubiquitous concept of "imagined community."[28] Anderson argues that the nation is what we, its citizens, imagine it to be. Andrew Higson offers a critique of Anderson's position, insisting that it refuses to give space to the "cultural difference and diversity that invariably marks [both] the inhabitants of a particular nation-state."[29] We, inhabitants of nation-states, do not share a unified vision of who and what we are. To dispel the myth, we must turn our attention to the question, Whose voices are heard within it?

Perhaps the imagined community might be better thought of as a mythic community. Like the American melting pot and the Canadian mosaic, the idea of national community is one of the great myths of our times. It allows us to foreground the social construction of our supposed national ideals but then buries the stratified nature of the nation. The myth of unified vision, suggested in the idea of imagined community, blinds us to the power necessary to shape the national imaginary in a world where nation, citizenship, multiculturalism and so on are experienced in so many different ways. One myth about Canada is that it is very diverse and totally accepting of all social differences while the U.S. is not. However, fewer than 10 percent of Canadians are not white, while over 25 percent of Americans are not white.[30] Rights and access to abortion are different in Canada than in the U.S., but while there are no firm statistics, about 50 percent of Americans (or almost 150 million) are thought to be pro-choice. We need to be careful that we do not confuse what are differences rooted in social and political history with essential differences between individuals within nations.

Simonetti also makes comparisons between the two series that seem somewhat arbitrary. For example, she argues that "neither show is above moralizing,"[31] by discussing how *90210* deals with a pregnancy scare and *Degrassi Junior High* with the death of a character's parents at the hands of a drunk driver.[32] The pregnancy episode, Simonetti relates, ends with Brenda (Shannen Doherty) saying that she (implying the audience) should not have sex if she cannot "take the consequences."[33] A better comparison might have been made with the *Degrassi* episode where eighth-grader Spike (Amanda Stepto) discovers that she actually is pregnant. While Spike does not offer a line of dialogue as explicit as Brenda's to the audience, she really does not have to; the consequences of her decision to have sex are right there for us to see. Brenda is not pregnant and so she does not actually have to face the consequences of her actions, at least not today; what she has to face is the possibility that if she continues to have sex — at least unprotected sex — she may at some point have consequences to face.

As with many moral issues taken up on *90210*, there are not a lot of stakes here. Once Brenda discovers she is not pregnant, the incident is more or less forgotten; Brenda goes on to have plenty of sex in later years. Spike, by contrast, decides to have a baby, and her pregnancy and attempts to manage motherhood and school remain central to the *Degrassi Classic* (and even the *TNG)* narrative. The difference here seems less national than narrative: *90210* may be moralizing, in the sense that it seems to offer a correction to the morals of its audience and characters, but *Degrassi* is not saying that if you have sex you deserve what you get (not so subtly hinting towards a pro-abstinence view). Rather, the moral of the *Degrassi* story seems to be that it is important to be well informed before you have sex, because there may be real consequences to face if you do not, which, to me, is not moralizing.

The interpretation of the drunk driving episode as suggesting Wheels's parents *deserved* to die as retribution for minor, and very normal, parental irritation is a stretch. Perhaps Simonetti meant that Wheels is guilt-ridden because he had been complaining about his parents, and feels that his anger somehow brought on their misfortune. But compare this to an episode of *90210* in which Dylan's (Luke Perry) father Jack dies in a car bombing related to ties he has to the Mafia. In both cases we empathize with the young men who have to deal with the loss of their parent(s). But Jack's death is really a morality play about retribution for his criminal past, whereas the Wheelers, like their son, are shown to be victims. Further, the consequences for Wheels and Dylan are different. Dylan is very rich and lives on his own in a luxury hotel. Wheels, by contrast, has no money and is forced to live with his grandparents. In this case, as in the one described above, the difference between the two series is rooted in the narrative, not in essential differences in national identity, and Simonetti overlooks the very important question of genre. While *90210* may have been inspired by *Degrassi*, its formula is essentially that of a prime-time soap opera for a teen and youth audience, while *Degrassi* is a teen drama.[34] Soaps, especially in the American tradition, have tended to be full of hyperbolic characters and stories. While the lessons may be taken from everyday life, the ways in which the stories are told are not. *90210* may aim to educate as well as entertain, but it is not going for authenticity in the same way that *Degrassi* is, which is offering, as a drama, a "slice-of-life," while *90210* is offering something "larger–than-life."

Simonetti makes this connection, but she links it to essential cultural differences between Canadian and American teens. Contrasting American dreams with Canadian didactic realism, she argues: "American teens firmly believe in dreams, whereas their Canadian counterparts believe in sobering lessons."[35] Simonetti continues by suggesting that these different strategies can be linked to American entrepreneurialism and Canadian caution. While there are certainly differences between the shows, this particular dichotomy seems forced. If anything, many *90210* narratives stress the inherent danger of the outside world. Although the characters may sidestep consequences to their risky behaviours (including jail and death, as well as pregnancy and disease), they are very often victims. Simonetti's suggestion that *90210* narrates the American dream identifies that dream as exclusively based on money and class privilege. The dreams of the characters on *90210* all require material wealth, something that most of them never actually have to dream about because they are born with it. *DC* offers more sobering lessons in that there are *actual* consequences that its young characters have to face as their stories unfold. But many of its stories point to the value in taking decisive risks, even against great odds. Because *DC* takes place in an urban, working- and middle-class space, the risks its characters take may be less dramatic than those available to the extremely privileged characters on *90210*, but they are there nonetheless.

Simonetti continues this argument by suggesting that Americans embody "persistence and idealistic pursuits" while, once again, Canadians exhibit caution, refusing to take risks. She writes: "While obstacles melt away in front of Americans, they keep Canadian dreams in check."[36] But *Degrassi's* characters often fight for their dreams, and, I would argue, their willingness to face seemingly insurmountable obstacles suggests that they can also be idealistic. Often, this idealism emerges in response to fights against various forms of oppression: Melanie (Sara Ballingall) overcomes her discomfort with her body to help the girls defeat the boys' soccer team in a swim meet; Spike successfully returns to school after having a baby; Michelle (Maureen McKay) leaves home after discovering her parents are racist; Lucy (Anais Gronofsky) successfully completes a feminist horror film and later battles for the recognition of girls' sports; and Dwayne (Darrin Brown) fights for his right for respect after his friends and classmates discover he has contracted the AIDS virus. In each case, the characters' struggles demonstrate a desire to take risks, engaging, at times idealistically, with many complex social issues. On *90210*, as in most soap operas, the characters are wealthy, have exciting jobs and meet celebrities, but they also experience an enormous amount of violence and tragedy in their lives, and fear of the dangers that lurk outside their doors is as much a part of the narrative as the idea that the world is each of theirs for the taking.

Simonetti argues that *90210* presents hegemonic values, while *Degrassi* "defies hegemony"; this argument is made primarily in relation to the two series' representations of class, race and politics. The dichotomies the author creates between the two series are as follows: *90210* has class divisions while

Degrassi has none; *90210* has racial tensions while *Degrassi* is multicultural; *90210* is sexist while *Degrassi* is "unfailing [in its] criticism of patriarchy, systemic sexism, and gender-defined expectations."[37] Let me begin with the question of class. *90210* is primarily about the wealthy, and the way it questions class often focuses on relative poverty: the upper-middle-class teens cannot compete with their multi-millionaire classmates, although in the early years of the show, Andrea (Gabriella Carteris), a poorer student, provided some contrast, as did several guest characters. Simonetti asserts that class differences do not appear on *Degrassi*, as if sharing "a nondescript middle-class lifestyle" is somehow not hegemonic.[38] But while class is not a central concern of the series, it does make its presence felt. In one episode, for example, Yick (Silus Synasasy) feels frustration over being a Vietnamese boat person and feels further marginalized after the mother of his best friend, Arthur (Duncan Waugh), wins the lottery. But we are also visually cued to the class differences between other characters as we get to know more about them, such as where they live, what they wear, the professions of their parents and so on.

While racism on *90210* may be "implied by the absence of visible minorities," Elizabeth Waiters argues that several storylines on the series try to provide role models about interracial friendship to its audience.[39] However, there is a pervasive whiteness or segregation in the cast of *90210*, while the cast of *Degrassi* includes more visible difference. This makes the few episodes of *DC* that specifically treat questions of racism much more powerful. When BLT (Dayo Ade) reacts to being called a racist name, or Lucy explains the pain of being called an "oreo," the audience experiences these things through the eyes of core characters with whom they have relationships, as opposed to through the eyes of characters introduced for a few episodes to teach the core characters about tolerance, an issue Simonetti also raises.[40] *DC* also deals with questions about immigration and ethnicity; several first generation characters fight with their parents about being allowed to *be* Canadian, whereas the unified American identities of the *90210* characters are never questioned. The greater visible difference of core cast members, often found in Canadian drama, is due at least in part to the existence of public policy through the mission of the Canadian Radio-television and Telecommunications Commission to maintain "the development of broadcasting services that reflect the cultural and linguistic plurality [that] is an essential part of the Canadian social structure."[41] Both

Degrassi and *90210*, however, have trouble getting past conventional taboos, like showing interracial relationships. Both series highlight the problematic nature of these relationships, and most characters end up with partners of the same race.[42]

On the issues of hegemony and resistance, I tend to agree with Simonetti, although I remain unconvinced that these are necessarily rooted in essential nationalistic differences. It is true that *Degrassi* takes a critical position on sexism, incorporating many storylines in which its young female characters actively name and fight against patriarchy.[43] This is due to *Degrassi*'s on-going commitment to empowerment and social justice, something its producers have fought for continuously, which perhaps has been more central to the tradition of youth programming in Canada than in the U.S., and persists to this day. Left-leaning American producers have difficulty finding forums in which they can fully articulate their political viewpoints and visions; this is particularly evident on network television, but it is also true on cable. While sex and violence may have attained relatively high levels of acceptance on both sides of the border, issues like abortion, interracial relationships, non-heterosexual sex, systemic privilege, fat phobia and pervasive sexism and racism are almost never touched upon in a systemic way.[44] Canadian series have had greater facility getting some of these issues to air, and they have tended to elicit weaker reactions from Canadian audiences. But is this because of some intrinsic and essential difference? Or is it rooted in the very different histories of television's development in our respective nations and in the very different political and economic powers that can and have been brought to bear on producers in order to ensure that only certain views can be seen on the small screen?

Simonetti writes that it is "Canada's lack of a collective dream that explains its tolerance for diversity," suggesting that "this tolerance has come to be associated with Canadian identity."[45] There is truth in this assertion, except that what Simonetti is talking about once again is the cultural myth of the Canadian mosaic and the American melting pot. Americans, she claims, have a single dream, assumedly one in which all traces of social difference disappear with the achievement of social privilege and financial success. Canadians, by contrast, are seen to have no such aspirations and to embrace no such fantasy of assimilation; indeed, all Canadians are valued regardless (or precisely because) of the socio-cultural differences they are encouraged to maintain. But by invoking these essential qualities, Simonetti reinforces the myth of essential difference. She suggests that these two series do not appeal to viewers cross-culturally, yet *Degrassi* was seen across the U.S., despite the fact it aired exclusively on PBS, and was used in many classrooms as an educational tool. *90210* aired in Canada for ten years, and many people I know watched it religiously (including me). Simonetti suggests that the series' "glamorous lifestyles tend to irk *Canadians*,"[46] but E. Graham McKinley, in her pioneering 1997 study of *90210* and the construction of (American) viewer communities through talk about television, found that "most viewers called the characters' lifestyle, with its extreme wealth, 'unrealistic.'"[47] McKinley notes, however, that while her interviewees accepted and even enjoyed this unrealistic glamour, they could not tolerate when the characters and storylines were presented or were resolved unrealistically. Interestingly, it is this insistence on narrative closure, no matter how unlikely, that Simonetti sees as being intrinsic to the show's American dream ethos and which made it, in theory, popular with American but not Canadian teens.

That is not to say that differences between being American and being Canadian do not exist, but that the differences are cultural constructions, ones that are slippery and constantly changing. I agree that the way that *Degrassi* and *90210* complete their story arcs is very different. Censorship in the U.S. is far more pervasive than in Canada and is dealt with by, for instance, earmarking only minor or transient characters for negative experiences, or by removing the need for central characters to deal with the real potential consequences of their actions.[48] So while Brenda avoids dealing with her potential pregnancy, Spike, Erica (Angela Deiseach) and Tessa (Kristen Bourne) each experience not only the moment of crisis but all the moments after it as well. Likewise, on *90210* Donna (Tori Spelling) becomes extremely angry at her mother's racist attitudes towards her friend D'Shawn (Cress Williams, who is African American), but on *Degrassi*, Michelle actually has a relationship with BLT, and leaves home rather than accept her father's racist views. The narrative strategies the series deploy are different. However, as Rebecca Haines points out in "That White Girl from *That Show*" in this volume, Canadian viewers did not easily accept Michelle and BLT's interracial relationship, and quite a few complaints about the story arc were received, belying the myth of Canadians' acceptance of social difference.

HAS THERE BEEN A CONVERGENCE?

Have things changed since 1994, the year Simonetti's article was published? Few successful teen series have followed *90210* in their specific focus on the wealthy and the glamorous, with the exception of the 2003 series *The O.C.*, which is also a prime-time soap but does not focus exclusively on teens. *Dawson's Creek* (1998–2003) and *Felicity* (1998–2002) were both dramatic series and focused on more "realistic" teens, at least in terms of class, yet had many of the same narrative issues Simonetti identifies in *90210*. Critically acclaimed series like *My So-Called Life* (1994–95) and *Freaks & Geeks* (1999–2000), both of which only lasted one season, were actually quite close to *DC* in terms of their characters and narratives, though there were many taboo topics they did not touch on. Several supernatural series, most notably *Buffy the Vampire Slayer* (1997–2003), have received enormous amounts of critical acclaim, much of it focused on taboo breaking, especially around issues of gender and sexuality. Buffy has also eschewed traditional narrative closure and simple moralizing; its characters often have to face the consequences of their actions. So perhaps there has been a kind of media convergence in both directions, with American series taking on more realistic issues (even if sometimes in supernatural guise) and Canadian series taking on a bit of their southern neighbour's glamour.

While there have been a variety of Canadian teen series produced since the early *Degrassi* series went off the air, the one I would like to mention here is *Degrassi: The Next Generation*. Changes in television production have allowed some of the visual differences that were so noticeable between *DC* and *90210* to fade. Thus, *TNG*'s cast is more generally upper middle class, attractive and well dressed. Narratively, *TNG* is somewhat more like *90210* in that it tends to have more storyline closure and its characters are more likely to find ways to conquer the odds on their way to the "Canadian" dream of fame and material success. While many discussions of *DC* have focused on its recognizable (inherent) Canadianness, viewers do not immediately identify *TNG* as Canadian, often believing that the series is filmed in Los Angeles or Florida.[49] Unlike *DC*, *TNG* airs on an American cable network. Viewers on both sides of the border connect to the show, its characters and the situations they find themselves in; American viewers have actually petitioned for The N to stop censoring the series before it airs in the U.S. Yet, despite the more conservative climate and the move towards

"American-style" narrative and production values, *TNG* has retained *DC's* critical perspective on social issues and continues to take risks in its story-telling. The U.S. censorship of the new series reflects different values within media cultures in both countries, but does it reflect inherent cultural differences between our two nations? According to Stephen Stohn:

> The British are very concerned about sex ... [But] they have this notion, the watershed notion that before a certain time you do not air anything about sex. Sex is very difficult because kids shouldn't be aware that it exists, I'm overstating the point, but *Degrassi* is problematic to them in a way that is not so problematic with the Americans or Canadians. Drug use is a very sensitive issue for Americans in particular, and not so much on the Canadian side and not so much in Britain.[50]

Does this reflect essential differences? If so, what does it mean that American audiences seems to so fully embrace the show as Canadians have embraced series like *Buffy* and *The O.C.*?

Perhaps television provides us with a reflection of the shifting, porous, multiple and never complete view of the myth upon which our nations were founded and which continue to be circulated. Simonetti's comments as she moves into the final pages of her article continue her essentialist trajectory. She suggests: "Unlike Americans, the future doesn't belong to Canadians."[51] What does this mean? Doubtless, she is correct in asserting that both series "bear the ideological imprint of their respective cultures,"[52] although I would replace "the" with "an"; there is no single, unified national ideology, just as there is no singular imaginary community of Americans or Canadians. We cannot assume we know how audiences understand any of these texts, nor can we presume Canadians and Americans will read them in particular, unified ways.

One thing is certain, despite their differences, *Degrassi* and *90210* were incredibly successful television series in their nations of origin, in that of their nearest neighbour and in a variety of other nations around the world. Since the two series first aired there have been many changes in media production, in the global market and in our understanding of nation and of television. The continuing differences between some of the narratives that can be produced for Canadian and American television suggests that there are national differences in media production, if not between "Canadian" and "American" as monolithic identities. Simonetti's argument that *DC* and *90210* represent essential differences between Americans and Canadians is problematic; it ignores the similarities between these two nations' peoples, and the marked differences between the different people within each nation. Her insistence that "*Beverly Hills 90210* celebrates the pursuit of dreams, persistence, individualism, hegemony, and materialism; *Degrassi Junior High* extols caution, tolerance, collectivism, multiculturalism, and egalitarianism," and that these somehow reflect the essential qualities of Americans and Canadians, does not do justice to either nation or either series.[53] As the top executives who have worked on *Degrassi* for the last twenty-five years insist, both stories are a necessary part of both our viewing cultures.

NOTES

1. Kate Aurthur, "Television's Most Persistent Taboo," *The New York Times,* 18 July 2004, 1. Retrieved July 22, 2004, from www.nytimes.com.

2. John McKay, "*Degrassi* Worries U.S. Teen Channel," *Montreal Gazette,* 20 July 2004, D1.

3. Rebecca Eckler, "Confessions of a Teen Drama Queen," *National Post,* 24 July 2004, TO3.

4. Marie-Claire Simonetti, "Teenage Truths and Tribulations Across Cultures: *Degrassi Junior High* and *Beverly Hills 90210*," *Journal of Popular Film and Television* (Spring 1994), 38.

5. Yan Moore, interview with author, Toronto, ON, May 2002. Although Yan is one of the creators of *TNG* and continues to write for the show, he is more of a consultant on the series, leaving the day-to-day writing to the new stable of young writers. The story about the American network's desire to centre *Degrassi* around a wise old woman, the "Bill Cosby character" (Stephen Stohn, interview with author, Toronto, ON, May 2002), was mentioned in almost every interview I conducted with Yan Moore, Linda Schuyler and Stephen Stohn.

6. Yan Moore, interview with author, Toronto, ON, February 2003.

7. Linda Schuyler, interview with author, Toronto, ON, February 2003.

8. Linda Schuyler, interview with author, Toronto, ON, May 2002.

9. Audrey Fisch, "Abortions in TV Land," *Salon.com* (March 8, 2000), 2. Retrieved July 20, 2004, from salon.com.

10. Michele Byers, "Race In/Out of the Classroom: *Degrassi (Junior High)* as Multicultural Context," in Charmaine Nelson and Camille Nelson, eds., *Racism, Eh? A Critical Inter-Disciplinary Anthology of Race in the Canadian Context* (Concord, ON: Captus Press, 2004), 298–315.

11. Moore, interview, May 2002.

12. Joan Nicks, "*Straight Up* and Youth Television: Navigating Dreams without Nationhood," in Joan Nicks and Jeanette Sloniowski, eds., *Slippery Pastimes: Reading the Popular in Canadian Culture* (Waterloo, ON: Wilfred Laurier University Press, 2002), 149. *Straight Up* (1996–98) was a gritty teen series created by documentarians Janis Lundman and Adrienne Mitchell. It was seen by some to look at a darker, more urban side of teen life than the *Degrassi* series.

13. Aniko Bodroghkozy argues that *Seinfeld* intentionally moves away from the politically invested series of the previous decades, focusing on "middle-class baby boomers obsessively involved in the mundanity of their everyday lives, thoroughly divorced from the larger social and political realm," its character "in no way touched by movements for social change" (243). But this creates a false historical dichotomy. Issues are not at the forefront of many *Seinfeld* episodes, but certainly they are there, including political issues like abortion, anti-Semitism, female contraception, marriage, circumcision and, more generally, what is considered appropriate social behaviour in a wide range of circumstances. See Aniko Bodroghkozy, *Groove Tube: Sixties Television and the Youth Rebellion* (Durham, NC: Duke University Press, 2001).

14. Glyn Davis and Kay Dickinson, *Teen TV: Genre, Consumption and Identity* (London: The British Film Institute, 2004), 5.

15. Nicks, "*Straight Up*," 149–150.

16. Anabela Carneiro, "A Teen Anthem for Television: *Straight Up*, The Next Wave for TV … Exploding the Teenage Myth," *TG Magazine* (1996), 2. Retrieved July 30, 2004, from www.tgmag.ca.

17. Stohn, interview, May 2002.

18. In *Teen TV*, Davis and Dickinson point out that the idea that "quality" is often central to "the academic championing of certain teen series" (7). Thus, comparisons of teen series often rest on a desire to laud one by pointing out its inherent differences from others.

19. Rachel Moseley, "The Teen Series," in Glen Creeber, ed., *The Television Genre Book* (London: The British Film Institute, 2001), 41–43.

20. Mary Jane Miller, "Canadian Television Programming in English." *The Museum of Broadcast Communications.* Retrieved September 22, 2003, from www.museum.tv.

21. Other series, including some earlier ones like *Room 222, Welcome Back Kotter* and *The Facts of Life*, focus on the school as a site of adolescent development. But teachers in these cases sometimes simply replace parents in generational conflicts with teens. Some series, such as the more recent *Boston Public* (2002–04), are more

interested in the lives of a group of attractive teachers than in the students they work with. In series like *DC* and *Saved by the Bell*, the school is a primary site of narrative action that centres on students.

22. Stephen Stohn and Linda Schuyler, interview with author, Toronto, ON, February 2003.

23. Moore, interview February 2003.

24. Moore, interview May 2002; Moore, interview February 2003.

25. Aniko Bodroghkozy, "As Canadian as Possible ...: Anglo-Canadian Popular Culture and the American Other," in Henry Jenkins, Tara McPherson and Jane Shattuc, eds., *Hop on Pop: The Politics and Pleasures of Popular Culture* (Durham, NC: Duke University Press, 2003), 572.

26. Simonetti, "Teenage Truths and Tribulations Across Cultures," 38.

27. Ibid., 39, 40.

28. Benedict Anderson, *Imagined Communities* (London: Verso, 1991).

29. Higson cited in Ira Wagman, "Wheat, Barley, Hops, Citizenship: Molson's 'I Am (Canadian)' Campaign and the Defense of Canadian National Identity through Advertising," *The Velvet Light Trap* (Fall 2002), 78. See Andrew Higson, "The Limiting Imagination of National Cinema," in Mette Hjort and Scott Mackenzie, eds., *Cinema & Nation* (New York: Routledge, 2000), 63–74.

30. Statistics Canada, "Visible Minority Population, By Age Group (2001 Census)." Retrieved April 2005 from www.statscan.ca; and U.S. Census Bureau, "Overview of Race and Hispanic Origin," *Census 2000 Briefs and Special Reports* (March 2001). Retrieved April 2004 from www.census.gov.

31. Simonetti, "Teenage Truths and Tribulations Across Cultures," 40.

32. Incidentally, the article suggests that Alex's parents die in a car crash, when it is actually Wheels's (Derek Wheeler) parents. Neil Hope played Wheels during all the *DC* years, as well as the character Robin "Griff" Griffin on *The Kids of Degrassi Street* (*KDS*). Alex Yankou (John Ioannou) was part of the *Degrassi* ensemble, though a more secondary character. John also played Pete Riley on *KDS*.

33. Simonetti, "Teenage Truths and Tribulations Across Cultures," 40.

34. See Rachel Mosley, "The Teen Series," in Glen Creeber, ed., *The Television Genre Book* (London: The British Film Institute, 2001), 41–42; John Tulloch, "Soap Operas and their Audiences," in Creeber, ed., *The Television Genre Book*, 55–56.

35. Simonetti, "Teenage Truths and Tribulations Across Cultures," 40.

36. Ibid.

37. Ibid.

38. Ibid.

39. Elizabeth D. Waiters, "*90210* in Black & White and Color: Inter-Ethnic friendship on Prime Time Television," in Murray Pomerance and John Sakeris, eds., *Pictures of a Generation on Hold: Selected Papers* (Toronto, ON: Media Studies Working Group, 1996), 205–224.

40. Simonetti, "Teenage Truths and Tribulations Across Cultures," 41.

41. The Canadian Radio-television and Telecommunications Commission, "A Broadcasting Policy Reflecting Canada's Linguistic and Cultural Diversity," Public Notice CRTC 1985–139 (Ottawa, July 4, 1985). Retrieved April 2004 from www. crtc.gc.ca.

42. This is also true of *TNG*, which has several non-white characters in its core cast. While at the start of season one, Ashley (Melissa McIntyre, who is white) starts out dating Jimmy (Aubrey Graham, who is Black), she eventually ends up with Craig (Jake Epstein, who is white), while Jimmy ends up with Hazel (Andrea Lewis, who is a woman of colour). Likewise, Liberty (Sarah Barrable-Tishauer, who is Black) spends almost three seasons mad about J.T. (Ryal Cooley, who is white) but ends up with Towerz (Travis Donegan, who is Black). While Emma (Miriam McDonald, who is white) begins dating Chris (Daniel Morris, who is Black) in season three, almost nothing is done with this storyline.

43. See my chapter "Have Times Changed?" in this volume.

44. Many American cable series, especially many airing on HBO, are considered groundbreaking in their portrayal of taboo subjects — and in many respects, they are. But even a series like *Sex and the City*, which features more sex than just about any series aired on television, is ambivalent in its discussions and representations of abortion and interracial relationships.

45. Simonetti, "Teenage Truths and Tribulations Across Cultures," 41.

46. Ibid. Emphasis added.

47. E. Graham McKinley, *Beverly Hills 90210: Television, Gender and Identity* (Philadelphia: University of Pennsylvania Press, 1997), 93.

48. Simonetti, "Teenage Truths and Tribulations Across Cultures," 41.

49. Stohn, interview May 2002.

50. Stohn and Schuyler, interview February 2003.

51. Simonetti, "Teenage Truths and Tribulations Across Cultures," 42.

52. Ibid.

53. Ibid.

SOMETIMES A FANTASY:
DEGRASSI AND TEENAGE
ENTERTAINMENT IN AMERICA

Tom Panarese

SINCE ORIGINALLY AIRING in the 1980s, the *Degrassi* series has gained a cult following. This is not just true in the series' native country of Canada but also in the over forty countries in which *Degrassi* has been shown. In the United States, the Public Broadcasting Service (PBS) aired *Degrassi Junior High* and *Degrassi High* at the same time they were being aired in Canada by the Canadian Broadcasting Corporation (CBC). However, while the series never really achieved the widespread popularity of other American television shows, its approach to portraying teenagers and the issues they encounter was ahead of its time.

Several factors have contributed to *Degrassi*'s overall lack of popularity with its American audience. Most of the series' American fans hail from the specific regions of the country where the shows have been available on PBS affiliates. Many have also watched *Degrassi Junior High* and *Degrassi High* as part of an educational curriculum, and that, together with their PBS presence, may have given the shows an unintended stigma. The programs lacked much of the escapism found in the teenage-oriented entertainment produced in the 1980s and 1990s, particularly American television shows that were popular among that audience. Still, those who were devoted viewers of both *Degrassi Junior High* and *Degrassi High* remain fans and have fond memories of the programs' stories and characters, as well as the lessons they taught. Many still enjoy *Degrassi* via the Internet, where along with many other 1980s creations, the shows have enjoyed a small renaissance. Some fans have rekindled their love for the original series by watching its latest incarnation, *Degrassi: The Next Generation*; however, the success of that show owes more to marketing to today's teenagers than to the nostalgia of fans for the original series.

The brainchild of Kit Hood and Linda Schuyler, *Degrassi* began in the late 1970s and early 1980s as *The Kids of Degrassi Street*, which did not have much exposure in the United States but was popular enough in Canada to warrant another series from the two producers. Taking many of the actors from *The Kids of Degrassi Street*, who were at the time the age of junior high-school students, Hood and Schuyler cast them in *Degrassi Junior High*. The program began airing in Canada on January 18, 1987, and was introduced to the United States through PBS six months later. *Degrassi High* followed the show's characters to high school and ran from 1989 to 1991. Boston-based WGBH co-produced the shows, and the station's logo appeared in the bumpers before and after each episode. Several major-market PBS stations aired the series, including WNET in New York, WTTW in Chicago, KQED in San Francisco, KCET in Los Angeles, as well as stations in Dallas-Fort Worth, Cleveland, Indianapolis, Milwaukee, Philadelphia and Detroit. Additionally, the programs were available to cable television customers near the Canadian border in cities such as Seattle and Buffalo, as they had access to CBC programming.[1]

However, as widely available as *Degrassi Junior High* and *Degrassi High* were, they never were extremely popular in the United States. Shown during prime-time after-school viewing hours in some cases, the shows faced strong competition from other regional and local programming, as well as from cable television. For example, in the New York/New Jersey area, WNET aired back-to-back episodes of *Degrassi Junior High* and *Degrassi High* at 5:00 and 5:30 p.m. after the popular kids game show *Where in the World Is Carmen San Diego?* for much of their original run, eventually moving the shows to Sunday mornings. It also showcased each of the shows during its pledge drives. PBS would air an episode and give a behind-the-scenes look at that show's stars and characters before pitching, "If you'd like to see more of Joey Jeremiah, call in your pledge." However, local television stations, such as Fox-affiliate WNYW and then-independent WPIX, aired reruns of popular sitcoms from 5:00 to 8:00 p.m.[2]

For example, WPIX aired a late-afternoon and early-evening lineup that provided a smooth transition from children's to adult programming by following a two-hour Disney cartoon showcase with episodes of teen-oriented programs such as *Saved by the Bell, Beverly Hills 90210* and the teen soap opera *Swan's Crossing*. Beginning at 6:00 p.m., the station aired reruns of a variety of classic and contemporary shows. Over the years, these included *Star Trek, The Twilight Zone, The Wonder Years, Charles in Charge, Full House, Family Matters, Happy Days* and *Cheers*. Many of these shows remain popular and accessible through cable reruns — Nick at Nite and TV Land currently own the broadcasting rights to *Happy Days, Cheers* and *Charles in Charge*; TBS airs *Saved by the Bell* every morning; and *Beverly Hills 90210* is an FX mainstay. Meanwhile, *Degrassi Junior High* and *Degrassi High* have all but disappeared from American airwaves.

Degrassi: The Next Generation (*TNG*), however, has fared better as part of tween-oriented The N, where it is extremely popular.[3] AAC Kids™, the international distributor for *TNG*, has touted the show's success both in Canada and abroad, saying, "*Degrassi: The Next Generation* has proved a huge ratings winner for CTV in Canada, where it was the #1 Canadian drama in 2001, currently the most popular show on Noggin in the U.S., and ABC in Australia — where it was the number one show in the core tween demo."[4] This tween demographic has proven to be very valuable over the past few years because of its purchasing power. Market researcher Packaged Facts has conducted studies of tweens' buying power and their subsequent value to advertisers, and has shown that tweens have the potential to spend $35 billion per year.[5] As a result, cable channels such as The N have cultivated programming that speaks directly to this demographic. Sarah Tomassi Lindman, vice-president of programming and production for The N, says *TNG* appeals to tweens because of the same things that were considered valuable aspects of the original *Degrassi* series. For instance, "The great thing with *Degrassi* is that the casting is all age specific, so 13-year-olds play 13-year-olds. Shows like this are why we think of The N as a place for kids to graduate to when they're ready to move on to the next stage."[6] A recent *Entertainment Weekly* article notes that "the Canadian high school drama *Degrassi: The Next Generation* built a rabid stateside following with what creator Linda Schuyler calls its 'brutal honesty.'"[7]

EDUCATION VERSUS POPULARITY

When *Degrassi Junior High* and *Degrassi High* originally aired in the U.S., there was no pretense of ad revenue-based programming, as PBS did and continues to air all of its shows commercial free, relying on member support, grants and fundraising for revenue. PBS's adult programming appeals to a more sophisticated audience — many of its prime-time shows feature in-depth news coverage, the fine arts or science. Its children's programming is educational. Shows such as *Sesame Street, Mr. Rogers' Neighborhood, 3-2-1 Contact* and *The Electric Company* specialize in teaching kids both basic academic and social lessons. PBS's presence in the lives of teenagers was relatively unheard of in the 1980s, and as part of its educational mandate, the network created supplemental materials that were made available for classroom learning. Included within these materials were discussion and activity guides for teachers, program description fact sheets and a student newspaper. According to WGBH editorial content manager Sonja Lattimore, the teacher guides, which were available for each season of *Degrassi Junior High* and *Degrassi High*, featured a program synopsis for each episode, discussion questions, suggested activities, recommended reading and additional resources.[8] The aim was to use the show to teach the topics focused on in individual episodes, with the materials guiding in-class discussion or, in the case of the student newspapers, connecting directly to teens. Each student newspaper consisted of sixteen pages of articles that also tied into the episodes' topics (dating, sex, AIDS and so on) and included details and background information on the show as well as trivia quizzes and other games.

Additionally, in-depth materials called the "*Degrassi* Health Curriculum" were produced for educators who were using the series as an introduction to a more in-depth discussion of teen issues. For instance, the curriculum included background information on topics such as alcoholism, relationships, AIDS, dating abuse, sexual orientation and teen pregnancy. They provided student lessons, reading lists and resources for students and their teachers.[9] These educational aspects were touted as the show's strong point and were used in stateside marketing — for instance, there was a supplement that ran in the *Seattle Times* and in other newspapers that had an approach similar to the student newspaper. However, even though *Degrassi* served as a fine example of how PBS reached an adolescent audience, it struggled to keep an audience that had grown out of *Sesame Street* but wasn't quite ready for *Masterpiece Theater*. This dilemma was shared by much of the industry, including major networks and cable channels. What was popular among a teenage audience changed as the audience itself grew and abandoned the mainstays of its childhood for television shows that were "more grown up." For example, the eight-year-olds of the 1980s who watched Nickelodeon were obviously not watching the channel by the 1990s; they had moved on to MTV.

But even MTV, which is often cited as a paragon of youth culture, has not been immune to the dynamic youth market. For example, during the mid-1990s, its ratings dipped and the channel began to lose viewers because, while the market had matured, the channel had not. As a result, MTV conducted enormous market research and repositioned itself to appeal to a fresh group of teenagers as opposed to those who had been teenagers and were now abandoning the channel.[10] PBS has historically had this problem. While it did attempt to bridge its demographic gap with programs such as *Degrassi Junior High* and *Degrassi High*, the 1998 Roper Youth Report illustrates that there was an enormous drop-off of PBS viewing among children, despite statistics proving that children who watched PBS throughout their youth were more educated:

> This year, 34% of the sample indicated having viewed PBS in the week prior to being interviewed. This percentage is highest among children ages 6 and 7: almost six in 10 (57%) had watched PBS in the past week. Viewing of PBS declines among 8 to 12 year-olds (37%) and among 13 to 17 year-olds (21%) although a sizeable portion continue to watch public television throughout their youth.[11]

In the years following the Roper Report, PBS aired some programs designed for teenagers, including the entire reality series *American High*. The Emmy award-winning show, which had aired on Fox before being cancelled after four episodes, followed the real lives of several students at Highland Park High School in Highland Park, Illinois. However, PBS was still stuck with the stigma of being "educational," and therefore "uncool," something *Degrassi* cast member Darrin Brown acknowledged: "In Canada, *Degrassi* was a prime time show, but in the United States it was not as recognized. Possibly because of the stigma associated with American public television." However, he does go on to note that in certain areas such as Chicago, Boston and Miami the show did have a strong following.[12] Although PBS's educational value was praised by the Roper Report, which noted that children who were eight to seventeen years old and watched PBS were more likely to be interested in science, crafts, cooking and computers, it obviously hurt *Degrassi Junior High*'s and *Degrassi High*'s potential to become enormously popular in the United States, because PBS was considered "uncool."

"Cool" is the elusive goal for many teen advertisers. As pointed out in "The Merchants of Cool," a special report on PBS's series *Frontline*, advertising recognizes the enourmous potential of the teenage and tween market. Rachel Dretzin, one of the special's producers, notes that teenagers, especially in the last decade or so, have become the key market for advertisers because of their number (there are approximately 33 million teenagers in the United States), their wealth (they spend in the range of $100 billion each year) and their access to media (75 percent have a television in their bedroom). These facts add up to marketability. "Despite a lifetime of bombardment," Dretzin says, "teens are still less inured, and more plugged in [to] marketing messages through the media than any other demographic."[13] The irony of that marketability, however, is that teenagers do not pay as much attention to brand names as might be expected. They respond, instead, to "cool" and, as a result, boutique consulting companies have been established for the sole purpose of reading this market.

Dee Dee Gordon and her company, Look Look, are a team of corporate spies, mostly made of former "cool" kids, who study adolescents in order to predict what can be sold to them. "We look for kids who are ahead of the pack and influence what other kids do," she notes. "We look for the 20% that are gonna influence the other 80%."[14] This philosophy is predicated on the idea that if a company can discover a trend or subculture while it is still underground, they can be the first to bring it to market. Of course, being that the market is enormously dynamic, once marketers discover "cool" and bring it to the mainstream, it stops being "cool." So, in an attempt to combat this paradox, marketers, even though they are considered "uncool" by their targets, create stereotypical images that are used to sell various products such as clothing, music, movies and soft drinks to American teens and tweens. For example, the female image, called the "midriff" and the male image known as "the mook" are basic teenage stereotypes. The "midriff" is a sophisticated, almost sexualized girl who appeals to the fact that girls often mature faster than boys. The "mook" is the typical adolescent boy — more prone to childish behaviour and usually oblivious to the attitudes and interests of his female counterparts.[15] *Degrassi: The Next Generation* and its initial popularity with American audiences reflect this marketing strategy.

One of *TNG's* main characters, Emma Nelson (Miriam McDonald), is a typical midriff. The daughter of original *Degrassi* character Spike (Amanda Stepto) who became pregnant during the second season of *Degrassi Junior High*, Emma is a typical eye-rolling fourteen-year-old girl. In the show's fall 2001 premiere episode "Mother and Child Reunion," she shows how weary she is of immature boys such as J.T. (Ryan Cooley) and Toby (Jake Goldsbie) by becoming involved with Jordan, a sixteen-year-old boy she met over the Internet. "Girls are so much more mature than boys," she says. "That's why I like Jordan. I've never had a boyfriend so smart, so thoughtful." Jordan, however, turns out to be a pedophile who is appealing to "midriff" characteristics, and he kidnaps her at a Toronto hotel. Her friends suspect something is wrong, and once they discover the truth, they tell Spike, who heads with the police to the hotel. Emma, thankfully, is rescued before she can be harmed.

MARKETING THE CONTENT

"Mother and Child Reunion" is an updated version of the "don't always trust strangers" lesson that was a moral of the *Degrassi Junior High* episode "Taking Off," where the character Wheels (Neil Hope) is picked up while hitchhiking and nearly sexually assaulted. The lessons for *Degrassi: The Next Generation* (*TNG*) have been updated to reflect the times without being watered down. The show's production, however, is different — *Degrassi Junior High* and *Degrassi High* were shot on location in the greater Toronto area, but *TNG* is shot in a studio and on a backlot and the set décor is purposely more stylish. For example, the Nelsons' house, one of the primary sets, is painted in brighter colours, a contrast to the many darker sets of *Degrassi Junior High* and *Degrassi High*. While interior decorating tastes may have changed since 1987, the producers may have been taking a style note from *Saved by the Bell*, which purposely created bright sets because it aired Saturday mornings against other networks' cartoons.[16] While *Saved by the Bell* is often ridiculed for its lack of realism, it was stylish and did contain enough of the elusive "cool" element to run for nearly a decade and to spawn an entire genre of Saturday-morning sitcoms. During the 1990s, NBC gradually replaced its Saturday-morning cartoon programming with a block of teen-oriented sitcoms it called "T-NBC." *Saved by the Bell* (and its own "next-generation" show *Saved by the Bell: The New Class*), *California Dreams, City High, Running the Halls, Just Deal* and *Hang Time* were among the offerings that began to air in 1993. Currently, NBC's Saturday-morning programming features a mix of animated and live-action shows aimed at both children and teenagers.

The classic *Degrassi* series' realism was valued by many of its fans, including Shelby Wilson of Memphis, Tennessee, who says, "Seventh-grade students can identify with most every episode and have some excellent discussions. They really seem to gain insight into how they act and especially into how others act because every character on *Degrassi* is someone they know (usually themselves)."[17] LeJarie Battieste of Los Angeles, citing Spike's pregnancy storyline, mentions the lessons that *Degrassi Junior High* taught through the show's realistic portrayals of teenage situations. "I basically learned that as a young kid you aren't alone," she says. "I came from a small school where young girls were already having babies so I knew a lot about that already but I was so pleasantly surprised to see it on *Degrassi* because at that time and even now there were no TV shows dealing with teenage pregnancy and interracial dating."[18] The programs' focus on topic such as sex, drugs, dating, work and abuse reflects the creators' philosophy: "Real kids talking to real kids from the heart."[19] Epitome Pictures, *TNG*'s production company, reiterates this on its Web site:

> It is easy to forget that programs like *Degrassi*, which seem relatively tame to-day, explored teen Canadian issues in a realistic and non-judgmental manner never before attempted in television. Our broadcast partners, CBC and PBS, also deserve credit for having faith in what was then a new method of story-telling, and putting the series in prime-time.[20]

GENERATION X AND THE TEEN FILM

The generation of teenagers that comprised *Degrassi Junior High* and *Degrassi High*'s core audience came of age in the 1980s, and their reluctance to readily bow to marketing concepts and trends brought about the label

"Generation X." The name itself comes from the title of a novel by Douglas Coupland. In fact, one of the chapters of Coupland's novel is titled "I Am Not a Target Market."[21] Ironically, while it would seem that Generation X would be drawn to entertainment that depicted teenage life in a less-stylized, more-pessimistic manner, much of America's landmark teen entertainment of the 1980s and early 1990s had an element of what was "cool."

Films such as *Fast Times at Ridgemont High*, *Sixteen Candles* and *The Breakfast Club* touched teenagers on an emotional level and presented very deep storylines, but also had slick soundtracks and good-looking casts. In *Fast Times*, for example, Stacey Hamilton (Jennifer Jason Leigh) has an abortion; however, for many, the most memorable parts of the movie are Linda's (Phoebe Cates) nude scene and the antics of the stoned surfer character Jeff Spicoli (Sean Penn).[22] Similarly, while John Hughes directed several brilliant films that touched teenagers on a very personal level, they had a slick, stylish packaging. For instance, *Sixteen Candles*, Hughes's directorial debut, combines honest pubescent angst with slapstick comedy and a pop-song-laden soundtrack. The film also marked the first time that Hughes cast Molly Ringwald, and her performances in three of his films resonated with audiences. Jonathan Bernstein sums up the actress in his book *Pretty in Pink: The Golden Age of Teenage Movies*:

> How does Molly Ringwald express mortification? Let me count the ways. The rolling of the eyes. The chewing of the lips. The appalled exhalation. The jaw dropping in disbelief. The flinching. The lowering of the head signifying a wish to be swallowed up by the earth.[23]

Ringwald's performances are very often genuine portrayals of the expression and behaviour of teenage girls. In *Sixteen Candles*, she plays an awkward teen who is so unnoticed that her own family forgets her sixteenth birthday, leading to a comedy of errors and her constant state of mortification. In *The Breakfast Club*, Ringwald's character, Claire, is the prissy, popular prom queen who is stuck in detention on a Saturday with four other students. Hughes's script eschews the slapstick prominent in *Sixteen Candles* and leans towards melodrama. The characters begin the day unfamiliar with one another, having come from different cliques; however, by the end of the film, they expose themselves via confessional monologues. The "geek" of the group, played by Anthony Michael Hall, sums up the film's overall message at its end in his essay to Mr. Vernon, the assistant principal who lords over them:

Dear Mr. Vernon: We accept the fact that we had to sacrifice a whole Saturday in detention for whatever it is we did wrong, but we think you're crazy for making us write an essay telling you who we think we are. You see us as you want to see us: in the simplest terms, in the most convenient definitions. But what we found out is that each one of us is a brain, and an athlete, and a basket case, a princess, and a criminal. Does that answer your question? Sincerely yours, The Breakfast Club.[24]

But as much as the characters touch the audience, there is still a sheen of style and "cool" about them that shows that Hughes is very aware of the conventions of Hollywood. The film's climax has the main characters sitting in a circle on the floor of the high-school library pouring their hearts out. At the end of this string of confessionals is Alison's (Ally Sheedy) confession that she is in detention that day because she "had nothing better to do."[25] The characters then erupt in laughter, which leads to an extended dance montage, which suggests that while the students are struggling to deal with adult problems, they are still kids. It also helps set up a "happy" ending. After the dancing subsides, Alison, who has been eyeing Andy (Emilio Estevez) throughout much of the day, is taken by Claire to a back room for a last-minute make-over. When she emerges, she goes from "ugly" — oversized sweater covering her clothes, face hidden behind a mop of hair — to "beautiful." Bernstein considers this particular moment to be heartbreaking; it is also indicative of how often entertainment for American teenagers straddles harsh reality and escapist fantasy. "The remaking of Alison stands as *The Breakfast Club*'s biggest blunder," he notes. "Before, she was a unique and unnerving character. After, she was just another simpering, pretty high-school girl with the hots for a jock. You may think you hate Courtney Love but imagine how cheated you'd feel if she cleaned up her act."[26]

Hughes's films mixed honest storytelling with the flash and style of 1980s youth culture and spawned an entire genre of imitators; however, that genre's appeal did not last long. By the late 1980s, teen films were being made in lesser number and those that were did not fare well at the box office.[27] In fact, the most significant late-1980s teen film is decidedly anti-Hughes. Written by Daniel Waters and directed by Michael Lehmann, *Heathers* presents the social structure of a suburban high school with the same stark comparisons as *The Breakfast Club*, but takes the inter-clique conflict to satirical heights by making it literally a matter of life and death.

Veronica Sawyer (Winona Ryder) is the "unofficial" fourth member of the most powerful clique at Westerburg High, the Heathers — a trio of girls with the same name who do not discriminate in their wish to make everyone else feel smaller than they are. Early in the film, Veronica is conflicted by her own popularity (especially because it is by proxy — she is friends with the three girls), but keeps any thoughts of deviating from the orders of best friend Heather Chandler (Kim Walker), to herself.

That is, until newcomer rebel character Jason, "J.D." Dean (Christian Slater), comes to Westerburg. The two become romantically involved and shortly after send Heather Chandler to her death by tricking her into drinking a mug full of drain cleaner. This is the first of three killings, all of which are made to look like suicides. At first, Veronica is empowered by how she and J.D. take down Heather Chandler, as well as star football players Kurt and Ram. However, she begins to regret her actions as the supposed suicides become a media spectacle and these reprehensible characters become martyrs. Further problematic is her moral dilemma — killing, even if there is a point to be proven or revenge to be had, is wrong. While J.D. is an obvious psychotic who finds no problem with his actions, Veronica eventually sees that he is as poisonous as the Heathers and turns on him. *Heathers* concludes with her thwarting his grand scheme to blow up the school (instead, he straps the bomb to his chest and commits suicide). This climax follows a rant from Veronica's mother that is almost a direct response to The Breakfast Club's letter to Mr. Vernon. Veronica, annoyed at how the media has turned teen suicide into the topic du jour, laments, "All we want is to be treated like human beings." Her mother responds:

> Treated like human beings? Is that what you said, Ms. Voice of a Generation? How do you think adults act with other adults? Do you think it's just like a game of doubles tennis? When teenagers complain that they want to be treated like human beings, it's usually because they are being treated like human beings.[28]

Bernstein agrees with the assessment that the film, though an over-the-top satire (the symbolism of the characters' clothes is obvious — the Heathers wear primary colours while Veronica and J.D. are often clad in black), is a gritty shot at Hughes, especially at the happy endings his films have. "Released in 1989 ... it stands as an unanswerable Last Word," he notes. "*Heathers*, in fact, killed the genre that inspired it stone dead."[29]

FANTASY ON TEEN TV

Television geared for teenagers during the same era underwent a similar struggle — the most popular teenage shows have been sitcoms and dramas with photogenic casts and an emphasis on style over substance. Further complicating matters is the need to adhere to the conventions of story-telling found in sitcoms and one-hour dramas. *Saved by the Bell*, which premiered on NBC in the late 1980s, is the archetype of American teen television shows.[30] The students of Bayside High School are clean-cut and face problems that are solved within each half-hour episode. Many of the topics covered were common teen problems, but whereas *Degrassi Junior High* had an episode about teen pregnancy that had a lasting impact on one of its characters, when *Saved by the Bell* handled an issue, there was little lasting impact on any of its characters. Its most famous episode is one of its few attempts to deal with a serious issue: drug addiction. However, instead of a character having problems with alcohol, marijuana or cocaine, Jessie Spano (Elizabeth Berkley) becomes addicted to caffeine pills.[31] Her particular problem is solved by the end of the episode and is only mentioned once again — in a clip show.[32]

On the wildly successful Fox series *Beverly Hills 90210*, important issues are handled during the sixty-minute timeframe, but there are also long-running storylines. For instance, an early episode features Brenda Walsh (Shannen Doherty) finding a lump in her breast. Within sixty minutes, she has a biopsy and gets the results (it is benign). However, the story also serves to enforce the show's main storyline — Brenda's relationship with "rebel" character Dylan McKay (Luke Perry). Some of the characters do have long-term problems; however, the solutions are often contrived. One of the show's main characters, Donna Martin (Tori Spelling), has a learning disorder, but is able to overcome this problem and fulfill West Beverly Hills High's graduation requirements. However, she is inebriated at the senior prom and barred from graduating. Instead of following through on Donna's actions by showing their consequences, the storyline wraps up within two episodes, as Brandon Walsh (Jason Priestley) leads a massive protest and is able to convince the school board to let Donna graduate.

These are just a few examples of some of the issues that *Beverly Hills 90210* dealt with over the course of its decade-long run. Its spot in prime time allowed it to touch on issues that were heavier than *Saved By the Bell*'s caffeine pill problem. *Beverly Hills 90210* was the most popular teen show in the 1990s because it was a soap opera that utilized production elements its executive producer, Aaron Spelling, is famous for — flashy sets, stylish characters and situations that could only happen in Beverly Hills. In fact, that show was so much of a fantasy that most of the cast was well beyond their teen years when it began airing. The world of West Beverly Hills High School could be traumatic, but its traumas were less real than those faced by the middle-class teenagers of *Degrassi Junior High* and *Degrassi High* and more in tune to the wealthy adult trauma of *Dynasty*. On *Degrassi Junior High*, Wheels's parents were killed by a drunk driver; on *Beverly Hills 90210*, Dylan McKay's father was murdered because he was about to testify against some powerful men he once worked for. But the creators of both television shows were well aware of *Beverly Hills 90210*'s emphasis on style. As Kit Hood notes:

> I truly hate it when people compare *90210* to *Degrassi*. We had entirely different concepts and appealed to different audiences. Aaron Spelling knew how to market *90210*. Linda [Schuyler] and I were not experienced in marketing. Our emphasis was providing moralistic integrity. The *Degrassi* series was never about making money. Toronto is not Hollywood, we do not have the same mentality or resources.[33]

That is not to say that all American television programs featuring teens have been stylized escapist fantasies. Two of the most notable teenage shows of the 1990s were NBC's *Freaks & Geeks* and ABC's *My So-Called Life*. *Freaks & Geeks*, which aired during the 1999–2000 television season, was a critically acclaimed look at life at a high school in 1980. Premiering in a season rife with teen shows and 1980s nostalgia, *Freaks & Geeks* had both these elements to its advantage; however, it was cancelled before all seventeen episodes could be aired. *Freaks & Geeks* centred on the two children of the Weir family: intelligent sixteen-year-old Lindsay (Linda Cardellini), who begins hanging out with burn-outs, and puny Sam (John Francis Daley), a freshman who is constantly picked on while forever longing for a date with a pretty cheerleader. The program tried to appeal to teenagers, as well as to the twenty- and thirty-somethings who had been teenagers in the 1980s.[34] But instead of relying solely on nostalgia to tell its stories, *Freaks & Geeks* had complex stories showing its characters facing consequences for their actions. In the first episode, Lindsay runs afoul of her guidance counsellor when he catches her cutting class; while he hands out an official school punishment, the real consequence is how this contributes to her deteriorating relationship with her parents. Mr. Weir (Joe Flaherty) is watching his brainy, well-behaved daughter go down a path that is completely different from what he planned, and like most parents confronting their teenagers, can do nothing but lecture and yell.

Meanwhile, Sam and his friends Neal (Samm Levine) and Bill (Martin Starr) face what is a timeless problem for scrawny, puny and otherwise awkward ninth graders: jocks and bullies. One of the funnier moments of the series occurs when the boys are forced to shower in gym class. After much protest, Sam relents. On his way to the shower, he is confronted by one of the class bullies, who takes Sam's towel and pushes him into an empty hallway. Sam, now naked, walks quickly to his locker to get his extra pair of shorts, but just then, the bell rings and he ends up streaking the school. Another hallmark of the show was its realistic depiction of a high-school crush. From the show's first moments, the audience knows that Sam would do anything to go out with Cindy Sanders (Natasha Melnick), a pretty cheerleader. She is nice to him, but there does not seem to be any hope — until the episode titled "Smooching and Mooching," in which Cindy decides that she wants to go out with Sam and tells Bill to ask Sam to invite her to a party. At the party, the two make out in a dark bedroom. Had this been *Beverly Hills 90210*, Sam would have quickly become accepted in all cool circles and his geek friends would have fallen by the wayside and been written out of the show, much like David Silver's (Brian Austin Green) friend Scott (Doug Emerson), who became so unnecessary after David became popular and began dating Donna that the producers killed him off in the second season. Instead, Sam is absolutely miserable while dating Cindy because they have nothing in common — he does not enjoy the company of jocks and cheerleaders. So, he breaks up with her.

Freaks & Geeks did not sugarcoat its stories, which also contributed to its cancellation. An anonymous posting on the Web site *Jump the Shark*,[35] while making a derisive comment about *Freaks & Geeks*, sums up the American television viewing experience well, when the author says:

> You see everyone thinks for him or herself of dreams of success not failure. People dream of being rich, not poor. People dream of being handsome and pretty not ugly and homely. The general public out there wasn't willing to watch a TV show about three young kids being social outcasts and nerds who

would lose a great deal of the time. For some this would bring back bad memories of their own awkward youth. *Freaks & Geeks* in other words wouldn't be too pleasant to watch. One poster said that the execs who cancelled *Freaks & Geeks* were the types that weren't freaks or geeks in high school, the types who threw bottles at the kids who hung out at Radio Shack, the types who considered and made these kids the source of comedic entertainment for their own cool crowd. Point well taken! That is exactly why *Freaks & Geeks* also failed, does anyone one think that the nation at large should now laugh at these three young nerds now that this "cool crowd" is the country itself? Does anyone think that people who are nerds, or geeks, or just socially slow to develop something to laugh at? Entertainment? It is not.[36]

Similarly, ABC's critically acclaimed program, *My So-Called Life*, which aired during the 1994–1995 season, was an honest look at the experiences of fifteen-year-old Angela Chase (Claire Danes). Angela, like *Freaks & Geeks*'s Lindsay Weir, is a "good" girl who has begun hanging out with someone who her parents disapprove of — the unpredictable Rayanne Graff (A.J. Langer). Angela is a very real character for the audience, mainly because at the time, Claire Danes was the same age as her character and well-versed in the typical expressions of exasperation and embarrassment of a fifteen-year-old girl (in fact, Danes was often compared with Molly Ringwald).

A Return to Reality

My So-Called Life is the one American television program that has come closest to capturing the realism of the classic *Degrassi* series. There are differences in the way the shows present their stories — Angela's parents are significant to her stories and often have plots that parallel their daughter's, and Angela provides voice-overs that serve as an inner monologue. But much like *Degrassi Junior High* and *Degrassi High*, *My So-Called Life* features characters making decisions and learning lessons that do not disappear after the end credits. Many of the choices the main characters make have long-lasting effects on both who they are and how strong their relationships are with other characters. Angela is in constant conflict with her mother and is beginning to doubt the integrity of her father, who she at one point catches giving the brush-off to another woman. Had the series been allowed to continue beyond its nineteen-episode run, the Chases' marriage may have fallen apart, which is one of the most traumatic ways for a teenager to realize her parents are fallible.

Another important storyline centres on Rayanne's drinking problem. The child of divorced parents, she lives with her often-absent mother. Rayanne's upbringing is the complete opposite of Angela's, and her uninhibited way of living is appealing, especially considering Angela has been brought up in a very stable nuclear family. However, Rayanne's appeal slowly loses its luster. At her birthday party, she mixes drugs and alcohol, and it's not until Angela desperately calls her mom that she's saved. After that incident, Rayanne attends counselling and Angela's interaction with her is awkward, especially as Angela begins seeing Jordan Catalano (Jared Leto). In the episode titled "Betrayal," which takes place seven episodes after Rayanne's overdose and the end of Angela and Jordan's relationship, an off-the-wagon Rayanne sleeps with Jordan. Her friendship with Angela is therefore dealt a fatal blow, and the fallout reveals that while Angela openly admired how free Rayanne's life was, Rayanne admired her friend's sheltered home life. The girls' mutual friend, Rickie (Wilson Cruz), explains this to Angela towards the end of the episode: "I mean, face it … she's always partly wanted to be you. And in a way, I think this was her screwed up way of, for one night, kind of pretending she was you."[37]

Complex relationships often played out in a similar fashion on *Degrassi High*. Since the show was a true ensemble of characters (whereas *My So-Called Life*, even though it had a considerable supporting cast, still focused on Angela), when a character dealt with an issue or a trauma, the effect was not only immediate but also far-reaching. In the two-part episode "A New Start," Erica (Angela Deiseach), having lost her virginity to someone she met while working as a summer camp counsellor, discovers she is pregnant. When Erica confides to her twin sister, Heather (Maureen Deiseach), that she thinks she may be pregnant and is considering abortion, they have the following exchange:

Heather: "But abortion's wrong. You remember what the minister says. How do you think mom and dad would feel? I thought you were anti-abortion."

Erica: "Well, I am."

Heather: "You have to talk about it. It's horrible to think of those babies dying every day in the killing centers."

Later in the episode, Erica begins a discussion about the topic in class (although she does not reveal her predicament), and an argument among the students ensues, with several giving contrasting views on abortion. Shortly thereafter she decides to have the abortion, and even though she is vehemently against the choice her sister has made, Heather accompanies her sister to the clinic at the end of the episode's second part. Much like Rayanne Graff's near-overdose, Erica's abortion has a lasting effect not only on Erica but also on a few of the characters surrounding her.

In "Everybody Wants Something" (three episodes later), Erica is confronted by and gets into a fight with Liz (Cathy Keenan) because of the abortion. Liz is vehemently against abortion (as it was almost her fate; her father did not want her mother to have her). This ideological difference and the subsequent fight strains Heather and Erica's friendship with Liz. Much later in the season, in "Natural Attraction," Erica begins dating again and this causes Heather to fear her sister will have another abortion, and she is so disturbed that she has nightmares. When she finds Erica and her new boyfriend making out at a school dance, she launches into a tirade:

> This is how it began with Jason! You're going to do it again, aren't you? Just like the summer! You don't care what happens! You don't care what you did! Everything is you, you, you! You don't care how I feel!

When she returns home later that night, Erica talks to her sister about the tirade and the abortion. Heather's anxiety was caused out of concern for her sister and because she violated her personal beliefs when she accompanied Erica to the abortion clinic. She cries about having believed she helped murder a child, and while Erica does argue with her, she also offers to help, suggesting Heather see the counsellor she has been seeing ever since the abortion. By spanning most of the season and touching several characters personally, a very controversial and complex issue was humanized without being patronizing, and it also served as a catalyst in the evolving relationship between the sisters.

In the real world, however, the storyline's complexities were almost lost among the controversy of the topic. When "A New Start, Part Two" originally aired in Canada in 1989, the episode concluded with Heather and Erica going to an abortion clinic and being confronted with a crowd of anti-abortion protesters. The freeze-frame ending the episode featured Erica entering the building while a protester held up a plastic model of a fetus. PBS, however, believed that the image was too graphic for American audiences. Abortion was rarely broached on network television and never in regard to adolescents. Knowing they were dealing with a highly controversial subject, the show's writers clearly presented both sides of the debate. The episode's ending was truncated, and when "A New Start, Part Two" aired on PBS in 1989, it ended with a freeze-frame close-up of the sisters' faces as they approached the clinic. PBS was criticized for weakening the episode, despite keeping most of the subject matter intact. The CBC seemed to show more trust in the program's audience being able to draw their own conclusions from an open-ended episode.[38] Some American fans appreciate the open-ended nature of the show's episodes. "What I liked about *Degrassi*," says Jennifer Smothers, who watched the show growing up in Michigan, "was that it always showed both sides of an issue. It really made us think about every angle and it never really gave easy answers."[39]

In addition to cutting the end of "A New Start, Part Two," PBS edited the *Degrassi* finale, the two-hour movie *School's Out*, cutting the "foul" language used in the movie's climactic scene, as well as some of the sexual content throughout the movie. This sort of editing has not been isolated to *Degrassi* on PBS. *Freaks & Geeks*, *My So-Called Life* and *Degrassi: The Next Generation* have all been victims of editing that is akin to censorship. In 1999, *My So-Called Life* aired on cable television's Fox Family Channel and several scenes depicting suggestive dialogue or situations — even those concerning sex between consenting married adults — were cut from the rerun episodes. In 2001, the channel (now ABC Family) aired all seventeen episodes of *Freaks & Geeks* but heavily edited the show because of references to drug use and some language (words such as "ass" and "bitch," which are allowed on network television, were censored). *TNG* is often edited and recut before broadcast on The N. In 2004, the network refused to air the two-part episode "Accidents Will Happen," in which Manny (Cassie Steele) becomes pregnant and decides to have an abortion. However, unlike simply editing the show, as with "A New Start," the entire episode did not air. According to The N executive Meeri Park Cunniff, "It's a serious episode and the summer [schedule] is all light-hearted."[40] This decision by The N led to protests on the network's Web site message boards as well as letters and phone calls to its offices. One fan wrote a letter to *Entertainment Weekly*, saying:

I was shocked when I read that The N, a network ballsy enough to show *Degrassi: The Next Generation*, might not air the episodes ... I was especially amazed that they would blame the decision on tone, while they're showing a story line in which Terri lands in the hospital after a beating from her boyfriend. I have enjoyed the show because it has tackled difficult topics ... However, if these episodes never air, I will lose respect for a network I thought was willing to take chances.[41]

Fantasy over Reality

Despite not being as popular in the United States as other television shows, whether it be due to its isolation on PBS or America's taste for fantasy over reality, *Degrassi Junior High* and *Degrassi High* continue to have a strong fan base. Says Natalie Earl, "I became an obsessive *Degrassi* fan because it was the only program that portrayed teenagers in a realistic and gutsy sense. I mean, back in the 1980s, what other teen drama featured skinheads, punks, and goths as main characters?"[42] Earl and Toronto-based fan Mark Polger were responsible for giving *Degrassi* a significant presence on the Internet during the late 1990s. (See Mark Polger's essay in this volume.) They interviewed as many former cast and crew members as they possibly could and constructed Web sites that overflowed with nostalgia. Earl's site has since closed, but any *Degrassi* fan who does not have immediate access to old *Degrassi* episodes can scour Polger's site for pictures, sounds, episode summaries and even virtual tours of the sites where the *Degrassi* series was filmed. Series creator Kit Hood praised Earl in an interview, saying "one of the things I admire about you Natalie is that you are paying tribute to *Degrassi* because it brought you happiness as a teenager."[43]

Other fans have not been as proactive in their admiration for *Degrassi*, but still treasure their memories just as much as Earl and Polger. In spring 2003, with the assistance of Polger and his *Degrassi* Web site (which has unofficially become the premier source for fans interested in the classic *Degrassi* series), a survey was offered to American fans who wished to share their experiences of "growing up" with *Degrassi*.[44] In addition to asking these fans for basic information on how old they were when they first watched *Degrassi Junior High* or *Degrassi High* and what cities they lived in at the time the shows aired, the survey requested testimonials in order to ascertain what the shows' statewide audience took away from their viewing. For example, Henry Soto of New York City notes what was, for him, one of the longest-lasting influences of the show: "I learned that I wasn't the only one having problems growing up, that I was normal. All kids/teens have trouble during those years and it helped me deal with some of the ones I was experiencing."[45]

In fact, many of the American fans felt a kinship with the *Degrassi* characters because of this realism. Tracy Merrifield, who watched *Degrassi* in California and Washington, cites the story of Spike's pregnancy as a part of the show with which she deeply identified, and notes that "the episodes covered so many different aspects of this issue and did so in a manner that was informative but not preachy."[46] Seth Saeger of Bethlehem, Pennsylvania, adds, "As a kid, the few episodes that I did see had the impact of opening my eyes to issues that I never knew existed."[47] Tara Fetty wrote, "I was the same age as the characters and when the show was on, my parents were separated and I lived with my dad. It was hard for him to talk to me about some things you would talk to a teenage girl about. I learned by watching the show the dangers of unprotected sex and taking drugs … it made it easier to talk to dad because I was already familiar [with the issues]."[48] And Daniel Mesa recalls, "I remembered being actually a bit shocked by the show sometimes because it was so raw. It was amazing to experience this show as a teen, growing up right along with them."[49]

Kit Hood notes that, while producing *Degrassi*, letters from fans who were deeply affected by the show were a huge source of energy and inspiration. "It was the touching fan letters that gave me the motivation to get through rough days," he says. "There were times that the pressure would escalate, especially when the kids were being rowdy and non-compliant. The fan letters prevented me from exploding at everybody. It was encouraging to read how we touched their lives. Teenagers would actually make major decisions based on our show. For that reason, we tried to cover as many issues as possible."[50]

Many other American fans offer similar testimony as to how the *Degrassi* series influenced their lives, both when the shows originally aired and more recently through the Internet, old videotapes and through its current incarnation, *Degrassi: The Next Generation*. Moreover, *Degrassi* has been referenced in movies and songs. San Francisco-based punk/ska band Skankin' Pickle recorded the 1994 song "I'm in Love With a Girl Named Spike." The song pays tribute to *Degrassi High*, specifically the character Spike, even making a *Beverly Hills 90210* comparison.[51] Lead singer Mike Park, who wrote the lyrics, dedicated the song to Amanda Stepto, and met her on one of the band's trips to Toronto. Another ska act, Headboard, covered the song "Everybody Wants Something," adding rap and horn arrangements to the simple melody originally performed by fictional *Degrassi* band The Zit Remedy.[52] "I love *Degrassi!*" proclaims Headboard's Glenn Rubenstein. "I got to know the show when my eighth grade English teacher showed it to us ... Their band [The Zit Remedy] and the stuff they did early on inspired a lot of our early career (like make tapes, harass radio stations, try to play at your school, et cetera)."[53]

Filmmaker Kevin Smith is especially proud of his experience with *Degrassi Junior High* and has made references to the show in three of his movies, most notably the 1997 film *Chasing Amy*, which features this exchange between two characters, Holden McNeil (Ben Affleck) and Banky Edwards (Jason Lee):

Holden: "What do you wanna do tonight?"

Banky: "I don't know. Get a pizza. Watch *Degrassi Junior High*."

Holden: "You got a weird thing for Canadian melodrama."

Banky: "I've got a weird thing for girls who say 'aboot.'" [54]

Smith has also written at length about his obsession with *Degrassi Junior High*, which he watched when he was a convenience store clerk in Leonardo, New Jersey:

I've often tried to figure out why I liked it so much ... I think it had something to with high school in general, a time that — until [his first film] *Clerks* took off — I assumed were the best years of my life. The show calls to mind an era when one's largest crises were wondering when you were finally going to get to third with a girl, or the possibility of a shitty grade in gym. And any program that helps you forget you're jockeying a register — even for an hour — has to be brilliant TV.[55]

★

This is *Degrassi Junior High* and *Degrassi High*'s lasting legacy. The shows and their philosophy of presenting "real kids talking to real kids from the heart" has proven to be groundbreaking. Though there is still a significant amount of adherence to style over substance on prime-time shows aimed at teenagers (such as on Fox's hit *The O.C.*), the philosophy of The N and its programming proves that more attention is being paid to the other side of that coin. On its official Web site, The N claims to be a network with real programs for real kids: "The N on TV is different than any other network. Because all of the shows on The N are about the way life really is and the stuff that really matters ... The N is not just *for* you, it *is* you."[56] Mark R. Hill of Lancaster, Ohio, an avid fan of *Degrassi* since *The Kids of Degrassi Street*, summarizes the *Degrassi* experience perfectly when discussing *Degrassi: The Next Generation*: "I'll have to say I was skeptical, but have ended up liking [*TNG*] quite a lot. The young cast is capable and interesting. The new half hours move along quite fast and are almost as involved and complex as the originals. I don't think there's a more realistic youth drama on TV today."[57]

NOTES

1. When the Canadian cable channel Showcase aired *Degrassi* reruns in the 1990s, many of the people in these areas had similar access.

2. In the late 1990s, WPIX became New York's WB affiliate.

3. "Tween" is a term used to describe what has become a powerful demographic in recent years: the nine to fourteen year olds.

4. Chris Aylott, "AAC KIDS™ Brings 22 New Episodes of *Degrassi: The Next Generation* at MIPCOM 2002," Alliance Atlantis Communications Press Release, 16 September 2002.

5. Shirley Brady, "Are Kids Tuned In?" *Cable World,* 9 September 2002.

6. Ibid.

7. Neil Drumming, "Cutting Class," *Entertainment Weekly,* 11 June 2004, 19.

8. Sonja Lattimore, e-mail to author, 30 June 2004.

9. Ibid.

10. "The Merchants of Cool." *Frontline*. Prod. Rachel Dretzin and Barak Goodman. PBS, WNET New York, 2000.

11. "Children Who View PBS 1998 Roper Youth Report — Update." *Corporation for Public Broadcasting*. Retrieved June 11, 2003, from http://stations.cpb.org/system/reports/ researchnotes/109/.

12. Natalie Earl, "Darrin Brown (Dwayne) Interview." *Degrassi Online*. Retrieved May 29, 2003, from www.degrassi.ca/interviews.

13. "A Talk with the Producers of 'The Merchants of Cool.'" *Frontline*. Retrieved June 11, 2003, from www.pbs.org/wgbh/pages/frontline/shows/cool/etc/producers.html.

14. "The Merchants of Cool." *Frontline*.

15. Ibid.

16. "Saved by the Bell." *The E! True Hollywood Story*. Prod. Michael Lynn, Los Angeles. December 2002.

17. Shelby Wilson, e-mail to author, May 1, 2003.

18. LeJarie Battieste, e-mail to author, April 30, 2003.

19. Joan Nicks, "Degrassi," *The Museum of Broadcast Communications*. Retrieved May 15, 2003, from www.museum.tv/archives/etv/d/html/degrassi/degrassi.htm.

20. Linda Schuyler and Stephen Stohn, "Canadian Television Policy Review — Call for Comments." *Epitome Pictures*. Retrieved May 15, 2003, from www.epitomepictures. com/ crtc.html.

21. Douglas Coupland, *Generation X: Tales for an Accelerated Culture* (New York: St. Martin's Press, 1991), 17.

22. Cates's nude scene had such an effect that, according to director Amy Heckerling, video store owners would complain that because that particular scene on the video tape was paused so frequently the quality of the film on the tape had been damaged.

23. Jonathan Bernstein, *Pretty in Pink: The Golden Age of Teenage Movies* (New York: St. Martin's Griffin, 1997), 67.

24. *The Breakfast Club*. Dir. John Hughes (Universal Pictures, 1985).

25. Ibid.

26. Bernstein, *Pretty in Pink,* 67.

27. With the exception of the comedy *Career Opportunities*, Hughes all but abandoned the genre by the 1990s, finding success with the *Home Alone* franchise.

28. *Heathers*. Dir. Daniel Waters (New World Entertainment, 1989).

29. Bernstein, *Pretty in Pink*, 180.

30. The NBC show *Square Pegs* ran early in the 1980s and only lasted for two seasons. However, its influence on other teen television shows is questionable; it would have remained obscure if not for the success of its lead, Sarah Jessica Parker.

31. This episode is so much of a punch line that Dustin Diamond, who played Screech, laughed at the storyline on *Saved by the Bell: The E! True Hollywood Story*.

32. A clip show is an episode of a television program wherein one or several characters reminisces about the past and those memories are shown via segments from earlier episodes.

33. Natalie Earl, "Kit Hood Interview, Part 2." *Degrassi Online*. Retrieved May 15, 2003, from www.degrassi.ca/interviews.

34. In fact, many of the episodes have their origins in real embarrassing events in the life of series creator Paul Feig, who details them in his book *Kick Me: Adventures in Adolescence* (New York: Three Rivers Press, 2003).

35. "Jump the Shark" is a phrase used to describe the moment when a television show begins to decline in quality. The Web site *Jump the Shark* is a database of television shows where people are able to voice their opinions about when a particular show began to decline. The phrase itself is named after a moment on the show *Happy Days* when Fonzie jumped a shark on water skis while wearing his trademark leather jacket. Although it is more a matter of opinion, it is widely considered that this was a sign that *Happy Days* was in decline.

36. "Freaks & Geeks." *Jump the Shark*. Retrieved May 15, 2003, from www.jump-theshark.com/f/freaksandgeeks.htm.

37. "Betrayal," *My So-Called Life*. Prod. Marshall Herskovitz and Edward Zwick. ABC. WABC New York, 12 January 1995.

38. Nicks, "Degrassi."

39. Jennifer Smothers, e-mail to author, April 28, 2003.

40. Drumming, "Cutting Class," 19.

41. Annie Clark, "N Out of Sync," Letter to the Editor, *Entertainment Weekly*, 9 July 2004.

42. Stefan Dubowski, "Degrassi Reunion Brings International Fan Base," *Arthur: The Trent University Student and Community Newspaper* (1999).

43. Earl, "Kit Hood Interview, Part 2."

44. The site's mailing list, which is maintained by Polger and called "The *Degrassi* Digest," currently has 1,127 members from several countries.

45. Henry Soto, e-mail to author, April 27, 2003.

46. Tracy Merrifield, e-mail to author, April 28, 2003.

47. Seth Saeger, e-mail to author, April 28, 2003.

48. Tara Fetty, e-mail to author, April 30, 2003.

49. Daniel Mesa, e-mail to author, April 28, 2003.

50. Earl, "Kit Hood Interview, Part 2."

51. Michael Park, "I'm in Love with a Girl Named Spike." *Sing Along with Skankin' Pickle* (Dill Records, 1994).

52. The Zit Remedy, later The Zits, consisted of *Degrassi* characters Joey, Wheels and Snake.

53. Natalie Earl, "Interview with Glenn Rubenstein of Headboard." *Degrassi Online.* Retrieved May 15, 2003, from www.degrassi.ca/interviews.

54. *Chasing Amy*. Dir. Kevin Smith. (Miramax, 1997).

55. Kevin Smith, "Obsession Confession: *Degrassi Junior High*," *Details*, November 1996.

56. "About the N." *The N*. Retrieved May 15, 2003, from www.the-n.com.

57. Mark R. Hill, e-mail to author, May 4, 2003.

CHAPTER 3

DEGRASSI THEN AND NOW:
TEENS, AUTHENTICITY AND THE MEDIA

Sherri Jean Katz

THE WORLD HAS CHANGED A LOT since Joey, Snake and Wheels first burst through the doors of *Degrassi Junior High* and into our living rooms. Televised representations of teenagers have become more prevalent; the Internet has evolved into a medium that facilitates self-expression; and the teen-targeted media landscape has become far more complex. Of course, while these changes have taken place, there has been a definite transformation in the way specific concepts, such as "authenticity," are communicated though the television production process.

Authenticity is that quality of *perceived believability or realness* that makes television viewers buy-in on a fundamental level to what is happening on-screen, even as they are quite aware of the presence of constructed characters and written scripts. Authenticity enables viewers to identify with television characters and their situations, vicariously confronting new experiences and trying out different personalities. While the "essence" of authenticity is strong characters and drama that viewers find compelling, there are specific tools used in the production process to communicate this quality of real-ness. For example, as I discuss in this chapter, *Degrassi Junior High* featured a very raw visual appearance and this production choice was a tool that helped to communicate its authenticity.

In this chapter, I compare *Degrassi Junior High* and *Degrassi: The Next Generation* in order to illustrate that the tools used to convey authenticity have changed while the underlying essence of the series has remained the same. Both programs were created with a specific mission: to realistically present teen issues from the teen perspective.[1] Therefore, methodologically, it is important to analyze both shows within their respective production environments to illustrate which tools were used to convey authenticity in each show. It is also important to characterize the behaviour of fans, because the ways in which fans respond to the programs illustrate the effectiveness of these tools.

While the work of Henry Jenkins, Susan Murray and Christina Slade has furthered our understanding of teen fan communities in general, my analysis is challenged by the lack, prior to this volume, of scholarly writing focusing specifically on *Degrassi* fans.[2] Therefore, it is necessary that I incorporate some personal observations into the analysis of *Degrassi Junior High*, while at the same time acknowledging the methodological limitations of such an approach. The analysis of *Degrassi: The Next Generation* highlights the current online behaviour of fans, yet such an analysis is challenged by the anonymity of the Internet. For example, online bulletin-board postings can only be attributed to screen names, and it is not possible to verify the age, gender or nationality of fans through their online discourse. For the purposes of this chapter, I assume that their self-presentations are accurate.

Believable Identities

In her work *The Real Thing*, Christina Slade illustrates teen television audiences as "actively interpreting the content of television." She found that "children watch and make sense of television in complex and generally uncharted ways."[3] Henry Jenkins has coined the term "cultural convergence" as the tendency for teens to use "different media (such as television and the Internet) and their contents in relation to each other,"[4] and he notes that this practice creates online forums that permit an "interpretive and creative community actively appropriating the content of television."[5] Jenkins illustrates that through these online bulletin-board communities, viewers take ownership of the television product, asserting their own opinions, debating with one another and questioning the decisions of the producers, creators and distributors. They illustrate an understanding that media artifacts are manifestations of corporate decision making, and they simultaneously engage in an adoration of the product itself and a reinterpretation of it.

In her analysis of the television program *My So-Called Life*, Susan Murray illustrates how female teen fans seek a "narrative world through which they can come to an understanding of and give voice to their individual adolescent subjectivity."[6] She notes how the American Online bulletin board for the show became a platform for female teens in the U.S. to interact. They spoke of "Angela's [the central character] life [as] being just like their own, containing the very contradictions, ambivalence, and angst that they [were] experiencing."[7] Although they cognitively knew that Angela was not a real person, she nevertheless became real for them. They spoke of Angela as though she were a friend, imitated her clothing style, empathized and identified with her concerns and fought to "save her life" when the ABC network executives planned to cancel the program.[8]

As noted above, the presence of multidimensional characters with whom the viewers can identify is an essential element in establishing authenticity in teen dramas. Another parameter is stories that speak to adolescents' deepest concerns or what we might call the "teen condition." While this is not meant to suggest that all teens everywhere have the same concerns, face the same exact issues or interact in the same cultural environment, they do all engage in the socially constructed process of becoming adults and taking greater agency in and responsibility for their decisions. It is empowering for teen viewers to watch characters confront the teen condition, even if the specific issues the viewers and characters are dealing with differ, because viewers can vicariously negotiate their own agency through the actions of the characters. Some shows achieve this authentic quality without working on the terrain of everyday life. For example, in *Reading the Vampire Slayer* and *Fighting the Forces: What's at Stake in Buffy the Vampire Slayer*, several theorists illustrate how the television program *Buffy the Vampire Slayer* veils the teen condition in a series of complex metaphors, allowing authenticity to reside in a world populated by vampires, demons and the supernatural.[9] In *Degrassi*, however, the overriding mission to present issues realistically requires that the series appear to be "true-to-life."

While strong characters and drama that the viewers find compelling define the essence of authenticity, different television programs use different tools to communicate it. Therefore, it is necessary to contextually analyze *Degrassi Junior High* and *Degrassi: The Next Generation* within their respective production environments. In the mid-1970s, an eighth-grade schoolteacher, Linda Schuyler, and a former video editor and child actor, Kit

Hood, teamed up to make educational videos. They turned the children's 1979 book *Ida Makes a Movie* by Kay Chorao into a film on a budget of $17,000 U.S.[10] This launched *The Kids of Degrassi Street* (1979–85).[11] Working with the CBC and partially funded by Magic Lantern (a learning video and technology business) and private investors, Schuyler and Hood produced more episodes on a budget of $70,000 CAD each through their production company Playing With Time.[12] By 1986, they had produced twenty-six episodes of *The Kids of Degrassi Street* and were ready to take their next step.

That next step was *Degrassi Junior High*, created with the specific intention of presenting an unflinching look at teen issues from the teen perspective "in an intelligent and non-condescending manner."[13] The program was their response to what they recognized as a "scarcity of quality programming for adolescents."[14] Kate Taylor, the former associate director of children's and cultural programs for PBS who is also a former junior-high-school teacher, worked as an independent producer with Schuyler and Hood to secure funding in the United States. Once partnership between the CBC and WGBH Boston (PBS) was secured, the program began filming in the summer of 1986 and first aired in Canada on January 18, 1987. *Degrassi Junior High* ran for three seasons (forty-two episodes), after which the show was renamed *Degrassi High* and ran for two more seasons (twenty-eight episodes).[15] In early 1992, a two-hour televized movie entitled *School's Out* ended the series. That same year, the CBC aired *Degrassi Talks*, a documentary-style program in which members of the cast facilitated open discussions on important topics, such as alcohol, depression, drugs and sexuality with teens across Canada.

In Canada, *Degrassi Junior High* initially aired at 5 p.m. on Sundays, but due to a strong critical response, it was moved to the prime-time slot of Mondays at 8:30 p.m. The program attracted an audience of 1.2 million,[16] representing a "15 percent share of English-speaking Canadian viewers and 31 percent of viewers 12 to 17."[17] *School's Out* captured an audience of 2.325 million Canadian viewers.[18] In the U.S., *Degrassi Junior High* aired primarily in daytime or early access time slots on 250 PBS stations, representing 94 percent coverage of the U.S. public broadcasting market and earning "an average cumulative rating of 1.7," which corresponded to over 1.53 million households, during its second season.[19] The series aired in more than forty countries and won numerous awards, including two International Emmys and nine Gemini Awards.

Producing Degrassi

Degrassi Junior High was funded by the Canadian Broadcasting Corporation and Telefilm which provided two-thirds of the production budget, and by the Corporation for Public Broadcasting, public television stations, the Carnegie Corporation and other U.S. foundations which provided one-third of the funds. By its fourth season, the budget for the program had increased to "approximately $228,800 (U.S.) per episode."[20] In 1989–90, Playing With Time "raked in $4.5 million (CAD) in revenues."[21] In analyzing how authenticity is achieved, it is important to consider the decisions that the creators/producers made with respect to the show, and in the case of *Degrassi Junior High,* they insisted that the program maintain the same raw look even as the budget increased. The low-budget production values were maintained because they were a tool used to convey authenticity.

For example, the cast members in *Degrassi Junior High* were not professional actors. Rather, they were everyday kids in a repertory group who looked and acted like the normal teens they were. Creator Linda Schuyler has insisted "the entire company [was] nonunion for philosophical, not financial reasons."[22] Pat Mastroianni, who played the fedora-wearing Joey Jeremiah throughout the show's run, explained: "When I was younger, I was basically playing an exaggerated version of myself. We didn't really have the skills early on to separate ourselves from our characters, so the writers wrote each character closest to the person playing them."[23] In real life, these kids attended public schools, travelled on Toronto city buses, suggested ways to make the scripts believable and offered a variety of perspectives because of their varied economic, family and ethnic backgrounds. The repertory company cast was tremendous, and the fifty members sometimes played lead and sometimes played supporting roles.

The raw style in which *Degrassi Junior High* was shot communicated its authenticity. The show was filmed on one 16mm camera, entirely on location in an actual unused school building, Vincent Massey Junior School in Etobicoke, Ontario.[24] The images were not slick. One feels like a fly on the wall taking in the scene as the camera pans awkwardly and characters walk into and out of frame. Despite the use of colour in the set's décor and the actors' clothing, for example the red and blue lockers and Hawaiian print shirts, *Degrassi Junior High* had a muted and raw appearance. In the 1980s, the gritty style in which the show was filmed had a connection to "real life" because it was similar to the style of documentaries. These were the days before slick reality television shows like *Survivor* presented "reality" in an overly produced and highly orchestrated visual package. In his article "Performing the Real: Documentary Diversions," John Corner argues that the "extensive borrowing of the 'documentary look' by other kinds of programs, and extensive borrowing of nondocumentary kinds of look ... by documentary ... have contributed to a weakening of documentary status" and a "postdocumentary culture" in which reality can be portrayed without raw and gritty footage.[25] As an example, *The Real World*, which at one time used raw footage and sparse New York City and San Francisco apartment settings, now seeks to convey "reality" through crisp images and overly decorated, colourful mansions. The visual format used to communicate "real life" has changed since the days of *Degrassi Junior High*.

It is into this changed environment that Schuyler and partner Stephen Stohn launched *Degrassi: The Next Generation* (*TNG*). The program began airing during the 2001–02 season on Canada's largest private broadcaster, CTV, and on The N in the United States, which reaches 35 million households with programming targeted to tweens and teens after 6 p.m.[26] *TNG* has been successfully licensed in several other countries, including Britain, France and Australia by AAC Kids™. The show has won six Gemini Awards, a Young Artist Award for Best Family Television Series and a Young Artist Award for Best Ensemble, and Schuyler has been honoured with an Ingenuity Award for her work in Canadian television.

In creating *TNG*, Schuyler, Stohn and writer Yan Moore had the very same mission as they had with *Degrassi Junior High*: they sought once again to show teen issues authentically from the teen perspective. However, due to the changes mentioned above, they chose not to use low-budget production values and a raw visual format to communicate that "realness." For example, the everyday kids of *Degrassi Junior High* have been replaced in *TNG* by professional actors, many of whom have been auditioning and working since they were young children. Siluck Saysanasy who played Yick in *Degrassi Junior High* notes that the new cast members "go to schools for the performing arts and already have acting careers."[27] Stacie Mistysyn who played Caitlin adds: "They have dressing rooms, makeup and wardrobe, a studio ... We never had that stuff."[28] The names of the new cast members appear during the opening credits; they are a closed cast of regular stars as opposed to a large evolving ensemble group. In a comparison of the two programs, using two very similar episodes about school elections and sibling relations, *Degrassi Junior High*'s twenty-six-minute "Kiss Me Steph" episode featured thirty-three speaking repertory members, while *The Next Generation*'s twenty-two minute "Family Politics" episode featured sixteen speaking characters.

The Next Generation also has a sharp, slick visual appearance. The school and clothes look bright and colourful despite the fact that costume designer Kim Gibson actually "grays down the wardrobe with oatmeal-coloured dye so colours don't pop."[29] The school is actually a permanent studio with a back lot and not a real school building as was used in *Degrassi Junior High*. *TNG* is also filmed using more extreme close-up (XCUs) shots of cast members. Instead of a raw look, it became clear to the creators that "making the new show current [meant] creating a computer savvy environment."[30] They launched the new program as a joint television/Internet project and also set the show within a magnet school for CyberArts. Explaining this decision, Schuyler notes: "If we were going to bring it back as The Next Generation, we couldn't ignore the presence of the Web, both in our stories of the kids' lives and for us to have a forward-thinking website connected to the show."[31]

Technologically Savvy

The producers of *TNG* chose to use technology, both on and off-screen, in order to communicate the authenticity of the program. Specifically, the tools include media immersion in the classroom, which is representative of the viewers' own mediated world, and the Web site www.degrassi.tv, which is used to promote the "believability" of the characters and as a platform for cultural convergence. Onscreen, the characters in *TNG* differ in a fundamental way from the characters in *Degrassi Junior High* through their relationship to and their use of technology. *Degrassi Junior High*'s Snake is now a media immersion teacher who leads his students in designing HTML sites and editing music and photos digitally, but the characters are also learning how to navigate a complex media landscape. For example, Emma learns that the Internet can be a dangerous space when she is cyberstalked in the episode "Mother and Child Reunion," and Manny learns that e-mail must be used responsibly after embarrassing her teacher and Emma in the episode "Weird Science." As noted, today's teens are deeply immersed in complex and evolving technological environments and, thus, the premise of media immersion in the Degrassi Community School is an important tool used to communicate authenticity.

While technology helps to illustrate a realistic environment with true-to-life issues onscreen, *TNG* uses it as a tool off-screen as well. Toronto's Snap Media, a partner in *TNG*'s creation and development, operates the degrassi.tv Web site — its set-up cost was $1.2 million CAD, and it has $300,000 CAD per year as an operating budget.[32] While many Web sites associated with television programs showcase cast bios, press links and episode guides, www.degrassi.tv also invites fans to enroll as students of the Degrassi Community School. As virtual students, fans receive online guidance counselling, report cards and help with homework; they also compete against other homerooms in intramural games, set up lockers, trade d'mails with the characters and chat on classroom bulletin boards. The site is moderated and has a strict code of conduct, encouraging participants not to release personal information. As of June 2002, over 54,000 Canadian fans had registered, and as of July 2003, there were over 200,000 online students in total. "The vast majority of these visitors were girls aged thirteen to seventeen, who visited three to five times a week and stayed from thirty minutes to two hours." In a ten-month period, virtual students wrote well over 200,000 d'mails, 46,000 detailed journal entries and 225,000 classroom bulletin-board messages.[33] Fans can also sign up to receive text message updates on their cell phones and pagers. The site has remained very popular with fans of the show. In April 2005, while original episodes of *TNG* were not airing in Canada or the U.S., www.degrassi.tv attracted 60,459 unique visitors who together explored 4,460,737 pages of the Web site (that is, they clicked on several different pages, each of which counts as a page visited) over the course of 204,235 visits. Each visitor remained on the site for an average of 776 seconds.[34]

The Web site is a tool used to convey the multidimensionality of the characters, heightening the fans' emotional connection to the characters. For example, the "characters" post locker-journal pages for their virtual classmates to read, and onscreen moments are extended through interior monologues posted in these journals, which in turn provide deeper insight into and facilitate an in-depth look at the characters' emotions. "Take My Breath Away," the episode in which Manny and Craig go on a first date, ends the day after the date at his locker when he breaks up with her. Manny's reaction onscreen is captured by a hurt look as the camera shot freezes and the episode ends. But Manny's story did not really end there; in her locker journal entitled "I Thot He Liked Me!" she expands the narrative beyond the episode's last scene by expressing her feelings:

> I'm all confused cuz 1 minit we are having a gr8 time and the next minit (or day — whatever!) he's dumping me and the part that sux the most is that i totally still like him and i don't even know what i did to change his mind. but I still like HIM! He wuz the 1st guy who I ever really liked and who liked me too.[35]

While the characters' postings in some way enhance the idea that they are "real people" with real emotions, they also highlight the "real" issues that comprise the teen experience. In the above example, Manny expresses anguish over a situation many real teens face. Hazel's acceptance of her ethnic heritage, Ashley's drug use and Paige's rape are some of the very serious stories that have been expanded and contextualized online through the locker journals. For example, in response to learning that Paige was raped, Hazel posted:

> It's scary what going through something like that can do to your sanity — she says she brought it on herself which is an incredibly sad thing to hear. She said "no," and NO means NO. I wish I could help her. I wish I could go back in time and prevent it from ever happening ... Even though it didn't happen to me, I feel like it kinda did.[36]

As noted above, multidimensional characters that seem like real people and true-to-life stories that address our greatest hopes and dreams, our deepest fears and anxieties comprise the essence of authenticity in television dramas. These two elements are at the soul of *Degrassi Junior High* and *The Next Generation*, and a comparison of the two shows illustrates that fundamental issues and teen rites of passage have not really changed, although the environment in which they occur has. For example, *Degrassi Junior High* had an episode "Rumour Has It" in which gossip about a teacher was spread throughout the entire school. In *The Next Generation*'s "Rumours and Reputations," cell phones, two-way pagers and e-mail are used to spread a rumour about a teacher at a speed never imagined in the original. These new characters have some of their most important confrontations over e-mail and instant messaging. Indeed, it is no accident that in the first and second season, the opening montage of *TNG* began with Emma clicking into the school's Web site, a stark juxtaposition to *Degrassi Junior High*, which began with an anonymous student picking up books.

Even so, the characters in *TNG* are not really all that different from the generation that came before them in that their media immersion cannot replace face-to-face communication. When Jimmy feels neglected by his parents in "Coming of Age," he does not go online; he runs to Ashley's home, plays big brother to her step-brother Toby and eats dinner with her family. When Manny, J.T. and Toby discover that Emma's been cyberstalked in "Mother and Child Reunion," it is up to her mother and Snake to save her in person.

CREATING "REALNESS"

In *Degrassi Junior High,* characters died, went to jail, became pregnant, suffered tragedy, contracted AIDS, tried drugs, were abused, had abortions, played in bands, fought, competed and fell in love. Drama in the real lives of the cast members provided material for the show. For example, "several parental deaths helped precipitate 'Can't Live With 'Em,' about the death of one character's parents and his continual struggle to deal with the tragedy."[37] Today, teenagers confront similar concerns and *The Next Generation* has addressed many important issues, including drug use, bullying, homosexuality, abortion, self-mutilation (cutting) and racism. Updates are often needed to make episodes fit into the current cultural environment; for example, Ashley tries ecstasy instead of acid, and Jimmy tries Ritalin instead of caffeine pills. Teens also face new issues, like Emma's experience of cyberstalking, but many of the underlying rites of passage have not changed: Joey, Snake and Wheels of *Degrassi Junior High* borrowed Snake's parents' car for a little joyride, while in *TNG* Craig and his friends borrowed one of the cars at Joey's dealership.

Susan Murray notes that in creating "realness," a show needs to "skillfully navigate through complex social and personal issues without entering into clichés [or] easy wrap-ups,"[38] and one of the defining qualities of *Degrassi Junior High* was that the non-linear evolution of the stories "often left the drama open-ended."[39] *The Next Generation* also seeks this complex structure; however, concern by Viacom over the highly serious nature of some episodes has led The N to hold back episodes and create sixty- or ninety-minute edited packages in which the issues find resolution or the consequences are shown. For example, The N combined "Jagged Little Pill," in which Ashley tries drugs, and "Karma Chameleon," which illustrates some of the consequences this had on her social life, with cut-in warnings about the dangers of drug use. Similarly, three episodes which address Paige's rape over a six-month period were combined into a ninety-minute package. The re-edited packages interrupt the show's sense of "realness" because the open-ended storylines are replaced with easy wrap-ups and because secondary plot lines involving other characters are shown out of order.

As noted above, true-to-life storylines and multidimensional characters are the essence of authenticity, but the measure of authenticity is the extent to which fans "buy-in" and behave as though the characters and stories are real. An investigation of the fans of *TNG* illustrates how www.degrassi. tv promotes the characters and stories as authentic. The "characters" send personalized e-mails and write bulletin-board postings to their virtual classmates asking for advice with the issues they face onscreen. Many fans respond to the characters as though they are real friends by offering the sought-after advice, identifying with their problems and addressing them as peers. For example, when the character Emma wrote about her mother and her teacher dating, responses from fans included, "Hey, Emma — Of course at first it'll seem hard fer you, but then l8ter on you'll get use to it"; "I totally understand ur problem, almost the same thing is happening to me"; and "Emma I know how you feel. I would feel weird."[40] Occasionally, virtual students attempt to break through the constructed reality with comments like, "People your responding to a character from the show degrassi like it's a real person! Is it just me or have you all gone mad?"[41] The truth is that these teens are not crazy. They recognize that they are not writing to a real person named Emma, but it does not matter. They have chosen to "buy-in" to the constructed reality and behave as though the characters and drama are "real." These fans often adopt similar screen names on the site in order to imitate the character with whom they most identify.

The bulletin boards on www.degrassi.tv foster Jenkins's concept of cultural convergence. The site is a forum where fans debate the onscreen drama, connect it to their off-screen lives and appropriate the content of the television show in an empowering way. For example, when *The Next Generation*'s Emma stood up to her principal and was suspended in "Fight For Your Right," the classroom discussion board invited virtual students to discuss how well their own principals consider their concerns. The responses were expressive, with some students offering detailed accounts of how they sought successfully and unsuccessfully to enact changes in their real-world schools.[42] These teens use the site to consider their adolescence and their agency, the "teen condition," within the context of what is illustrated through the onscreen drama, and they gossip about the characters as they would their own school classmates.

Teenagers responded to the characters and storylines in a similar way fifteen years ago. For example, while growing up in Long Island, New York, my neighbour and I watched the show together and would often talk about the characters, cheer and criticize their actions and compare *Degrassi* with our own school community. During one particular discussion, upon hearing the name Spike, my mother actually interrupted: "You're talking about *Degrassi*? I thought you girls were talking about the kids you know." But, of course, we did "know" them, as authentic characters in true-to-life situations, and we had come to accept them as "real." We were even annoyed when the terminology Grade 7 and Grade 8 were used because in the United States we used 7th Grade and 8th Grade and that minor detail would occasionally remind us we were outside a constructed reality and outside a somewhat different national and cultural reality as well.

But, unlike the teens of today, we did not have an organized fan community in the United States in which to share our opinions. *Degrassi Junior High* was a bit of a secret obsession: everybody watched it, but nobody knew anybody (aside from maybe a sibling or a best friend) who admitted to watching it. On the *Jump the Shark* Web site, worldwide fans of the program express similar recollections and also acknowledge how the use of everyday kids and compelling stories communicated the show's authenticity:

Wow! Finally, I'm glad to know that other people have watched this show.

Degrassi High ruled the closet TV planet in Australia — no one admitted watching it until i left high school.

The *Degrassi* series was always a very unique show, especially to me and my friends, who grew up in Toronto, where the show was filmed, and were the same age as the characters in the show. Back then, NOBODY admitted to watching the show, yet you'd go downtown and see a particular store or park and say "Hey, that's the store where Joey bought those condoms" or "that's the bridge Stephanie contemplated jumping off." The ultimate realization that ALL kids my age were watching the show was the day after the premiere of *School's Out*, the made-for-TV *Degrassi* movie.

The best thing about the show was that the people were real ... they were real students who were basically playing themselves. They dealt with real issues like AIDS when people were afraid to talk about such things.[43]

Of course fans of *Degrassi Junior High* have now found that larger community. Online mentions of the show appear to date back to 1990 on the listserv rec.arts.tv, while a designated *Degrassi* listserv, alt.tv.degrassi, was active by 1996.[44] An unofficial online digest, www.degrassi.ca was started in 1997, and a Web ring linking several fan sites was created the following year. Today, fan sites, fan-fiction collections and eBay auctions assure that *Degrassi Junior High* is well represented online and that precise details about the program are still discussed and remembered.

CAPTURING TEEN VOICES = AUTHENTICITY

Although the "essence" of their fandom is the same, teenagers today are far more empowered than fans were fifteen years ago, and that strength goes beyond just having a community in which to discuss *Degrassi*. We all know we are in the midst of what has been termed the "digital revolution." We have moved aside our audio tapes to make room for CDs, and we have banished our videotapes in favour of DVDs. But the real meaning of the digital revolution is far more complex. Teenagers understand a world that is theirs to reformat — they manipulate images and audio tracks with their computers and they overpower corporate music labels through peer-to-peer sites. As Jenkins notes, "Sociologists are starting to refer to the 'N Generation,' the 'Net Generation,' or 'Gen.com,' children who have come of age in relation to interactive technologies and digital media and who operate under the rather bold assumption that they can be active participants shaping, creating, critiquing and circulating popular culture."[45] Indeed, these teens can even tell the producers of *TNG* what to do and how to do it by interacting through www.degrassi.tv with Stephen Stohn, who uses the handle ExecProducer:

> For "U Got the Look" I think/hope it MIGHT have something to do with Terris modeling, which was a plot they kind of dropped last season after a really interesting start. Ive always hoped they [would] do more with that and show her character more.
>
> — Melanie (30 June 2003)

Exec, ATTENTION, EXEC, ATTENTION,

Suicide is a real problem in teens today. Starts with depression and ends up some one takes their life. I think there should be an episode where you bring in a character who is depressed [who] moves to degrassi school ...

— Lonnie06 (2 July 2003)

hmmm, wonder what the title means? Wonder if someone took my suggestion about Emma meeting her dad or not? Wait 'n see I guess.

— alleycat12380 (23 May 2003)

Exec producer this is for you I saw a picture of the season 3 cast ... Ashley looks so pretty now ... is she going back to her old style again?

— Eponine22 (9 August 2003)

Spike shouldn't die. Yeah death is a major issue but that has already been touched on with Craig's parents. And as much as I like the character of Spike, there has been so much attention put on her as far as going out with Mr. Simpson, marrying him, and carrying his baby. Yeah it would be a good plot twist, but really the line has to be drawn.

— TheRealDaria (20 June 2003)

And teens recognize this power:

I personally take it for granted, but I just thought about it, and I realize that by being a member of .tv I have the opportunity to discuss plot lines and questions, among other things, with the Executive Producer of the show, and then contact the cast directly ... amazing.

— californiachic (6 June 2003)

These teens also recognize the structures of corporate control, and they use the site to react against them. For example, fans in the U.S. have used the online forum to criticize and complain about The N's decision to re-edit controversial episodes, split seasons and delay episodes that have already aired in Canada. When one Canadian viewer told her virtual classmates, "I just saw the (season 3) commercial today! I was so excited to see it all play out," viewers in the U.S. reacted by exclaiming, "I hate the N," "The-N sucks," and "They hide the real degrassi from us ... they treat us like we can't handle everything."[46] Similarly, reacting against The N's decision not to air "Accidents Will Happen," a two-part episode in which Manny finds out she is pregnant and has an abortion, American viewers wrote, "I was very upset to find out that there was a whole episode that the the-n wouldn't show … Is anyone else outraged about this?"; "I think it was stupid they didn't show it here"; and "That is what happens in real life and people need to see that."[47] Another viewer noted in her locker journal: "They censor out background images and some things the characters say sometimes … I'm just upset that they edit it and I don't get to see the show the way it was meant to be seen."[48]

Of course, the bulletin-board interaction illustrates another way in which the site communicates authenticity. The writers of *The Next Generation* can mine the journal and board entries of the virtual classmates to capture an authentic voice for the program. They can analyze speech patterns and read the journals to learn the concerns of everyday teens. By noting how the audience responds to the numerous polls they circulate, by reading their personal journals and by keeping track of the message boards, the writers of the show have access to a tremendous amount of information about real-life teenagers. Whereas Schuyler once derived the teen perspective by chatting with the fifty members of *Degrassi Junior High*'s repertory company, the Internet now opens the potential for hundreds of thousands of fans to provide that perspective. Sometimes, the input is even directly solicited by producer Stephen Stohn:

> Jody Colero (the Music Supervisor) and I could use your thoughts here: What artists/groups music do you think would be played at a rave, one that had participants as young as, let's say hypothetically, Chris (his older brother would be the DJ) and Craig and Emma and Manny? Thanks! P.S. There is real difficulty in getting the rights to a lot of hiphop and [rave] music — there are so many samples embedded in the songs that it is sometimes almost impossible to contact everyone involved and get the necessary rights — so any thoughts could genuinely be helpful.[49]

Not only do they see their suggestions worked into the drama, some virtual classmates find their handles onscreen. *The Next Generation*'s television advertising spots on The N have featured message-board comments from fans gossiping about which characters belong together, which characters they like best and what they think will happen on the show. Ending with the taglines "If your life were a TV show, this would be it" and "*Degrassi* is just like real life," these spots are yet other tools through which authenticity is communicated. The N's house copy, "You're in The N: Real, Life, Now," reiterates the message.

In his analysis of *Dawson's Creek*, Will Brooker concludes that "participation in a TV show's extra-textual discourse (may not rise to the expression of) folk art."[50] However, in the case of www.degrassi.tv, many virtual classmates approach the role of cultural producer in the tradition of folk art or bricolage. In addition to developing plot ideas and advertising copy and reprocessing the drama that is shown, the participants write and submit articles for the Degrassi Community School's paper *The Grapevine* and design their own locker pages, which feature polls, personal interest icons, slide shows and personal journals in which they sometimes post original poetry and fiction. The virtual classmates are not only accepting the authenticity of the program, they are actually contributing to the tools that communicate it.

But what does this participatory and creative sphere *really* mean? Through the juxtaposition of *Degrassi Junior High* and *Degrassi: The Next Generation*, we can see an environment transformed. A real school building is now virtual and fifty teenagers have evolved into hundreds of thousands as fans who have stepped inside the very structures through which authenticity is conveyed. Despite these changes, *Degrassi* reminds us that the essence of authenticity and the soul of adolescence are the same as they were when Joey, Snake and Wheels first burst through the doors of a school and into our hearts.

NOTES

1. "How It All Happened," *Degrassi: The Next Generation Official Website*. Retrieved October 8, 2002, from www.degrassi.tv.

2. See Henry Jenkins, "The Poachers and the Stormtroopers: Cultural Convergence in the Digital Age," *Red Rock Eater News Service* (July 1998). Retrieved August 15, 2003, from http://commons.somwhere.com/rre/1998/The.Poachers.and.the. Sto.html; Susan Murray, "Saving Our So-Called Lives: Girl Fandom, Adolescent Subjectivity and My So-Called Life," in Marsha Kinder, ed., *Kids' Media Culture* (Durham, NC: Duke University Press, 1999); and Christina Slade, *The Real Thing: Doing Philosophy with Media* (New York: Peter Lang, 2002).

3. Slade, *The Real Thing*, 9, 15.

4. Jenkins, "The Poachers and the Stormtroopers."

5. Henry Jenkins, "Media Consumption," *Faculty Page: Massachusetts Institute of Technology.* Retrieved August 15, 2003, from http://web.mit.edu/21fms/www/faculty/henry3/.

6. Murray, "Saving Our So-Called Lives," 227.

7. Ibid., 226.

8. Ibid., 221–235.

9. Roz Kaveney, ed., *Reading the Vampire Slayer* (New York: Tauris Parke Paperbacks, 2002); Rhonda V. Wilcox and David Lavery, eds., *Fighting the Forces: What's at Stake in Buffy the Vampire Slayer* (New York: Rowman and Littlefield, 2002).

10. Kirsten Beck, "The Greening of Degrassi," *Channel* 9 (November 1989), 62.

11. *Kids of Degrassi Street* featured different characters and a different mission than *Degrassi Junior High*. It is therefore not included in my comparison.

12. Mark Polger, "Degrassi History." *Degrassi Online: The Unofficial Degrassi Website.* Retrieved August 25, 2003, from www.degrassi.ca/History/.

13. Shanda Deziel, "New Kids on the Block," *Maclean's*, 15 October 2001, 59.

14. Patricia Hluchy, "Singing the Puberty Blues," *Maclean's*, 19 January 1987, 54.

15. Throughout this chapter, *Degrassi Junior High* is used at times to refer to both *Degrassi Junior High* and *Degrassi High*. No distinction is made between the two programs as they featured the same characters and the same general mission.

16. Ian Allaby, "Films and TV: Linda Schuyler and Kit Hood," *Canadian Business* 63 (September 1990), 60.

17. Beck, "The Greening of Degrassi," 64.

18. "School's Out," *Degrassi: The Next Generation Official Website.* Retrieved August 25, 2003, from www.degrassi.tv.

19. Beck, "The Greening of Degrassi," 64. One rating point represented over 900,000 households in the United States in 1988, and therefore the U.S. audience of the show can be calculated at over 1.53 million households during this time.

20. Beck, "The Greening of Degrassi," 64.

21. Allaby, "Films and TV," 60.

22. Beck, "The Greening of Degrassi," 63.

23. Ben Doherty, "School Ties," *Newcastle Herald* (Australia), 13 September 2002, 5.

24. Beck, "The Greening of Degrassi," 63. A different school was used for *Degrassi High*. It was an unused building on the campus of Toronto's Centennial College.

25. John Corner, "Performing The Real," *Television and New Media* 3, no. 3 (August 2002), 255–263.

26. "The N," *Viacom*. Retrieved July 31, 2004, from www.viacom.com.

27. Deziel, "New Kids on the Block," 60.

28. Ibid., 60.

29. Bernadette Morra and Keith Beaty, "What's Hip on Degrassi Street," *The Toronto Star*, 23 August 2001, D4.

30. "How It All Happened," *Degrassi: The Next Generation Official Website*.

31. Mark Dillon, "Master Classes Cover Gamut of Content Creation," *Playback*, 10 June 2002, 34.

32. Judy Monchuk, "Innovative Degrassi Web site to expand into Australia, U.K.," *Times Colonist* (Victoria), 16 June 2002, B6.

33. Ibid.

34. This statistical information was provided by Stephanie Cohen, director of communications and marketing of Epitome Pictures, in an e-mail interview with the author, May 5, 2005.

35. sMiLeYgUrL, "I Thot He Liked Me" (December 1, 2002). *Degrassi: The Next Generation Official Website*. Retrieved February 1, 2003, from www.degrassi.tv.

36. daSpiritQT, "NO means NO" (April 13, 2003). *Degrassi: The Next Generation Official Website*. Retrieved July 31, 2003, from from www.degrassi.tv.

37. Beck, "The Greening of Degrassi," 65.

38. Murray, "Saving Our So-Called Lives," 226.

39. Marie-Claire Simonetti, "Teenage Truths and Tribulations Across Cultures: *Degrassi Junior High* and *Beverly Hills 90210*," *Journal of Popular Film and Television* 22 (Spring 1994), 41.

40. Agent363 (8 October 2002); babysparks (6 October 2002); and sunkizz (7 October 2002), "My Mom + My Teacher = My Hell." *Degrassi: The Next Generation Official Website*. Retrieved October 10, 2002, from www.degrassi.tv.

41. Vitch (7 October 2002), "My Mom + My Teacher = My Hell." *Degrassi: The Next Generation Official Website*. . Retrieved October 10, 2002, from www.degrassi.tv.

42. The Pollster (8/27/03), "Does Your Principal Listen to Students' Complaints?" *Degrassi: The Next Generation Official Website*. Retrieved August 31, 2003, from www.degrassi.tv.

43. "Degrassi: Junior High," *Jump the Shark*. Retrieved August 31, 2003 and July 31, 2004, from www.jumptheshark.com. The postings on *Jump the Shark* are anonymous and undated. The site does not use screen names.

44. This data was obtained by a search in *Google: Groups*, which has archived listserv activity. Retrieved August 25, 2003 and August 1, 2004.

45. Jenkins, "The Poachers and the Stormtroopers," 2.

46. dbStardust (19 August 2003); 1SeAnsFaN1 (20 August 2003); DegrassiDiva14 (19 August 2003); and Killavrilnow (20 August 2003), "Next Season Commercial!!" *Degrassi: The Next Generation Official Website*. Retrieved August 31, 2003, from www.degrassi.tv.

47. Emma 445 (31 July 2004); Camui (31 July 2004); and linerds (31 July 2004), "Who Here is from America??" *Degrassi: The Next Generation Official Website*. Retrieved July 31, 2004, from www.degrassi.tv.

48. amylin03 (journal entry 1 August 2004), "Degrassi in the USA." *Degrassi: The Next Generation Official Website*. Retrieved August 1, 2004, from www.degrassi.tv.

49. ExecProducer, Stephen Stohn (4 July 2003). *Degrassi: The Next Generation Official Website*. Retrieved July 19, 2003, from www.degrassi.tv.

50. Will Brooker, "Living on *Dawson's Creek:* Teen Viewers, Cultural Convergence and Television Overflow," *International Journal of Cultural Studies* 4 (2001), 469.

CHAPTER 4

CHANGING FACES:
WHAT HAPPENED WHEN
DEGRASSI SWITCHED TO CTV

Ravindra N. Mohabeer

WHILE SURFING THE TUBE for something to watch one evening in the summer of 2001, I was pleasantly surprised to find a *Degrassi High* rerun in prime time. Since we had a satellite dish, I first thought that I had stumbled upon a CBC station from the West Coast where it was still late afternoon. Alternatively, I thought that maybe I found one of the new digital channels that repurposes old shows. *Degrassi*, as a tried and true audience hit, certainly must rake in a nostalgic and loyal group of people like me who are in their early thirties. Among us are people tired of "reality TV," which does not reflect any sort of reality we experience in our own lives. Certainly not the type of reality that *Degrassi* had presented so well and for so many years.

At the first commercial break, to my surprise, I discovered that my local CTV station — a major network, no less — was airing the episode. Near the end of the show, I told my wife that she had missed a historical event. By being aired on CTV, *Degrassi*, that most public of schools, went private. By private, I mean that *Degrassi* moved from the publicly owned Canadian Broadcasting Corporation (CBC) to the privately owned Canadian Television Network (CTV), a part of the Bell-Globe Media group of companies.

Surely, *Degrassi* had gone private before this. For years, syndicated episodes of *Degrassi* had been featured on American cable stations including HBO, Showtime and the Disney Channel,[1] as well as on Canadian specialty channels. Sold, as it were, to television outlets hungry for content that would produce a good audience yield while featuring a family focus. *Degrassi* was used to fill a specific programming niche in their schedules, not necessarily to foster a sense of a Canadian youth identity. Each of these networks is, of course, a privately held enterprise. But, to the best of my knowledge, when *Degrassi* aired on CTV, it was the first time in Canada that it appeared in prime time on a "competing," privately owned broadcast network and not on the CBC, which had been its Canadian home since the late 1970s. It was interesting to consider the implications of *Degrassi* appearing on a "new" network. I wondered what the reasons were for this change and what the future might hold for the series.

What was even more interesting was not so much that *Degrassi* was on CTV but that it was on CTV during *prime time*. Despite the fact that the summer prime-time schedule is generally unpredictable and "second tier" in terms of offerings, prime time is still prime time. It is that part of the television schedule when only the best shows are put on display. This holds true despite a history and increasing variety of glitzy and hyped-up prime-time television flops. The bounty of less than stellar shows in prime time proves that the term "best" does not necessarily mean best "quality." Rather, from a television programmer's standpoint, "best" means most *potentially* able to draw in the greatest number of viewers. In this equation, artistic or social "quality" is subordinate to the ability to generate a large audience. Often, this is why you find so many similar shows on your television schedule at the same time in the same television season.

As big-money businesses, television networks are wholly dependent on generating the largest possible audience for each half hour of their programming day.[2] Indeed, as mostly publicly traded "private enterprises," television networks are obligated to their shareholders to ensure that audiences are generated to watch the programs they choose to run. For without an audience, networks have nothing to sell to advertisers, and advertising, of course, is a network's main source of revenue. Advertisers pay money to individual television stations or to their parent networks in exchange for the attention of the audience that tunes in to watch particular segments of programming. In this dynamic, the audience is not thought of as a "viewing public" with a desire for "quality programming," but as a commodity that is to be bought and sold; it is the "commodity audience." The term commodity audience refers to estimating the value of television time by calculating the number and types of viewers who watch a particular show. This places the *value* of a show not in the content of the show itself but in the show's ability to attract the attention of a viewing audience.

In practice, this means that if all of the networks decide to feature a medical comedy this season and one network in particular does not have one lined up, it runs the risk of loosing a chunk of its audience share. For each chunk of audience share lost, the amount that can be charged for advertising time decreases. It matters little if every network featuring a slight variation on a theme diminishes the possibility for variety or "quality" on television. What matters more is that audiences tune in to shows in large numbers. Without large numbers of viewers, advertising revenues go down and the out-of-pocket costs of staying in business go up.

In the wasteland of summer prime time, CTV might have seen *Degrassi* as a viable way of pulling in drama-starved viewers at a lower cost. It is, of course, cheaper to buy ready-made episodic programming like *Degrassi* that is proven to draw in a loyal audience in the bleak summer months of television than it is to make original programming that may or may not succeed in doing the same. When *Degrassi* first appeared on CTV that summer, fewer viewers were thought to be available; audience numbers do not matter and television programmers are not inspired to offer new first-run episodes or series until the fall. The episodic shows that are "new" to a network in the summer are often second-rate programs that could not find a place in the rough-and-tumble world of the fall-to-spring television season. Today, though, the availability of so many cheaper-to-buy American shows that do not fit into the limited number of prime-time hours during the first-run season make it easier to buy and air shows for the first time on Canadian networks in the summer. *Degrassi* in its first summer on CTV must have been seen as an episodic "cash cow" to tide the network over until the fall when cheaper, first-run, predominantly American programming could be bought to fill the same time slot.

THE DEGRASSI AUDIENCE

Degrassi was always a little bit different than anything else that was on television, Canadian or American. Whether or not it was seen as a hot commodity in television ratings, for me, *Degrassi* always eclipsed the frequent disappointment I felt when I watched each season's other supposedly best shows. Moreover, I came to know *Degrassi* long before I knew that my interest in following the saga of Spike's early teen pregnancy or the antics of The Zit Remedy meant that I was a part of a lucrative commodity audience. I became a committed member of the *Degrassi* audience because of what the show had to offer, not simply because of how the show was hyped and propped up by the network. *Degrassi* always had something to say, and that something always spoke directly to me. In fact, I would not characterize my relationship with *Degrassi* as something that has ever made me feel commodified. Perhaps CTV relied on the fact that viewers like me who had grown up with *Degrassi* would put aside their cynicism over the lack of variety on television, especially in the summer, and would not be distracted by the competing high-budget American programming on other networks. Instead, these viewers would tune in to something from their own golden age of television.

Though I had not followed the original *Degrassi* series on the Internet like many diehard fans, nor had I written slash fiction using the characters and storylines of *Degrassi* as fodder for my fantasies, over the years I never forgot my connection to the show. It sits in my mind as the embodiment of good youth-focused television. It is only the most profound of media experiences that creates this sort of affective resonance among its viewers, and shows of this sort are rare. Growing up in a North American media environment, characterized by rapid cuts (similar to an MTV montage) and polished storylines, *Degrassi* always felt like it existed both as a show and as a part of my life — bumpy, slow and rough around the edges. It is through this realistic and believable presentation of being a youth that *Degrassi* successfully carved out its place on the psyche of Canadians who came of age in the 1980s. I was happy to see the show featured so prominently, even if it was on CTV.

As a *Degrassi* fan, I had grown up alongside the kids from each of the series in first-run, and the fact that I had already seen almost every episode at least once didn't matter. I watched during what I thought was a one-time momentary lapse when *Degrassi* went private — bought by CTV to fill in a time slot, a time slot that in the fall would be occupied by something a fraction of *Degrassi*'s stature. I lent my attention to CTV, knowing that the station could sell it to its advertisers, enjoying this event as an anomaly. The next night, when I found *Degrassi High* on at the same time and on the same channel and saw commercials for *Degrassi: The Next Generation* (*TNG*), I realized that this was no momentary lapse. Rather, the presence of *Degrassi* on CTV that summer evening was indicative of something yet to come.

BECOMING A COMMODITY AUDIENCE

Greg Hughes says that the *Degrassi* television phenomenon is, arguably, one of the most successful media achievements to ever come out of Canada.[3] Its ability to speak *to* and *about* youth was not lost on the Canadian federal government's health and welfare division. In the 1991–92 television season, Health and Welfare Canada sponsored the creation of *Degrassi Talks* as a way to reach out to Canadian youth.[4] Even the federal government had come to see the *Degrassi* franchise as a powerful way to speak to Canadian youth. How then, did the move from the CBC, Canada's only national public broadcast network, to CTV, Canada's largest and oldest national private broadcast network, affect the series?

These two broadcast bodies have vastly different purposes and as a result present different sorts of programming. While it is unfair to characterize the move from public to private as having sold out the spirit of *Degrassi*, the new series *TNG*, which has aired exclusively on CTV, is characteristically different than the earlier versions. Make no mistake, this is not simply a matter of the times having changed. This difference lies in *TNG*'s association with CTV. Changes can be seen in the contrast between characters in the original series and *TNG*, in the various political and economic structures that underlie the funding of the various manifestations of *Degrassi* and in the spin-off merchandise and properties associated with *TNG*.

TNG is especially defined by its growing status as a commodity entity and not just as a television show, both because of generational shifts in viewing demographics and avenues for international redistribution and because of changes in the ways in which concepts of youth audiences and family audiences are administratively imagined. Although *TNG* has tried to stay true to its status as a unique Canadian product, by the end of its first season, it appeared much more plastic, generic and universal. From its gospel/ choral theme song, to the attractive, polished and decidedly more professional acting, the image of the average youth and the substance of average youth issues changed. All of this leads me to the conclusion that in moving from CBC to CTV, *Degrassi* went from being a social forum for and about *Canadian* youth to being a product for and about a generic and glamorized adult-take on a commodified youth culture.

In a review of *TNG* for *Shift Online*, Hughes says that not all *Degrassi* fans are happy with the new series:

> [*TNG*] has come under fire from some fans for not being true to its origins: a glossy visual style that contradicts the low-budget image of the original series, actors that are far too pretty to exist in real life, and characters that, well, aren't Joey Jeremiah. While some have attributed this to the shifting of the series from government-funded CBC to moneybags CTV, other fans have complained that *Degrassi: TNG* lacks characters that resonate with the audience as well as the old cast did.[5]

While Hughes summarizes two possible, seemingly opposite interpretations of *TNG*, he misses the obvious connection. The reason that the characters of *TNG* do not resonate with the audience as well as the old cast did *is* rooted in its association with CTV.

As a private network, CTV's purpose is decidedly different from that of CBC. In exploring this difference, I will make clear why the association of *Degrassi* with CTV has refashioned *TNG* into something that is only partially related to the earlier forms of *Degrassi*. *Degrassi* appeared on CBC from its first days to the cancellation of *Degrassi High* in 1991. Accountable to the Canadian public, the CBC professes to have a larger investment in promoting a unique Canadian experience than CTV does. The CBC's mandate is to tell

> Canadian stories reflecting the reality and diversity of our country; inform Canadians about news and issues of relevance and interest; support Canadian arts and culture; build bridges among Canadians, between regions and the two linguistic communities of Canada.[6]

The early days of *Degrassi* can be seen today as, perhaps, the last of a dying CBC era when shows were successful with the youth market because they told distinctively Canadian stories. Today, the CBC is often criticized for its limited success in producing and airing youth-focused television.

By contrast, CTV's approach to programming is more market than culture driven. While the following quotation is not the station's "mission statement" (it comes from an area of the Bell-Globe Media–owned CTV corporate Web site that describes what values they look for in a television program), it does reflect a BCE-CTV vision of "quality" television.

For BCE-CTV, television content is first directed towards the audience to which advertisers sell their products, and only secondly towards creating a shared media experience.

> CTV is a mainstream broadcaster in the business of making popular programming for the widest possible audience ... demonstrated audience appeal and/or market interest in the series will be key to decision-making, therefore, a renewed series is a more likely candidate for dramatic series extension funding. The extension will only be made on those series that would have otherwise received a 13-episode order.[7]

In order to qualify as a "viable candidate" for funding by BCE-CTV, a show needs to demonstrate that it is a "hit" among viewers. Again, being a hit does not mean that a show serves a particularly profound social or artistic function, but simply that it draws in enough viewers to maintain the interest of advertisers.

The same could be said of the CBC, inasmuch as it depends on advertising dollars for revenue. However, the approach of the CBC differs from CTV because of the manifest differences implicit in its value statements regarding programming. CBC is committed to speaking to Canadians about Canadian issues, while BCE-CTV is committed to speaking to Canadians as long as they are willing to tune in and be a part of a commodity audience. To be fair, this does not mean that BCE-CTV is not interested in telling Canadian stories from a Canadian perspective. What is more important for them as a private enterprise, however, is that these stories be ones that will encourage consistent audiences who will pay for their viewing with their attention.

For CTV, the addition of *TNG* to its scheduled programming is as much about tapping into a proven loyal audience as it is about telling stories about Canadian youth from a youth perspective. Had *Degrassi* not been as popular in its first several runs, and had it not enjoyed success in international redistribution and syndication, it is unlikely that CTV would have put as much effort into promoting *TNG*. From those summer evenings when I first discovered the impending return of *Degrassi* until long after *TNG* finally appeared in first-run during the family viewing zone of Sunday night, CTV promoted *TNG* ad nauseam. It was virtually impossible to tune in to any half hour of general CTV programming without encountering some reference to *Degrassi High*, the Web site www.*Degrassi*.tv or *TNG*. Interestingly, despite the heavy promotion, CTV and Epitome Pictures (the refashioned production company that represents part of the original creative team behind *Degrassi* and that is responsible for *TNG*'s production) could not count on a guaranteed audience for *TNG* in the way that CBC might have if the characters of *Degrassi* had gone to university in the early 1990s. CTV had to contend with a decade-long gap between the production of the old show and the new one that had not existed in the production periods prior to and in between *The Kids from Degrassi Street*, *Degrassi Junior High* and *Degrassi High*.

The decade-long gap that separated the last episode of *Degrassi High* and *TNG* meant that CTV did not have the natural progression of age that would transfer its familiar characters into a new school-based situation. As much as *Degrassi* always provided a lot of out-of-school contexts for its storylines, it was a show about youth who were connected by their shared experiences *in* school. Aside from that, CTV had a decade of youth-oriented television to compete with, largely spawned by the success of *Degrassi*. In planning for a next generation of *Degrassi*, there needed to be a school context for it to be taken seriously by viewers of the earlier series. At the same time, it would be difficult to reach a teen market if the central characters in *TNG* were all adults. It would be equally difficult to convince long-time fans that *TNG* had anything to do with the original series, aside from the name, without a connection to the old characters and storylines. It is this schism that is my biggest concern with *TNG*. In its new form, from the title alone, *The Next Generation* implies that it is and is not *Degrassi*. Including the word *Degrassi* in the title caught the attention of viewers of the original series, while *TNG* as an extension of *Degrassi* sold it as a program for youth. In some respects, *TNG* suffers from a schizophrenic location between two generations of viewers.

For *TNG* to successfully capture an audience, CTV had to draw in the *old* viewers who were caught up with the characters of the earlier series in order to introduce them to the next *Degrassi* generation, and at the same time it had to attract *new* viewers who were inundated by the myriad youth-focused television programs at their disposal. In this way, the decision to include old characters from *Degrassi* seems to have been as much about audience as storyline.

The way in which *TNG* has included old characters in the new show is clever, though somewhat predictable. Still, it reflects a particular attention to bridging audiences. In its pilot debut, *TNG* was introduced by way of a reunion of the old characters as a segue into a new life for a new *Degrassi* Community School and its new inhabitants. In August 2001, CTV viewers tuned in to reminisce with all of their favourite *Degrassi* friends. We all knew that these characters were now grown and would likely no longer be a part of a continuing next generation *Degrassi*. Nevertheless, we watched as Joey, Caitlin, Spike, Snake, Lucy and even Mr. Raditch were paraded in front of us, taking us back a decade in time as if it were yesterday. It was clear by the end of the pilot that only a few of the familiar "old-school" faces would be a meaningful part of the new school. This was made clear by designating the old characters "visitors" to the new school. Many of the familiar faces from earlier shows simply passed through as part of the reunion, while others were more clearly implicated as being part of the *next generation*. Three such characters included Snake, who had outgrown his Zit Remedy days to become a teacher; Mr. Raditch, who was to remain the principal of the new school; and Spike, who was the mother of Emma, *TNG*'s central character.

Part of the reason that the old guard made only a brief appearance is that *TNG* needed a more powerful tool than memory to crystallize the tween and teen viewers who only knew *Degrassi* as after-school reruns. This group may have connected with the old cast and characters but had come of age in a time of multiple teen dramas and a variety of *Degrassi*-like competitors. The *Degrassi* characters, with their 1980s big hair, pimpled faces, imperfect manners and incomplete acting skills, are a world apart from what most of today's youth have grown up seeing on prime time. The nostalgic viewing audience that long for the original *Degrassi* characters, though not to be dismissed, are not as lucrative as today's youth market.[8] It is estimated that, today, teens comprise a multi-billion dollar market segment that is increasingly separated from all other market niches. While it is true that nostalgic *Degrassi* viewers likely have the income to spend on products, it is really the teen market that drives youth-oriented television programming. Again, put in the context of the audience schism mentioned earlier, this presents an interesting challenge for *TNG*. For *TNG* to be successful, CTV needed a balance of *old* and *new* school to link these two disparate and seemingly irreconcilable groups of viewers.

Ironically, had it not been for the progressive thinking of the producers of the early *Degrassi* series, who pushed the envelope in terms of presenting "real" issues on television, CTV's attempt to take *Degrassi* into the year 2001 might not have worked at all. That is, if Amanda Stepto's character,

Spike, had not had a baby and struggled to raise her while trying to stay a part of the *Degrassi* community, it would have been difficult to credibly capture both a new and an old *Degrassi* audience. At least, it would have been difficult to capture the attention of an audience divided by a generation without alienating one generation for the sake of the other. This is not to say that all television shows fall into a generation-specific trap. What is most interesting about *TNG* is that it purposely, and forcefully, has tried to efface nearly twenty-five years of the evolution of television by uniting the old *Degrassi* with the new. This is ironic in that, at least within its first two seasons, *TNG* appeared to lack the depth of characters or storylines that made the earlier series so critically successful. In *TNG*, both characters and plot resemble the more glamorous and plastic American knock-off youth programs that followed the original *Dergassi* than they resemble the *Degrassi* of old. Emma, Spike's daughter, is the quintessential representation of what made the earlier *Degrassi* series successful, and what makes *TNG* different.

EMMA'S IMPORTANCE TO CTV

As a character, Emma, who is introduced in *TNG* as Spike's now middle-school-aged daughter, is the glue that holds the various strands of *Degrassi* audiences together. She embodies Spike's teenaged pregnancy and her struggle to complete high school, keep the baby and maintain connections with her friends, school and family. Emma is seen as both a hope for the future and a reminder of the past. She is the child that should not have been, the child who, through Spike's struggles, epitomizes the dilemmas of youth. In *TNG*, Emma represents the continuation of a classic *Degrassi* plot line, punctuating the question that remained in the minds of *old Degrassi* fans, Whatever happened to Spike's baby? She also embodies characteristics of long-gone members of the *Degrassi* community, for example, Caitlin's social conscience, the recurring goody-goody who acted as the alter ego of her friends. More important, though, she represents the social consciousness of the early series while also representing a social consciousness that reflects an idealized younger viewer of *TNG*.

This extreme social consciousness with its unwavering commitment on Emma's part, however, does not adequately represent the minute dilemmas and contradictions of being a youth in Canada. In *TNG*, Emma's precocious sociability acts as a conduit between viewers who are parents wanting their children to be mature and a more contemporarily youthful audience wishing to be rebellious and socially defiant. Emma is both of these extremes. In the pilot, Emma was readily able to act the part of the rebellious youth by sneaking out, meeting a stranger at a hotel and enlisting her friends to lie on her behalf. As a voice of reason, Emma is quick to identify the error of her ways, frequently judges others and acts as a bellwether for social causes (for example, her concerns over genetically modified foods that resulted in her protest in the cafeteria).

Contrary to the old *Degrassi* with its decentralized cast and rotating focus on different storylines and characters, Emma is the recurring figure in most *TNG* episodes during the first two seasons. Even when she was not featured in an episode's plotline, she was ever present as the underlying lynchpin that held old and new *Degrassi* viewers in place. While Emma's location as the central plot figure has shifted since seasons one and two, her role in capturing an audience and thus bolstering the other characters of the show — in essence grooming them for their own place in the spotlight — fashioned her as different than earlier *Degrassi* characters and made *TNG* seem to be less about the condition of youth and more about the spectacle of youth.

In this way too, Emma, epitomizes everything that makes *TNG* characteristically different from any other *Degrassi* of the past. As a character, Emma is over the top on just about every hot-button social issue. Even when she is not the immediate focus of an episode of *TNG*, she can be seen in cameos, organizing events, sitting in a classroom or disapproving the "negative" behaviour of others. She does not represent a range of emotions or the characteristically fluctuating demeanour of youth. She appears as a paper doll, created to represent a particular category of youth and to represent the adult voice of disapproval. Emma is the character in *Degrassi* who knows now what we wish we knew then. She acts with a passion and conviction for causes, presents a voice of maturity and "knows best," at least in comparison to the other children and youth on the show.

While Caitlin of *Degrassi Junior High* and *Degrassi High* can be seen as a parallel to *TNG*'s Emma, in Emma CTV has a particular caricature of the socially conscious, privileged youth created for the modern media. Perhaps her character borrows from the "good kid" image that pervades American teen dramas. Emma's eloquence, poise, flawless attractiveness and utter lack of fear represents an unrealistic version of youth that is more akin to the American self-actualized *After School Special* character than to a more "realistically" imperfect, pimple-faced, angst-ridden character of the earlier series.

Joan Nicks points out that part of the success of the earlier *Degrassi* series was the ability of the Playing With Time Repertory Company (PWT) to take ordinary kids who were not "professional actors" and allow them to be rough around the edges, naturalistic in their acting and believable in their speech. Nicks relates how,

> Yan Moore, head writer of the *Degrassi* series, tailored the scripts with the vital participation of the repertory cast, young people drawn from schools in the Toronto area. The situations, topics and dialogue were vetted in regular work-shops involving the young actors. In the interest of constructing valid actions and responses for the characters, this type of earnest consultation ensured that the *Degrassi* series would remain youth-centered, and that the drama's durable realist manner would avoid the plasticity common to television's generic sit-com families. Even as the actors grew within their roles over the first three series, and as new characters were added, a naturalistic acting style prevailed. If the acting at times appears untutored to some viewers, it remains closer to the look and speech of everyday youths than those of precocious kids and teens common to Hollywood film and television sitcoms.[9]

TNG is much more like the American-style youth programming than its predecessors. That is, in the first two seasons, *TNG* dealt with a new hot-button social issue every week, and the pace at which they unfolded made it seem as though *TNG* was more about touching the surface of the *in thing* rather than taking the *in thing* as a starting point from which to explore the complicated ways in which youth experience life. In many ways, *TNG* always seemed to resolve the issue in a way that American-style *After School Specials* did rather than being open-ended like the old *Degrassi*. Even the characters from the show's previous life who regularly appear as adults on *TNG* are there primarily to point out the folly of youth. *TNG* seems more geared towards describing normative behaviours than being a show about how confused and complicated the lives of youth remain. Today, *TNG* is envisioned as something to be sold to family audiences, not something that should speak to youth on their own terms.

For example, the first episode of *TNG*, "Mother and Child Reunion," dealt with how teens today live in a technologically sophisticated world that is often outside of the purview of adults. In that episode, Emma is lured to a hotel by a man she met on the Internet. It is not until she is at the hotel that she realizes the dangerous situation she is in. The episode was powerfully written and very dramatically edited to send home the idea that teens should be supervised while using Internet technologies. The moral contained a normative, family-value-oriented statement. It was aimed as much, or more, to parental viewers than to youth.

It is not fortuitous that the first episode focused on the Internet. In terms of commodity value and cross-platform repurposing, creating fear about "safe places" on the Internet was advantageous for BCE-CTV. Concurrent with the development of the television show was the development of the Web site, www.degrassi.tv (or degrassi.tv). To read the Web site's press releases, particularly those that list the number of awards and distinctions bestowed upon *TNG*'s Web companion, it seems as though the *Degrassi* Web portal is as valuable a commodity as the show itself. While it might seem unusual to portray the dangers of the Internet to try to drive viewers to the official *TNG* Web site, it really is not.

Not surprisingly, CTV's new parent company, Bell Canada Enterprises, has a large investment in the Internet both as a content and access provider (Sympatico). The cross-platform advertisement in the form of a "fan" at degrassi.tv is a deliberate attempt to create a Web life outside the show in order to maximize advertising knowledge and revenue for *TNG* and its parent companies. (According to the credit page at the site, BCE-CTV participated in the creation of the Web site along with Epitome Virtual Reality, Snap Media and other funders.) Through degrassi.tv, BCE-CTV has found a way of both enlarging the audience and tapping into the private connections that viewers may or may not be making with *TNG*. These connections can range from the feeling of wanting to belong to wanting to carry on the conversations and topics that are presented in the show through discussion boards. Those fans who really want to get the full experience can "decorate their own locker" in the virtual Degrassi Community School. Each of the interactive events on the Web site represents an opportunity to personalize the show by picking from (mostly) predetermined choices.

Today, one can literally receive a *Degrassi* message anywhere through the linking of degrassi.tv mail to Bell Mobility cellular services, another of BCE's major holdings. With viewers having the chance to be degrassi.tv members anytime and anywhere, someone who was once just a passive viewer can now extend the process of commodifcation by entrenching their commodification through participating in market research polls, disguised as "trivia," or by answering *Degrassi* surveys and questions of the day. Though viewers in the 1980s were not "passive," the construction of this companion Web site plays a strategic role in *TNG*. Rather than go to the "real youth" who act in the show for story ideas as Yan Moore did in the 1980s, *TNG* goes to the viewers/Internet/mobile users to find out what they want to see. Viewers have a chance to vote on their favourite endings or potential storylines via degrassi.tv and those who actually vote effectively act as an unpaid focus group on whom to test out the "sexiest" plot lines. This shift represents a move away from stories that speak to the complex social reality of youth to stories that position youth in a competitive television marketplace.

COMMODITIES & YOUTH MARKETS

More than anything else, CTV treats *TNG* as a hot commodity. Given the above example of how fans are drawn into the show and are offered ways of staying connected far outside the bounds of television viewing, it is clear that *TNG* has less to do with stories than with markets. Though it is a subtle one, the shift from a member of the "audience" to a member of the "market" is an important one. Despite the idea that all members of a television audience are conceived of as commodities to some extent, being considered a member of a market first means that the *TNG* television audience is less about television and more about consumption. This approach suggests that CTV treats *TNG* as a valuable tool for attracting the lucrative yet elusive youth market and subsequently the youth-directed advertising dollar. The use of television as a vehicle to display *TNG* is really only coincidental. In the end, the fact that *TNG* is on television once again reflects the attempt to conjoin old viewers with the new. To be sure, the old viewers are not the main targets of *TNG*. If this were the case, most of the spin-off marketing would be directed at nostalgia rather than looking forward. Clearly, it is not. Everything on degrassi.tv is directed at getting today's youthful "viewer" to participate in the *Degrassi* family of products across as many platforms as possible — TV, Internet, mobile phone and so on. Participants in the *TNG* experience are not encouraged to be nostalgic, but rather to contribute ideas about how to make *TNG* more lifelike.

Perhaps it is unfair to lament the passing of *Degrassi*, when in fact what we find in *TNG* is really a reflection of a new market reality. It is possible that had the earlier versions of *Degrassi* been hatched at a different time, they too would have been more market driven. This manifest difference between the old and the new alerts us to the fact that television has lost its ability to be a "stand-alone" medium of great importance. Like radio before it, television now sits in a position of secondary importance as a vehicle for large-scale social communication. In order for a modern television series to be popular, it must extend far beyond the confines of a cathode ray tube (or plasma screen) and into the rest of the media lives of its viewers. In this way, maybe *TNG* is more forward thinking than I have given it credit for. Where earlier forms of *Degrassi* attempted to become articulated into the lives of Canadian youth by using the then most powerful and prominent form of media to communicate ideas and issues in a way that few if any other shows did at the time, *TNG* uses television as a gateway. Through the door opened up by *TNG* the television series, the creators can access the lives of youth via the Internet and other forms of media that are slowly eclipsing television in terms of social and political importance.

CTV's *TNG* creates characters that, for lack of a better phrase, fit a mould. The purpose of these moulded characters is not simply to reflect the reality of finding similar characters in the lives of youth but to play on the perception that these characters exist in the real world in simple, neat and marketable packages. It is far easier to produce a J.T. Yorke who is a consummate clown, rarely ever concerned or effected by consequences, or an Emma Nelson who is always socially conscious and never tempted by the spoils of market society, than it is to reproduce a Joey Jeremiah. In characters like Joey, we found a class clown who used humour to mask a learning disability. In Caitlin, we found a social activist who constantly confronted family difficulties and inner struggles over being popular. In *TNG*, we find a class clown whose deep secret is an ability to sew — a secret treated humourously in order to complement his character rather than expose a youthful habit of hiding skills and passions that are not "cool." It is this lack of attention to the nuances of youth and the settling on fixed characters who seemingly serve singular purposes to *TNG*'s plot that makes it so different from the old *Degrassi*.

Both the storylines and the characters of *TNG* are developed to fit in with the programming environment — that is, the advertising and other shows that surround *TNG*. In this way, the show's purpose is not to tell complex and controversial stories about and for youth, but to tell stories that present a verisimilitude of youthful issues while not making too much noise or asking the audience to think too hard. It is precisely the ability to ask the audience to think that made earlier versions of *Degrassi* stand out and the lack of this that makes *TNG* blend into the rest of the programming week. What is interesting is that this "fitting in" has caused *TNG* to loose its edge. In the first two seasons, it enjoyed a position of prominence during the family programming hours on Sunday evenings. Poised as the lead show at the top of the 7:00 p.m. time slot, it was treated as an important show by CTV. Today, *TNG* enjoys a much less obvious star treatment. In the third season it was moved to the second half of the hour in a middle-of-the-week time slot, a location reserved for "weaker shows," and is being piggy-backed on "successful" American family sit-coms like *8 Simple Rules* or *Meet My Family*. *TNG* seems to have lost some of its luster at CTV.

What is most interesting about the move from Sunday night prominence to the second-slot on Wednesday night is that *TNG* is beginning to look more like the old *Degrassi* than the new. When it first arrived on the scene in 2001, the show aired with a glitz and glamour that was immediately different. But in its third season, with a return to the never-ending storylines, the constant attention to the liminality of youth and the more frequent reference to the old *Degrassi* cast, *TNG* might be turning a corner.

★

While it would be nearly impossible to make wholesale changes to the cast of *TNG*, the show seems to be reconnecting to its roots. The storylines, though still much more *After School Special* than *Degrassi Junior High*, have begun to reflect a greater level of complexity than was evident in the first two seasons. Despite this, *TNG* is still much more market driven, as is evidenced by the sponsor trivia and "audience polls" in which viewers are asked what they would like to see as the most "popular" endings to potential storylines rather than what they think would be more realistic outcomes. In the end, what will determine the fate of *TNG* will not be its ability to resonate with the audience the way that the earlier series did but CTV's ability to sell the idea of *Degrassi* to a new generation of sponsors.

In the end, it will be interesting to see if the contemporary youth audience will embrace a new version of the old *Degrassi*, pimples and all, or if they will abandon *TNG* for a more glitzy American version. Ironically, in trying to shape *TNG* to resemble sophisticated and over-the-top American youth programming, CTV might have created the seeds of its own disaster.

The reason that the older *Degrassi* was successful, both in terms of gathering an audience and in terms of creating a strong and significant television phenomenon, was because the shows were different from just about everything available at the time. *TNG*, however, has failed to mark itself as being different. In order to do so, it will have to remake itself into something that, at present, it is not.

NOTES

1. Joan Nicks, "*Degrassi,*" *The Museum of Broadcast Communications.* Retrieved October 2, 2003, from www.museum.tv/archives/etv/D/htmlD/*Degrassi*/*Degrassi*.htm.

2. I. Ang, *Desperately Seeking the Audience* (New York: Routledge, 1991).

3. G. Hughes, "*Degrassi*'s Next Generation." *Shift Online.* Retrieved October 2, 2003, from www.shift.com/content/web/382/1.html.

4. Nicks, "*Degrassi.*"

5. Hughes, "*Degrassi*'s Next Generation."

6. Canadian Broadcasting Corporation, "CBC Fast Facts: Mandate." *CBC.* Retrieved October 2, 2003, from http://cbc.radio-canada.ca/htmen/fast_facts.htm.

7. BCE-CTV, "CTV Benefits, Dramatic Series Extension: What Are We Looking For?" *BCE-CTV.* Retrieved October 2, 2003, from www.ctv.ca/servlet/ArticleNews.

8. N. Doherty and WGBH Educational Foundation. *The Merchants of Cool* (WGBH Educational Foundation, 1999). Video.

9. Nicks, "*Degrassi.*"

The Next Generation Goes Digital:
Technology, the Medium and the Message

Laura Tropp

ONE OF THE MOST PROMINENT differences between the earlier series of *Degrassi* (*DC*) and the current *Degrassi: The Next Generation* (*TNG*) is the way the teens on the show engage with technology.[1] All of the *TNG* episodes either feature technology in the background or as a key part of the plot, which provides a unique opportunity for analyzing how the program represents the changing role of technology in society and, particularly, in youth culture. Since *TNG* replicates the same educational-minded goals as *DC*, one can observe how the use and representation of technology in youth programming has changed over time. In *DC*, technology did not play a central role but was only one of many elements in the students' educational lives. In *TNG*, technology has shifted to become a ubiquitous presence that shapes their learning environment.

In the recent episode "Hot for Teacher" on *TNG*, the teacher, Mr. Simpson, lectures his students on Canadian scholar Marshall McLuhan and his famous aphorism "The medium is the message." McLuhan, inspired in part by another Canadian scholar, Harold Innis, argued that examining the content of media is not enough; it is as important to understand its context — that is, how the content relates to the particular characteristics of each medium. In the United States, scholars such as Walter Ong, Neil Postman and Joshua Meyrowitz have also explored how new technologies have affected society. Ong examines how cultures shift as they move from orality to literacy; Postman argues that the dominant medium of our culture helps to determine the way our society thinks about and understands our world. For example, Postman argues that widespread use of television promotes a tendency among viewers to see all aspects of society (education, politics, religion) in terms of entertainment. Meyrowitz, like Postman, explores how ideas about childhood and adulthood have shifted with the introduction of electronic media.[2]

Though these scholars wrote about media in the 1980s, their theories are particularly relevant today as the number and types of mediated experiences increase and as technology itself becomes a subject of popular culture. For these scholars, understanding the context of the media message — including when it was produced, the intentions of the producers and the characteristics of the particular medium — is just as important as interpreting the content. In this chapter, I apply the theoretical work of these scholars in order to explore how the media environment differs between *TNG* and the earlier versions of *Degrassi*.

NEW TECHNOLOGIES, NEW EXPERIENCES

McLuhan understood that technology is a way to extend the human senses, that it allows human beings to go further than their physical bodies will allow. For example, a telephone allows one to converse with others, though they are not physically present. In creating these extensions, one changes the environment in which one lives. *TNG* represents a world in which technology has become an accepted part of the characters' lives, yet the introduction of new technologies has changed how the characters understand their world. In the time between the airing of *DC* and *TNG*, technology shifted from being an occasional part of the plot to a central theme of the program. In *DC*, teens were often found roaming the halls of the high school or meeting in each other's homes. In *TNG*, the teens supplement these activities with spending time in the computer lab[3] or at a hangout named The Dot Grill. When technology appeared in *DC*, such as when Lucy loaned her camera to Joey and his band to make a music video, it became the centre of the episode "Everybody Wants Something." In *TNG*, however, technology is a constant presence: the teens own cell phones, play video games and work on and communicate through the school's computers.

The importance the program places on technology can be witnessed simply by comparing the opening credits of earlier versions of the series with *TNG*. In *DC*'s credits, all the characters were engaged with each other, shown talking, laughing, walking through their school or sitting in class-rooms. *TNG*'s opening credits add mediated technologies to these activities. In the first and second seasons, the credits began with Emma sitting at her computer sending an electronic message. The message became an animated envelope, which moved through the shots during the rest of the credits. The envelope flew past other students playing basketball, singing in a chorus and talking and having fun. Interspersed within these activities were additional mediated communications. Toby surfed the Web on a school computer, and Craig used a camera to take a team picture. The final shot of *TNG*'s credits mirrored *DC*'s (in this case, *Degrassi High*'s) by using a close-up shot of a pocket on the back of a teenage girl's jeans. The difference is that on *TNG* there was a cell phone in her pocket, and as the animated envelope swooped back into her pocket, she picked up the phone to retrieve a message.

The superimposition of the electronic message illustrates the omnipres-ence of this new technological environment. Face-to-face communica-tion is no longer the only or even primary way that teens communicate today. *TNG*'s opening credits sequence might feature teens engaged in in-terpersonal communication but an electronic message is permeating their activities, reshaping their environment and offering them new avenues of communication and information while they continue to pursue the tradi-tional activities of school.

In the opening credits of the second half of season three, the animated envelope is replaced by the frame of a video camera being operated by one of the students (Ellie). The characters continue to engage in their school activities, but now they also mug for the camera, demonstrating a height-ened awareness of the mediated communication in their environment. Sociologist Erving Goffman compares individuals interacting with one an-other to actors performing on stage as they try to create impressions and roles for their audiences.[4] Goffman's notion of role-playing is apparent in the opening credits: the students are not simply living their lives but also performing them. *TNG* illustrates, then, a new and different media envi-ronment in which the teens must face both the demands of being watched by and performing for the camera. The opening credits are only the begin-ning of *TNG*'s representation and use of technology. It is also used to reflect the changing teaching environment.

In the earlier versions of *Degrassi*, the students and teachers were the central figures. The classes, although progressive and student-centred (the students were active participants in discussions), still featured traditional rooms with the teachers standing at the front of the class and students sitting in rows watching them. While there are still many traditional classrooms, one of the classrooms prominently featured is the Media Immersion classroom, which places the students behind computer screens. This new classroom no longer solely focuses on the teacher–student relationship but on the technology within the classroom. The computer screen has replaced the chalkboard and, especially, the teacher as the centre of the students' attention. While Mr. Simpson loses some authority within the classroom (for technology has replaced him as the key figure teaching the students), his students respect him for his technological prowess, which they embrace. He encourages them to "use the technology and their imagination" and to "take technology to the next step." In fact, the students enjoy showing off their mastery of technology to him. For instance, in the episode "Jagged Little Pill," they construct a thank-you message using Flash animation to surprise him.

Technology has also influenced how students communicate with each other in class. In the *DC* episodes, teachers were frequently seen writing on chalkboards, and students were shown passing notes to each other or whispering to each other. For example, in the episode "Rumour Has It," teens passed on gossip about whether Ms. Avery, a favourite teacher, was gay by talking to one another inside and outside of class. Contrast this with the *TNG* episode "Weird Science," where Manny accidentally e-mails the entire Media Immersion class a "note" about Emma's mother dating their teacher, Mr. Simpson. In neither instance does the teacher seem aware of the rumours. Mr. Simpson finds out only when Emma says something out loud, and Ms. Avery learns about the rumour when Caitlin has a discussion with her. The interest students display in the personal lives of teachers and the spreading of gossip still exists, but in this new technological environment the technology allows the gossip to spread more quickly and more efficiently.

At the Degrassi Community School, technology has shifted from scarcity to abundance. In *DC*, technology was visible but only on an occasional basis. For example, Lucy had a video camera, but it was used in specific episodes as a plot device rather than an everyday part of the characters' lives.

Lucy used the camera to make video letters for her friend, L.D., in "Sixteen, Part Two," and Joey and his friends begged Lucy to use her camera to make a music video for their band in "Everybody Wants Something." Active use of media technologies was uncommon enough to be noticeable when it did occur. In *TNG*, however, the Internet and other new communication technologies are treated as everyday learning and communication tools; they are so plentiful that they have become ordinary. In every episode, for example, the characters use the Internet for research: Marco explores whether he is homosexual ("Careless Whisper"); Terri and Paige look up information on palm reading ("Cabaret"); Ashley goes online to order condoms ("The Mating Game"). In addition, the students have greater choice over how and when they use these technologies. Whereas in *DC* the principal controlled the use of the school intercom system, in *TNG* students produce a daily program of announcements that they broadcast via the school's television system.

While *TNG* attempts to raise awareness about issues of corporate sponsorship of and access to technology, it brushes over the question of whether schools or students need this technology in the first place. In the episode "Parents Day," Emma writes an editorial arguing that the computers in their school are not really free because of the advertising placed on them. She argues, "Students shouldn't be force-fed advertising when they are at school." Meanwhile, Sean's brother responds, "A free computer is a free computer," especially for his brother who is falling behind in school and does not have access to new technology at home. The show raises the issue of the digital divide, but it does not further explore class issues. Emma, as a member of the middle class, is in the position to reject advertising as a condition for technology use; Sean, a member of the working class, must accept access to technology based on the conditions of corporate sponsors. In any case, Emma continues to use computers and the question of corporate sponsorship becomes a non-issue. The fact is that for the students of *TNG*, technology has moved from the realm of the extraordinary to the ordinary. It has not simply become a way to "extend the senses," as McLuhan suggests, but a natural and inevitable part of the environment.

PUSHING BOUNDARIES

The influence of new technologies, and particularly the Internet, on the lives of the Degrassi students has changed how they relate to adults and how they access information. In *DC*, several episodes focused on the danger of teens interacting with adult strangers or gaining access to adult worlds by looking at pornography and buying condoms. In *TNG*, technology plays a central role as the teens test their boundaries in accessing information and acting independently; teens are more technologically savvy than adults, which sometimes leads to trouble.

In *TNG*'s pilot show, "Mother and Child Reunion," Emma meets a boy on the Internet who turns out to be an adult male who is a sexual predator. This theme is reminiscent of two previous episodes of *DC*. In "Taking Off, Part One," Wheels runs away and is propositioned by a man from whom he accepts a ride. In "What a Night," Stephanie gets in over her head while on a date with an older man, her soap opera idol. In both episodes, the teens manage to extricate themselves from these situations. In *TNG*, however, a technology that Emma trusts is used to deceive her; her bad judgement alone did not create her problem, and she alone cannot solve it. Her friends help Emma's mother save her by breaking into her e-mail account to find the location of Emma's "date." Through this experience, Emma learns not to trust everything she finds on the Internet, and the police encourage Emma's mom to keep the computer in a public area where she can keep an eye on it, while at the same time chastising her to "keep the cyberstalkers out of her room." The police seem to take more of an interest in the role of the computer as opposed to Emma, the actual victim. (While this topic is not followed up on in subsequent episodes, there is less use of the computer at home but just as much use of computers at school.)

Teens can also bypass adult "border controls." In the episode "Eye of the Beholder," Toby and J.T. disable a filter on Toby's family's computer in order to search out pornography online. Using technology to view pornography was also the subject of an episode in *DC* ("The Best Laid Plans"), in which Arthur and Yick tried to watch the pornographic video *Swamp Sex Robots*. However, unlike Toby and J.T., they never succeed in watching the video and their efforts to secure it in the first place were much more involved. They needed to find a way to obtain the video (stolen from Yick's brother), find a place to hide it (Yick's locker) and then find a place to watch it (Arthur's house once his mother and sister had left). Arthur and Yick are immersed in trying to access the technology while Toby and J.T. take this access for granted. Despite the fact that Toby's computer is located in his family's living room, he can still accesses porn by disabling the filter effortlessly. He says, "It's weird, I didn't search for this stuff before but as soon as Kate [his stepmother] installed the filter ..." Toby sees Internet pornography primarily as forbidden fruit. He desires it because the adults are trying to prevent him from having access to it.

Though trying to obtain pornography is not new for teens, the Internet makes it easier. Meyrowitz argues that the properties of different media technologies vary in their control of access to information, for example, "the complexity of print's code excludes all young children from communication in print. In a sense, print creates 'places' where adults can communicate among themselves without being overheard by children."[5] The Internet, like television, with its emphasis on the visual, allows children into worlds that used to be exclusively for adults. When teens use the Internet, they have greater access to "adult" information that previously was more difficult for them to attain. As Toby and J.T. illustrate, the adult world of pornography can be easily accessed from the family's living room, without ever having to leave the house to buy a magazine from an authority figure. There is no need to find a place to hide it, there is a degree of interactivity and the amount is endless.

Undoubtedly, between the old and new *Degrassi*, teens have gained more control and a greater ability to access an adult world. In the *TNG* episode "The Mating Game," Terri and Ashley use a computer to order condoms. Ashley tells Terri, "You can buy anything on the Net." This episode is reminiscent of a scene from "The Best Laid Plans" in which Wheels goes to a drugstore to make the embarrassingly public purchase of condoms from the store cashier in preparation for his date with Stephanie. Stephanie's mother is the cashier who sells Wheels the condoms; later they share an awkward moment when she realizes that he is her daughter's date. In "The Mating Game," Ashley's purchase over the Internet allows her to avoid contact with an adult who might intervene. Ashley's easy experience of buying condoms online contrasts with the experience of her boyfriend, Jimmy, who has an embarrassing moment at the store, much like Wheels did. Not only is Ashley empowered to buy birth control, she is also hip to the new technology that allows her to do so without being under the watchful gaze of an adult authority figure.

The parents, of course, are not untroubled by these technological experiences. In trying to reassert control, they find that they cannot ignore the technology but must embrace it. After Emma's incident with the online predator, she is still allowed access to the computer but only in a space visible to her mother. The boys are "punished" for looking at pornography by having to visit both female and male pornography Web sites with their parents. Here, the parents use the technology to teach Toby and J.T. a lesson about objectifying women while forcing them to include their parents in their technological experience.

At other times, the teens are given technologies as a way for parents to keep an eye on them. For example, when Emma needs to leave a party with her drunk boyfriend, she calls her mom for a ride home on the cell phone her mom gave her ("Message in a Bottle"). These new media technologies create a paradox, allowing teens greater freedom yet allowing parents to watch over their teens. In a *New York Times* op-ed, Joe Queenan writes, "Parents frantically trying to insulate their adolescent progeny from the all-engulfing darkness are resorting to tracking devices, hidden cameras, Internet monitoring software and even automotive transponders."[6] He argues that ultimately this may threaten the child–parent relationship as teens begin to resent parental intrusion into their lives through technology. In *TNG*, though, Emma and her mother are brought closer together because of the cell phone. Unlike the teens in *DC*, who had to extricate themselves from dangerous or uncomfortable situations, in *TNG* the teens' parents are just a cell-phone call away.

COMMERCIALIZING THE MEDIUM

McLuhan writes, "In the new electric Age of Information and programmed production, commodities themselves assume more and more the character of information, although this trend appears mainly in the increasing advertising budget."[7] The growth of consumerism over the past twenty-five years along with the increase in teens' purchasing power means that *TNG* exists in a more hypercommercial environment than its predecessors.[8] Not only is the program shown on traditionally commercial networks, but it has also begun to mimic the conventions of commercial television by hiring polished actors, exhibiting high production values and featuring characters and dialogue that promote an awareness and celebration of the television world itself, where consumption and fame are the norm.

In *DC*, Simon was the only character involved in the television world; he first appears in the episode "Eggbert" and is recognized by the other students for his work in a commercial. In "A New Start," he stars as the model for a Dude Jeans campaign. However, in *TNG*, several of the characters become focused on the celebrity ideal. Terri, an overweight teen, is upset about her body image until she becomes a plus-size model. She seeks out a solution to her self-image issues by becoming a commodity and a celebrity. In "It's Raining Men," J.T. stars in a commercial and hosts a launch party for himself. He says to his friend Toby, "The commercial might seem dumb, but it's a dream come true." The characters' dialogue includes references to popular culture and acknowledges their media savvy. In "It's Raining Men," Ellie describes a Zombie movie as "a clever critique of consumerism," and Spinner, as he helps his homosexual friend Marco get ready for a date, quips that he's "a straight eye for the gay guy," referring to the popular reality show *Queer Eye for the Straight Guy*.

Wanting to attain fame can also be a strong motivator. In "Basketball Diaries," Liberty learns how difficult it is to be an onscreen television personality when Ashley finally agrees to let her read on-camera, instead of always writing the scripts. When Ashley, who is "the face" of the school's televised announcements, at first refuses to let Liberty try it, Liberty says to her, "Anyone can read a cue card. A monkey can do your job." Once in front of the camera, Liberty learns that an anchor's job is difficult when she has trouble reading her lines; nonetheless, she becomes immersed in the celebrity-obsessed media environment and wants to become a celebrity, recognizing that fame is valued in a televisual world. This episode cleverly analyzes the constructed nature of the televised news medium. The audience learns that the professionals on news programs have skills and strategies for producing the news. The program teaches teens how to use these skills, but it also traps them by assuming this environment is a given. Liberty's goal is mastering the medium and learning to live with it, not without it, in order to attain celebrity status.

In contrast, *DC* played down "celebrity" status and focused more on being "real." It used real kids instead of actors, for example. The teens had acne, were too short or too tall, overweight or underweight, and reflected the imperfections that most humans face. *TNG* also promotes itself as being real, using advertising slogans like "If your life was a TV show, this would be it" to make this point. However, the actors on *TNG* are more polished than in *DC*; most have some acting experience. The *Degrassi* Web site advertises that teens can audition for the show, but they need to "send a photo and résumé detailing [their] acting experience."[9] In addition, on *TNG* imperfections among the student characters are highlighted as unique rather than natural. For example, the fact that Terri is overweight becomes the focus of two episodes ("Eye of the Beholder" and "Mirror in the Bathroom"). Furthermore, *TNG* has fewer actors than *DC* (the third season of *TNG* listed seventeen actors compared with twenty-six on the third season of *Degrassi Junior High*), which means there are fewer characters and thus less diversity in the storylines, transforming each of the characters into archetypes: Paige is the sexy girl, Toby is the computer nerd and J.T. is the short kid who compensates by being the class clown.

While both versions promote the show as "real," the definition of real has changed. *TNG* promotes its authenticity by mimicking a typical commercial television drama. Unlike *DC*, which was filmed in a real school, *TNG* is filmed in a studio,[10] allowing for better control of the set design, lighting and sound which produces a more polished look. While *DC* promoted its actors as no different than everyday teens by using non-actors, *TNG* publicizes its actors as celebrities. For example, in the U.S., The N sponsored a contest during *TNG*'s third season in which the winner would meet her/his favourite characters/actors on the set of the program as well as star in the show.[11] In *DC*, "real" kids were the norm; in *TNG* the "real" kid becomes extraordinary, placed in the program as a result of a contest for one episode rather than regularly included as a part of the program's structure.

McLuhan called this shift in definition a reversal within the medium. He writes, "The principle that during the stages of their development all things appear under forms opposite to those that they finally present is an ancient doctrine."[12] In other words, the show has come full circle. While *DC* was created in order to offer an educational alternative to the commercial fare on television, *TNG* inevitably takes on the style of commercial television, because it is produced in a hypercommercial environment.

EXTENDING TELEVISION: EDUCATION OR ENTERTAINMENT?

Neil Postman describes television as being most useful for entertainment as opposed to education. He argues, "Entertainment is the supraideology of all discourse on television. No matter what is depicted or from what point of view, the overarching presumption is that it is there for our amusement and pleasure."[13] Both *DC* and *TNG* attempt to counter this assumption and strive to be educational while also entertaining. But the producers are media savvy and have always acknowledged the limitations of using television for education. They have compensated by extending the show beyond the boundaries of the medium.

During *DC*, the producers distributed pamphlets and supplemental reading materials to teachers to encourage them to show the series in classrooms and to provoke discussion about the issues raised on the program. In *TNG*, the producers have shifted their attention from television in the classroom to creating an educational experience on the Web. With the creation of a *TNG* companion Web site, the producers are taking advantage of their new media environment to move beyond class materials provided to teachers.

Studies indicate that "children make virtually no distinction between the Web and television. A study of the media preferences and usage of 4,000 Americans aged 4 and up by MTV Networks [in 1997–98] found that, though technically sophisticated convergence may not yet be here, convergent behavior in kids has arrived."[14] The creators of the new *Degrassi* acknowledge on the program's Web site that when creating this version of the show, they felt a need to move beyond the television medium. Wanting to appear more current, they created what they describe as a "convergent TV/Internet project."[15] The *Degrassi* Web site is intended to stimulate further discussion on topics initiated by the show. When the show is played in the United States, the Web site address appears on the bottom of the screen, encouraging teens watching the program to visit it. Promotions during the show reinforce this message. For example, in an episode ("Dressed in Black") exploring romantic relationships, the characters themselves visit the *Degrassi* community Web site, something the viewers at home can also do. Once there, visitors are encouraged to debate the ideas being presented on the show, as well as "interact" with the show's characters. Thus, the Web site and the television program have a symbiotic relationship — each one promotes the other.

★

Neil Postman treats technology as a "Faustian Bargain," and writes, "For it is inescapable that every culture must negotiate with technology, whether it does so intelligently or not. A bargain is struck in which technology giveth and technology taketh away."[16] In this new media environment, technology provides both gains and losses for the culture using it. The teens viewing *TNG* not only are taught lessons about issues that each show confronts (the dangers of drugs, dealing with social pressure and so on) but also are introduced into a new way of seeing the world, one that emphasizes the technology within their environment.

On The N, *TNG* promotes itself during its own commercial breaks by using a text-message theme. The image on the screen features text that teens message back and forth about their excitement and anticipation of the program. This advertisement both reflects this generation's use of the technology and encourages its use. The show sends messages about how technology has the power to improve their lives: the teens have fun using the technology to create music of their own, work on school projects and communicate with friends, for example. Yet the program also demonstrates the potential danger of technology, leading them into worlds they are not ready for, getting them into trouble with authority figures or contributing to miscommunication.

The program also reflects the changing television environments between *DC* and *TNG* as the program's content mimics the new media environment in which the show exists. While both shows treat themselves as an educational opportunity for viewers, *TNG* succumbs to the biases of commercial television. *TNG* exists in a different medium environment and critical examination of both programs reveals how *TNG* is shaped by its new environment. *TNG* must appeal to teens who are more media savvy and comfortable with commercialism. Technology is a constant presence in the show, just as it is a presence in teen's lives today. Ultimately, though, the program sends the message that technology is an inevitable part of our culture. It implies that it is natural for the teens on the program, as well as those viewing it, to embrace new technologies. Thus, technology shifts from being simply a tool to help one achieve a goal to becoming a ubiquitous part of the environment. As Mr. Simpson says, "The medium is the message."

NOTES

1. *DC* is the abbreviation for *Degrassi Classic*, which encompasses *Degrassi Junior High* and *Degrassi High*. The series retains a cult following among viewers who, even today, regularly purchase their own copies of the shows or even bid for them on eBay. The title of the most recent series, perhaps coincidentally, bears a striking similarity to the popular *Star Trek: The Next Generation*, which, like its predecessors, offered viewers a chance to imagine a technological future of spaceships meeting and battling aliens from other planets.

2. See Walter Ong, *Orality & Literacy: The Technologizing of the Word* (New York: Routledge, 1982); Neil Postman, *Amusing Ourselves to Death: Public Discourse in the Age of Show Business* (New York: Penguin Books, 1985); and Joshua Meyrowitz, *No Sense of Place: The Impact of Electronic Media on Social Behavior* (New York: Oxford University Press, 1986).

3. For example, J.T. plays a virtual game of basketball during his free time in "The Charming Man." In "Coming of Age," Emma studies in the computer lab while Sean and Manny look up astrology Web sites.

4. Erving Goffman, *The Presentation of Self in Everyday Life* (New York: Doubleday, 1959).

5. Meyrowitz, *No Sense of Place*, 238.

6. Joe Queenan, "Electronic Leashes for Teenagers," *The New York Times*, 24 May 2001, F10.

7. Marshall McLuhan, *Understanding Media: The Extensions of Man* (Cambridge, MA: MIT Press, 1995), 36.

8. For an explanation of hypercommercial environments, see Robert W. McChesney, *Rich Media, Poor Democracy: Communication Politics in Dubious Times* (New York: The New Press, 2000), 34–35.

9. "Degrassi Fan Pages." *Degrassi Television Website*. Retrieved July 13, 2004, from www. degrassi. tv/fan.

10. Ibid.

11. This contest was promoted during the "non-commercial" breaks on The N.

12. McLuhan, *Understanding Media*, 34.

13. Postman, *Amusing Ourselves to Death*, 87.

14. Rachel X. Weissman, "The Kids are All Right — They're Just a Little Converged," *American Demographics* 20 (1998), 30.

15. "Behind the Scenes on Degrassi." *Australian Broadcasting Corporation Degrassi Television Website.* Retrieved July 16, 2004, from www.abc.net.au/degrassi/bts/happened.htm.

16. Neil Postman, *Technopoly: The Surrender of Culture to Technology* (New York: Vintage Books, 1993), 5.

ONLINE FAN FICTION:
IS SELF-EXPRESSION COLLABORATION
OR RESISTANCE?

Michael Strangelove

HER NAME IS ANNE. She was born in 1989. She lives in Yorba Linda, California. Her father is 45, her mother is 44. She has a stepdad, two sisters and two stepsisters. Anne's favourite television shows are *Degrassi: The Next Generation, One Tree Hill* and *Law and Order*. Her favourite movies: *Bang Bang You're Dead, The Breakfast Club* and *The Goonies*. Her favourite bands: Hanson, Evanescence and The Rasmus. Her favourite book is *Fearless* by Francine Pascal. Her favourite sports team is the LA Lakers. Her favourite drink is Dr. Pepper. Her favourite colours are black, red and blue. The people Anne most admires are the cast of *Degrassi* and her parents. How do I know all these things about Anne? Like many *Degrassi* fans, Anne made a personal fan site that celebrates her love of the television series.

Anne represents a new breed of fans that use the Internet for self-expression. Anne and other online fans are a marketer's dream come true. These fans willingly reveal their consumption patterns, their personal demographics and actively promote commercial media products — all for free and all online. This is the new generation of digital consumers and online fans who are rewriting the rules of audience participation in media culture.

Online *Degrassi* fans provide a unique opportunity to explore how the Internet community interacts with commercial media. This chapter discusses how *Degrassi* fans build online communities, how they extend the narrative universe of *Degrassi* by writing their own scripts and how they interact within official and unofficial *Degrassi* Web sites. It also provides an opportunity to explore how fans are positioned as collaborators within the corporate media system.

DEGRASSI'S ONLINE CULTURE

The various *Degrassi* television series have an international fan community, some of whom participate in online fan culture. Like Anne, these *Degrassi* fans make their own Web sites, engage in online group discussions, create role-playing games where fans pretend to be different *Degrassi* characters, join fan listings (Web sites that act as white pages, listing fan biographies and contact information) and over 50,000 participate in the official corporate site, www.degrassi.tv. Pirated copies of *Degrassi* shows are also being exchanged over peer-to-peer file exchange programs such as Kazaa. *Degrassi* fan Web sites largely consist of digital photographs of the series' stars, plot outlines, gossip and information about the stars, and songs from the show and about the show. Recent sightings of stars from *Degrassi* are also shared in great detail.[1]

The *Degrassi* community provides an example of how media consumption and audience participation is changing in the Internet era. As with all online fan communities, members of the *Degrassi* community are digital pirates. Their Web sites are littered with corporate intellectual property — images, video clips, songs and words from the television show. Although in many cases there has been no attempt to alter the meaning of the *Degrassi* material, this activity still amounts to the appropriation of intellectual property. Here we see one of the most common online activities — self-expression through the use of corporate cultural material. That this form of online behaviour is so prevalent should come as no surprise. Within capitalism, individuals are involved in life-long projects of self-construction through the selective consumption and display of goods derived from the marketplace. This can be seen throughout the *Degrassi* community when individuals display pictures of their favourite characters, create stories about these characters or create entire Web sites dedicated to their favourite character. The creator of one fan site explains how she identifies with the show because it mirrors the way she was in school:

The show has a definite 1980s essence — and, being a child of the '80s, I appreciate this. Spike and Lucy's layered outfits, Cindee's spandex, the lack of technology, even the music ... all spark memories of my ten-year-old days! For the most part, the show is still applicable to today (of course, some aspects come off as "dated", but not in a bad way ... and that's to be expected). Plus, *Degrassi* happened to be in its peak between 1988 and 1990, and those were like the coolest years of my life.[2]

In some instances, the cultural production of the *Degrassi* community — through the appropriation of *Degrassi* material — does not stray very far from the meanings embedded in the television series. This can be seen in the largest of the "homemade" fan sites, www.degrassi.ca, which is owned and operated by Mark Aaron Polger.[3] The site solicits fan fiction based on *Degrassi* but lists the following restrictions: "*Degrassi* World Fan Fiction must be consistent with the established *Degrassi* theme and style. Be moral and uplifting. You can touch controversial topics but keep it tame. Sexual descriptions need to be 'PG-13' rated. No profanity. No racist or prejudiced comments, obviously."[4] Polger provided the following explanation for why he insists on maintaining the PG-13 qualification on fan contributions:

> I like to make all content on www.degrassi.ca and its subsites "G" rated because I do not want to meddle in erotic *Degrassi* fan fiction. I do not want parents emailing me and telling me I am the webmaster who is corrupting their kids. I do not want to be accused of being a pedophile or pervert so it is easier to accept and edit non-explicit fan fiction.[5]

It should be noted that such restrictions on the publication of fan fiction on the Internet are rare (usually being found only on Web sites sponsored or owned by media corporations).

Erotic fan fiction constitutes one of the most prolific categories of online cultural production and is also found within the *Degrassi* community. It is impossible to restrict the type of literature produced by fans who have access to the Internet and have a strong desire to self-publish their own stories. Throughout the world of fandom, individuals rewrite scripts, write their own scripts, make their own mini-movies or transform heterosexual relationships within a plot into gay or lesbian relationships. Kirk and Spock, along with Xena, are favourite targets of this type of rewrite, known as "slash" and "femslash" fiction. Most of the cultural production by fans violates trademark and intellectual property laws, yet the law has proven powerless to stop this type of folk culture from becoming one of the Internet's most prominent features.

FAN FICTION: EXPANDING THE NARRATIVE

The *Degrassi* community produces a small but growing corpus of fan fiction, which is archived on sites throughout the Internet. New characters and situations are introduced, and the official storyline is altered in numerous ways, thus the "authentic" version is distorted. In one piece of fan fiction, Captain Joey and co-Captain Caitlin, Communications Officer Lucy, Science Officer Snake and other members of the *Degrassi* cast travel on the *Starship Degrassi* to the lost planet of the Hunks. Storylines like Lindsay Gordon's "The Tear-Eater: The Wrath of Tessa Camponelli" often explore romantic encounters between *Degrassi* characters and frequently express strong moral consequences:

> On the eve of Joey and Caitlin's first sexual encounter one would think that the world would be on their sides. After 5 years of dating, Caitlin (aka the Ice Princess) had finally decided to give her "flower" to her true love Joey. During a romantic dinner to celebrate their anniversary at the local Swiss Chalet (Caitlin took advantage of her discount), Caitlin hinted to Joey that tonight would be their special night. Passing a condom, which Lucy had previously shown Caitlin how to use on a banana, to Joey over the dinner table in a classy move, Joey grinned from ear to ear. He had been waiting for this moment for what seemed like forever. What Joey didn't know was that evil lurked close by ...
>
> Over the summer break, Joey had "hooked" up with a slutty little girl named Tessa "Tramponelli." Their sexual escapades ended abruptly when Joey impregnated her and donned a yellow t-shirt that appropriately stated "Born to Be Bad." Little did Joey know, Tessa "Tramponelli" was actually a practising Wiccan. That night, while crying on her bed with pink ankle socks, Tessa conjured up a spell that would ruin Joey's relationships forever! Emerging from the beaker of smoke and stench was a creature so horrible that Tessa quickly gave the monster its mission and sent it on its way. The worst was to come.[6]

Gordon's fan fiction also demonstrates how the *Degrassi* audience responds to the series' Canadian setting. As she points out, "The Swiss Chalet reference is due to the fact that in the movie, Caitlin worked at a restaurant that only Canadians would clearly recognize as Swiss Chalet (while Joey clearly worked at Shoppers Drug Mart)." Gordon based her story on the *Degrassi* TV movie, *School's Out:* "My story is a strange take on what could have happened had *Degrassi* been a bad 'B' horror movie." Reflecting on her love of *Degrassi*, she writes, "As many of my generation can profess, we have a strange fascination with *Degrassi*. Not because we feel it was an amazingly acted or written show, but because it was the only Canadian show geared to teenagers at the time. The characters were humorous, the acting lacking, and the storylines unintentionally funny."[7]

Fan fiction also celebrates the homosexual relationship between the two characters Marco and Dylan. Other sites, such as *Puppy Love* (degrassi. fanfic.cc), offer a wide variety of erotic stories based on *Degrassi* characters and storylines. These stories discuss heterosexual, gay and lesbian romance, rape, drug abuse, self-harm and death. Major characters are killed off, and wider social issues, such as school shootings, prostitution and pornography, are explored.

Often fan fiction challenges other fans to explore "unauthorized" aspects of the *Degrassi* universe. One fan had an uncomfortable experience with reading slash fiction but nonetheless continued reading fan erotica and found a new dimension in the imaginative world of *Degrassi* as a result, "Let me start off with saying that at first I thought I'd be uncomfortable reading femslash due to previous experiences with the regular slash. But, I actually really enjoyed this fan fiction. It brought up a side of Ellie and Paige's relationship I wouldn't be able to imagine on the show."[8] Perhaps as a personal reflection of the writers' life world, *Degrassi* slash and femslash stories frequently explore the first time a character has a sexual experience with a member of the same sex. Fan fiction, particularly among young writers, often draws heavily upon autobiographical experiences.

The Internet provides amateur writers with an opportunity for enhanced self-expression and artistic exploration. Aspiring writers uncertain about their talents can also remain anonymous: "Alright, I never post my stories in communities. Why? Because I think my writing is horrible and I hate it more than anything. But, despite the fact that I'm so nervous that I might be a little sick to my stomach, I'm posting this."[9] The anonymity enabled by the Internet has led to a entirely new level of self-expression within capitalism, and fan communities such as *Degrassi* are at the forefront of this phenomenon.

In the early years of the *Degrassi* community, its fan fiction rarely strayed beyond relatively tame scenarios of character X dating character Y. Generally speaking, the appropriation of commercial media products by the Internet community tends to involve the aggressive reworking of the material and its intended meanings (as demonstrated in Gordon's excerpt above). This did not occur within the *Degrassi* community until quite recently. In early 2003, *Degrassi* fan erotica was quite rare, whereas by mid-2004 there were dozens of such stories, including some explicit portrayals of homosexual lovemaking. It appears that the longer the *Degrassi* fan community exists, the more intensely sexual its fan literature becomes, and the more it departs from the PG-13 character of the television series itself. In response to the erotic "Craig and J.T.'s Sleepover," one fan wrote, "Big penis Craig is hot and I love how it makes me want to masturbate."[10] This is precisely the type of intellectual property violation that the entertainment industry is incapable of eliminating from the Internet's domain.

One area where *Degrassi* looms large is the commercial site www.The-N.com. This site's archives included 129,000 postings on *Degrassi* in mid-July 2004. Over one thousand new e-mail messages were posted daily by *Degrassi* fans at The-N.com. The-N.com also provides a space for hundreds of *Degrassi* fan fiction stories. On any given day dozens of brief fan fictions are posted and commented on by the *Degrassi* community. Many are very short, consisting of only a few dozen sentences. Here writers often post a story idea, ask for feedback and then write a brief script. Frequently a story will be posted in a serial fashion, with the author writing a small section, posting it to the group, receiving feedback, then posting part two, then receiving more feedback and so on until the story plays itself out. In some cases these exchanges between authors and their readers go on for days as a story slowly takes shape. In one instance, The-N.Com member Runaway891 (all members of the-N.com are anonymous) developed a *Degrassi* script during a four-month long exchange with fellow fans. It is not unusual for exchanges between writers and readers to continue for many weeks as the story unfolds. These exchanges often involve hundreds of e-mail replies from readers, some of whom occasionally are rewarded by being incorporated into the story.

Within fan communities, writing is often a highly social activity. Writers receive constant encouragement from group members, and in exchange the group gets an expanded narrative world. The story continues, the fan's imaginative world is more fully elaborated, and the collective identity of the fan community itself survives and grows in status. Fan writers often engage in a form of cultural resistance when they attempt to make a commercial narrative such as *Degrassi* more "real." One author wrote *Degrassi* slash because she felt that the sexual tension in the narrative was too predictable: "They have people hooking up that you would expect to hook up. I thought that if you put people together that didn't seem to likely to hook up, it would be cool (and I like erotic themes in my stories). When I put 'straight' people of the same sex together and make them have sex, it is very hot and I love that. Also, it creates a vivid picture."[11] Another author explored erotic themes in the *Degrassi* narrative because he felt that it was "wrong to think that people that age cannot and *do* not sometimes take part in the kind of situation I write about."[12]

In larger fan communities the total production of storylines may soon exceed the production volume of the media company that owns and produces the program. Here we see the foreshadowing of a fast approaching future when the volume of non-commercial cultural production within the Internet gains parity with or entirely exceeds the level of cultural production that is taking place within the commercial entertainment industry. Commercial media will find itself in increasingly intense competition with non-commercial (not-for-profit) fan productions that are often every bit as entertaining as commercial products. The cumulative effect of such a shift within media culture is as yet unknown, but, as will be explored further below, capitalism's ability to manage consumer perception and consumption habits is ultimately at stake.

FAN FICTION VS. INTELLECTUAL PROPERTY AND MEANING

The online community's production of fan fiction represents the appropriation of intellectual property and uncontrolled audience expression that currently plagues the broadcast industry and the commercial media sector. Online acts of appropriation are often described by media scholars as an attempt to deny corporations any sovereignty over the meaning of cultural products that constitute the consumer's world and self-identity. Every piece of fan fiction circulating online represents a challenge to the cultural authority of commercial media. As online fan communities expand, the cumulative effect of their cultural activity is a greatly expanded narrative that departs from the authorized version of the story. The end result is that the perception of the series among the online audience is no longer firmly in the control of the commercial media system. In this new age of online non-commercial cultural production, the audience's perception of commercial media products is increasingly influenced by collective meta-narratives produced by fan communities that operate outside the bounds of the capitalist mode of ownership and production.

The appropriative culture of the Internet is intensely aggressive in its hijacking of commercial media products because corporations are not only equally aggressive in saturating the mental landscape with their meanings but also aggressive in defending their claims to sovereignty over the interpretation and representation of their products and brands. Corporations attempt to monopolize cultural production within the Internet's economic system has led fan communities to challenge capitalism's cultural sovereignty. As corporations increase their level of control over cultural products, fan communities increase their resistance to the attempt to constrain their expression.

Trademark disputes over domain names is one example of the corporate attempt to maintain a monopoly over cultural production and meaning. In February 2000, Playing With Time Corporation (producers of *Degrassi*) contacted Mark Aaron Polger and asked him to transfer the domain names degrassi.ca and degrassi.org, which had been owned and used by Polger since 1998. Polger refused and was later served with a legal claim accusing him of trademark infringement and of using the *Degrassi* name in bad faith. The corporation dropped the suit (they subsequently created the official www.degrassi.tv site) and Polger remains in control of his *Degrassi* sites.[13] This is a rare instance of the individual winning a domain-name dispute against a media corporation (although in this instance the dispute never went to arbitration or litigation). While the dispute is in itself a minor incident, it is nonetheless indicative of a wider pattern of conflict between fans and media corporations.[14]

The *Degrassi* online community stands as a modest reminder of how fans resist the corporate control of meaning, whether they do it intentionally through resisting trademark claims (such as Polger did) or unintentionally through the act of creating fan fiction. Resistance in fan communities most often takes the form of a refusal to grant the production company sole rights in determining how a commercial product (television show, series, movie, book) is interpreted. We see this intent expressed when the 15-year-old Samantha writes on the site *Puppy Love* that she creates *Degrassi* femslash stories "to make Ellie and Ashley kiss, as is only right and proper."[15] With enhanced access to the means of cultural production (due to the arrival of the Internet), fans like Samantha can promote their own intrepretations over those of the series' producers. This is not to say that all fan-produced meanings stand in opposition to the commercial production system. The key issue is that when fan-produced meanings do oppose those of producers, there is little that the commercial media system can do to remove those meanings from the realm of the Internet and take them out of circulation.

Whether they intend to or not, online fan communities such as *Degrassi* represent a fundamental challenge to the authority of corporate media and a massive erosion of capitalism's ability to control meaning within the consumer's world. Online fan communities demonstrate that a new era of meaning-production has dawned, that a subversive "underground" symbolic economy is emerging from within cyberspace, and that the marketplace and the law are powerless to control the democratization of meaning-production that is taking place within the online community.

I am analyzing the *Degrassi* community from the perspective (which I will simply state and not defend here) that sees commercial media products as carriers of what Herbert I. Schiller described as a "diet of values," which propagates consumption patterns and other forms of belief and action congenial to the capitalist mode of social organization.[16] This "diet of values" is fed to commercial media's audience through highly controlled content. Even an apparently benign form of entertainment such as the *Harry Potter* series can promote capitalist values. The fictional universe of *Harry Potter*'s narrative has been criticized for celebrating the market while denigrating the state and socializing young fans into the notion that happiness is found in the consumption of branded consumer goods.[17] In this narrative, students prepare for a highly competitive social system that is characterized by a permanent state of war between good and evil where only the fittest survive and education is focused on the job market. The vast majority of cultural products that have their origin in the capitalist mode of production speak in the persistent voice of the market itself, *until the audience appropriates and rearticulates that voice.*

Within capitalism's dominant mode of cultural production the status of media content is carefully defended as private property through law.[18] It is further controlled through the structure of the commercial media system, which relegates the audience to the relatively passive position of receivers of fixed content meant for consumption and not appropriation, manipulation or rearticulation. For the most part, the majority of what the individual sees, hears and reads — the consumer's visual and auditory diet — has its origins in the marketplace in general and in media conglomerates in particular. An almost constant birth-to-death exposure to commercial media ensures that the individual more or less willingly participates in the capitalist social order. Fan culture is firmly situated within this context.

While the Internet has increased the autonomy of the audience, it has also enabled corporate media to extend its reach into the imagination of fans. *Degrassi*'s marketing strategy, for example, actively brings the fan deeper into the authorized storyline of the show. This occurs within the series' official site www.degrassi.tv. (which won Gemini awards in 2003 for best interactive and most popular site among Canadian television shows). This corporate site is a "virtual school" where fans can enroll and gain access to special features, such as occasional chat sessions with cast members. Users of www.degrassi.tv are assigned a homeroom, provided with their own "locker" and receive e-mail from the characters of the *Degrassi* series. I joined the degrassi.tv site and received a fictional e-mail from Mr. Simpson, the Media Immersion instructor at Degrassi Community School. Here is an excerpt:

> All your Media Immersion exams will be open book!
>
> Just kidding! I know I shouldn't toy with the students, but you'll have to forgive me for being a little punchy today. I'm on cloud nine because my cancer is in REMISSION!!
>
> That doesn't mean I'm out of the woods forever, but it does mean that for now, I'm in the clear. I can go back to living my normal life, albeit with a much, MUCH greater appreciation for the people I love and the experiences life has to offer …
>
> And as for my students! You wouldn't believe how much I'm looking forward to years and years of new faces coming and going through my classes … You may think of me as just a teacher, but your words and gestures made me consider you all a part of my extended *Degrassi* family.
>
> See you at school, for many years to come!
>
> Take Care,
>
> Mr. Simpson

By sending fiction e-mails, *Degrassi* brings the storyline of the television series into the lives of online fans and thus increases the interpenetration between the two mediums. Within commercial media productions, interactivity is often reduced to a marketing tool. Fans are invited to think of themselves as an "extended *Degrassi* family" and sympathize with a fictional character's personal struggle with cancer. The series was one of the pioneers of this type of marketing strategy, which, as can be seen by the above excerpt, involves creating a deeper emotional connection with the fan base. It is a brilliant strategy and has become one of the core marketing strategies among media companies. It is also fraught with moral dilemmas — to what extent is it harmless fiction or nefarious emotional manipulation by marketers and a media production company?

Aside from sending each other e-mail, users of the official *Degrassi* Web site have very little opportunity for the type of creative expression that otherwise characterizes online fandom. Here the production company is clearly intent on maintaining as much communicative control as possible. There is no central space for fan fiction within the official site and very little room for any personal expression beyond e-mail forums, which are carefully monitored. A considerable volume of fan fiction does appear within the e-mail forums, but absent are the erotic and violent themes found elsewhere on the Internet within the *Degrassi* fan community. Typical of all online fan communities, *Degrassi* fans exists in a relatively constrained fashion within the official corporate site, while simultaneously existing in a largely unconstrained fashion in other, non-corporate areas of the Web.

Although the extant body of *Degrassi* fan fiction is relatively small, the significance of such cultural production by fan communities is tremendous. The online *Degrassi* community demonstrates that fans are not constrained by the authorized meaning of a text. They rework corporate intellectual property to make new meanings.

CULTURAL CONVERGENCE AND COLLABORATION

When fans produce stories based on commercial media products, are they reduced to collaborators within the commercial media system, or are they challenging capitalism's cultural authority? Henry Jenkins, perhaps the most widely cited authority on the cultural analysis of fandom, positions fans as collaborators with the corporate media system. I believe his view represents a stunning misinterpretation of fans in the Internet era and is a gross misrepresentation of the trajectory of the corporate control of meaning. Jenkins wants to move beyond the "old rhetoric of opposition and co-option" but does so only by ignoring the oppressive nature of the commercial media system and by degrading those who actively resist corporate meanings. Those who do co-operate with commercial media are described by Jenkins as dialogic, affective and collaborative, while those who resist are negative, reactive, disruptive, ideological and confrontational.[19] Jenkins's theory of fan-based cultural production presents a picture of the online audience that fits well with corporate desire to control the collective imagination.

Borrowing from the economic trend of media convergence, Jenkins proposes that new media technologies may shift the position of the audience:

> One of the real potentials of cyberspace is that it is altering the balance of power between media producers and media consumers, enabling grassroots cultural production to reach a broader readership and enabling amateurs to construct websites that often look as professional and are often more detailed and more accurate to the original than the commercially-produced sites. In such a world, the category of the audience, as a mass of passive consumers for pre-produced materials, may give way to the category of cultural participants, which would include both professionals and amateurs. We will certainly need and value the contributions of skilled professional storytellers but we will also provide the tools to empower popular creativity, often in response to what the storytellers put before us.[20.]

In this vision of the future, Jenkins sees a form of "cultural convergence" wherein digital media technologies create a more participatory audience, "a world where all of us can participate in the creation and circulation of central cultural myths."[21] We see this more participatory culture emerging in the narratives developed by the *Degrassi* fan community and in the e-mails that degrassi.tv members receive from the show's fictional characters, like Mr. Simpson. Participatory online fan culture simultaneously frees the individual from the strict control of the official narrative while also bringing the fan more deeply into the authorized storyline.

The cultural convergence foreseen by Jenkins largely amounts to a more intense level of audience participation in new forms of *commercial media*. Audiences will act as junior partners to cultural industries. Analog audiences were passive audiences, whereas digital audiences are collaborators who actively participate in the economic system's production of culture.

It is curious that Jenkins's vision of cultural convergence favours the notion of collaboration. We can all agree that the balance of power between producers and consumers of meaning is shifting because of digital technologies. Yet describing the new position of the empowered audience as collaborative reinforces existing relationships within capitalism's meaning-production system. Media conglomerates remain in position as the dominant storytellers while the audience is permitted to occasionally colour outside the lines (consider the official *Degrassi* Web site). Jenkins does see enormous potential in appropriation as a cultural force, particularly when combined with the utility of the Internet. Yet his vision of the future of media culture exhibits qualities which I call "pre-Gutenberg."

Jenkins argues that the Internet's success as a cultural force ultimately depends on "the creation and maintenance of a shared cultural frame of reference, and for the present moment the most likely source of that frame of reference is the infrastructure created by centralized commercial media … All kinds of interesting cultural material is originating on the web, but most of it only reaches a larger community when it attracts the attention of traditional media."[22] Corporate media will continue to dominate cultural production, the audience will be repositioned as collaborators, and cultural material within the Web will only influence society's shared frame of reference when it is filtered through the corporate media system. Why we need or should celebrate a shared cultural frame of reference that is produced by the economy's propaganda system is not addressed.

Jenkins's pre-Gutenberg vision serves to validate capitalism's meaning production system. It reassures the owners and operators of the cultural industry that they will continue to be the gatekeepers of the mass mind — the Internet and its wired masses are no threat to the corporate control of capitalism's shared frame of reference. Jenkins understates just how much online fandom challenges the corporate control of meaning and the status of media products as property when he suggests that "fandom represents a potential loss of control over their intellectual property."[23] While corporations have won numerous domain name and trademark disputes against Internet users, they have lost control over digital media products and audiences within the Internet. What has happened is not a "potential loss of control" but a near complete breakdown of the concept of private property and the containment of audiences in cyberspace.

This issue of a "potential loss of control" may seem like splitting hairs but it is not. Describing the implications of online fandom requires that we correctly identify its context, and that context is best described as a decimation of the corporate control of meaning within the Net. The production company has no real control over how the online *Degrassi* community chooses to expand and rewrite the series' narrative. Jenkins's theory wrongly portrays the online audience as primarily collaborative when in fact its activity, when taken as a whole, is fundamentally subversive.

When Jenkins proposes a coming cultural convergence between the audience and the corporate-meaning production system, he implies that resistance will take a back seat to co-optation. For Jenkins, fandom is predominantly collaborative. These collaborative communities are early adopters of new media technologies and, as a consequence,

> their aesthetics and cultural politics have been highly influential in shaping public understanding of the relationship between dominant and grassroots media. Such groups seek not to shut down the corporate apparatus of the mass media but rather to build on their enjoyment of particular media products, to claim affiliation with specific films or television programs, and to use them as inspiration for their own cultural production, social interaction, and intellectual exchange.[24]

Jenkins is arguing that these early adopters of new media are also early adopters of a particular type of relationship between the grassroots and corporations. Fan communities show us the future state of the audience as a collaborator with the commercial myth-making machine. The cultural politics of media collaborators are projected as the vanguard of the coming cultural convergence. Yet the idea that the emergent media system of the digital era will render us willing collaborators with Disney, CNN, Fox, Rubert Murdoch, the Aspers, the Bronfmans and other media moguls is unlikely to sit well with many producers of grassroots media and fan fiction authors.

Jenkins's description of fan culture leaves one with the impression that the participants of fandom eagerly want to be embraced by corporate media as "active associates and niche marketers."[25] When Jenkins suggests, perhaps quite rightly, that fans want to share media power, he underestimates how this sharing of power with corporate media has the obvious potential to corrupt the collaborator and reduce the fan community to little more than another tool of the market. In the end, Jenkins's media theory serves to reassure the corporate sector that no real harm will come from Internet fan communities. If corporations embrace appropriative activity and use it to better market their products, then fans will make "commodity culture more responsive to consumers."[26]

Jenkins's theory of fan culture rests precariously on the highly speculative notion that corporations will willingly loosen their grip on intellectual property and the control of meaning that it grants. Yet the present trajectory of corporations, the state and intellectual property law indicates that precisely the opposite is taking place. Celebrating the notion of the audience-as-collaborator rings hollow when the balance of power within capitalism is only tilting further in the direction of corporations.

Consumer culture is far from being replaced by a new economic system that dissociates control of meaning from control of the production system (as is suggested by Jenkins). It has not been displaced by the wired economy. It has not been rendered obsolete by the digital age. Corporations are not about to relinquish control over commercial narratives and intellectual property. They show no signs of willingly relinquishing control over meaning.

At the centre of consumer culture stands meaning as the ultimate form of private property — the central organizing force behind all mass thought and action. On this point Jenkins's theory of a new balance of power within the media system falls apart. To believe that the owners and operators of capitalism will willingly share ownership of meaning with the audience is utopic thinking. It is also foolhardy. There is a cultural war in progress. Arguing that the audience should willingly settle for the position of collaborator with the most monstrous of myth-making machines is tantamount to insisting that it is okay to dance with the devil as long as we get to name the tune.

While it may sound wonderful when Jenkins claims that fandom points to the future state of the mass audience as "cultural participants," we must ask "in what are we called to participate?" This brings us back to Schiller's notion of the media system feeding us a diet of values that perpetuates the capitalist mode of social organization. Behind Jenkins's vision of cultural convergence I would suggest that what we really find is cultural assimilation; assimilation of the audience into the values and logic of the commercial media system. Resistance is futile, corporations own our culture, so let's co-operate and try and get a few of our own story ideas into the myth-making machine. All media theory is primarily a moral argument and

Jenkins's notion of collaboration strikes me as a moral failure. Here we are called to participate in the means to our own subjugation. By understating the culpability of the commercial media system in an unjust, destructive and violent economic system Jenkins makes collaboration sound like an ethical option, when perhaps what is really needed is a celebration and promotion of digital piracy, fandom appropriation and active cultural resistance.

★

Can we locate resistance within the fan community? In general, both resistance and co-optation occur within fandom. Fans engage in cultural resistance while simultaneously promoting commercial media products and expanding the audience and lifespan of these products. Yet, if we consider the enormous volume of production that takes place within online fandom it is clear that uncontrolled production by fan communities such as *Degrassi* challenges the cultural authority of commercial media and presents the marketplace with a battle over intellectual property that media corporations cannot possibly win. Thus, even without the explicit intention to resist the commercial system, fan-based cultural production presents a direct challenge to the control of meaning that stands at the heart of the economic system.

It should be noted that, regardless of the available legal mechanisms, the producers of *Degrassi* are quite powerless to control fan fiction within the Internet. Corporations as large and as powerful as Microsoft, McDonald's, Mattel and Lucasfilm (*Star Wars*) have proven incapable of regulating online cultural activity that erodes their brand meanings and intellectual property rights. When corporations attempt to assert intellectual property rights over fan communities the result is an inevitable backlash that leads to an even greater volume of intellectual property violations.[27] Online *Degrassi* fan fiction is here to stay. Whether they intend to or not, online fan communities such as *Degrassi* represent a fundamental challenge to the authority of corporate media and a massive erosion of capitalism's control over shared meaning. *Degrassi*'s online fan community demonstrates that a new era of meaning-production has dawned, that a subversive "underground" symbolic economy is emerging from within cyberspace, and that the marketplace and the law are powerless to control the democratization of meaning production within it.

NOTES

1. "Two Degrassi sightings: Aubrey Graham (Jimmy) was sighted two times. Wendy saw Aubrey Graham on Wednesday April 9th, 2003 at Eglinton station at about 6:40pm on an escalator. Steve saw Aubrey Graham at the Jewish Public Library of Toronto on Monday February 17th, 2003." Mark Aaron Polger, "Degrassi Digest," no. 155 (19 April 2003), *Degrassi Online: The Unofficial Degrassi Web Site*. Retrieved July 14, 2004, from http://digest-archive.degrassi.ca/DD155.htm.

2. Tamara Crista Tillinghast, "Why Degrassi," *Degrassi! Web Site*. Retrieved July 22, 2003, from www.angelfire.com/80s/degrassicanada/why.html.

3. I am indebted to Mark Aaron Polger for his helpful comments on sections of this article dealing with details pertaining to the online *Degrassi* community. Mark's work as a pioneer in the production and organization of online fan culture is precisely the type of effort that gets overlooked when "histories of the Net" are published, which typically focus on entrepreneurs, commercial products and the corporate sector. Those who understand the Internet realize that it is not corporations that built this system so much as individuals like Mark, who help give order to the Internet community's non-commercial cultural production. Mark's efforts, along with the online *Degrassi* community, are the type of cultural production that distinguishes the Internet as a historically unique phenomenon and that all but guarantees that the Net will have a dramatic effect on a social order that is otherwise firmly in the grip of corporate control. See Polger's chapter in this volume.

4. Mark Aaron Polger, "Degrassi World Fan Fiction." *Degrassi Online: The Unofficial Degrassi Web Site*. Retrieved July 23, 2003, from, http://degrassiworld.degrassi.ca.

5. Mark Aaron Polger, e-mail to author, 23 July 2003.

6. Lindsay Gordon, "The Tear-Eater: The Wrath of Tessa Camponelli," in *Degrassi World Fan Fiction*, No. 57. Retrieved July 10, 2004, from http://degrassiworld-archive. degrassi.ca /DW57.htm.

7. Lindsay Gordon, e-mail to author, 19 July 2004.

8. A Typical Freak's review of "Smoke on the Water," by Poeticquality, 30 May 2004. Retrieved July 16, 2004, from http://degrassi.fanfic.cc/reviews.php?sid=d&a=.

9. Poeticquality, "Freezing," *Puppy Love*, 17 March 2004. Retrieved July 10, 2004, from http://degrassi.fanfic.cc/viewuser.php?uid=6.

10. Andromeda Nichols' review of "Craig and J.T.'s Sleepover," by Degrassi Fan, 10 July 2004. Retrieved July 16, 2004, from http://degrassi.fanfic.cc/reviews. php?sid=30&a=. On July 16, 2004, *Puppy Love* (degrassi.fanfic.cc) contained thirty-eight stories and had seventy authors indexed. The stories where archived in four categories: Het (male/female relationships), which contained thirteen stories; Slash (male/male relationships), which contained nineteen stories; Femslash (female/female relationships), which contained three stories; and Gen (for fictions not focused on relationships), which contained two stories. Within the *Degrassi* fan fiction universe, slash fiction far outnumbered femslash fiction in mid-2004.

11. Debra Hardy, e-mail to author, 19 July 2004.

12. Degrassitngfan, e-mail to author, 18 July 2004.

13. For more details on the lawsuit, including the draft statement of the claim against Polger, see "Selected Article Index RE: Domain Name Dispute," *Degrassi Online: The Unofficial Degrassi Web Site*. Retrieved August 23, 2003, from http://www. degrassi.ca/domain-dispute.

14. For a survey of domain-name disputes and their implication for the symbolic economy, see Rosemary J. Coombe and Andrew Herman, "Culture Wars on the Net: Trademarks, Consumer Politics, and Corporate Accountability on the World Wide Web," *The South Atlantic Quarterly* 100, no. 4 (Winter 2001), 919–947.

15. Samantha (aka Sami), biographical note, *Puppy Love*. Retrieved July 17, 2004, from http://degrassi.fanfic.cc/viewuser.php?uid=11. Samantha maintains her own fan fiction site (www.vanishing-glass.Internet), which is a well designed and rich example of online self-expression by a 15-year-old online fan.

16. Herbert I. Schiller, *Culture Inc: The Culture Takeover of Public Expression* (Oxford: Oxford University Press, 1989), 33.

17. Ilias Yocaris, "Harry Potter, Market Wiz," *The New York Times*, 18 July 2004, A16.

18. Rosemary J. Coombe and Andrew Herman, *The Cultural Life of Intellectual Properties: Authorship, Appropriation and the Law* (Durham, NC: Duke University Press, 1998).

19. Henry Jenkins, "Interactive Audiences?" in Dan Harries, ed., *The New Media Book* (London: The British Film Institute, 2002), 167.

20. Henry Jenkins, "The Poachers and Stormtroopers," *Red Rock Eaters News*, 1998. Retrieved August 29, 2003, from http://commons.somewhere.com/rre/1998/The. Poachers.and.the.Sto.html.

21. Ibid.

22. Ibid.

23. Jenkins, "Interactive Audiences?" 165.

24. Henry Jenkins, "Quentin Tarantino's *Star Wars*? Digital Cinema, Media Convergence, and Participatory Culture," *Henry Jenkins' Web Site*. Retrieved August 23, 2003, from http://web.mit.edu/21fms/www/faculty/henry3/starwars.html. Jenkins's argument reads like an apology for fan communities: embrace the appropriative activity of fans, rein in the lawyers, hone your marketing strategies and fandom will increase the value of your commercial media products.

25. Jenkins, "Interactive Audiences?" 166.

26. Ibid., 168.

27. On the failure of corporations to control meaning within the Internet, see my book, *The Empire of Mind: Digital Piracy and the Anti-Capitalist Movement* (Toronto: University of Toronto Press, 2005).

PART II

BUILDING IDENTITY ON *DEGRASSI*

Only in Canada, You Say?
The Dynamics of Identity on Degrassi Junior High

Jennifer MacLennan

IT IS A TRUISM of rhetorical theory that a culture's public discourses both reflect and help to shape its view of itself. Such discourses, like all shared expression, are grounded on a foundation of "unquestioned beliefs" that the culture "takes for granted without hesitation."[1] Aristotle explained the phenomenon centuries ago, when he noted that commonly shared beliefs can provide an effective basis for persuasion: "because they are commonplaces, everyone seems to agree with them, and therefore they are taken for truth."[2] However, as pervasive and influential as they are, normally these "commonplaces" are neither made explicit nor overtly recognized; instead, they are simply assumed by the members of the culture "to be shared by every reasonable being," and function "typically without our being aware" of them.[3]

Thus, audiences are most readily persuaded by arguments that incorporate attitudes and beliefs that they have already accepted, since these arguments will sound like common sense to them. As Edwin Black explains, they are effective because they invite our participation, impelling us "not simply to believe something, but to *be* something"[4] — to fulfill, in effect, a cultural code that we have already embraced. These embedded arguments, known as enthymemes, appear routinely in overtly persuasive messages, such as election campaigns or advertising. However, what is less well recognized is that these same devices are equally pervasive and influential in other kinds of messages — messages that on the surface do not appear to be persuasive in intent. Television and film narratives provide an especially good example of popular forms that create such implicit arguments. By presenting us with a set of dramatized experiences anchored in the same network of "common-sense assumptions" that drive more explicitly persuasive artifacts, they invite our willing suspension of disbelief in exchange for the entertainment of a good story. As a result, they provide powerful vehicles for social and cultural identification, and a reliable source of insight into the culture that produced them.

This chapter argues that the popular Canadian television program *Degrassi Junior High* and its sequel *Degrassi High* provide just such a window into the Canadian ethos. That *Degrassi* is a significant Canadian cultural artifact cannot seriously be disputed. The show has attained both popular and critical acclaim, and remains "one of the highest rated Canadian-produced drama series ever," having won not only a Canada Award from the Academy of Canadian Cinema and Television but also "the Prix Jeunesse, the world's top award for children's programming; two International Emmies; three Children's Broadcast Institute Awards; several Gemini Awards; and countless others from all over the world."[5] As one fan notes, "The *Degrassi* series is Canada's best gift to the world since hockey... *Degrassi* rules!"[6]

AUTHENTICALLY CANADIAN

Like hockey, *Degrassi* is an unmistakably Canadian product. Indeed, as I will show, the show's authentic anchoring in its cultural context is what accounts, at least in part, for its broad appeal. Although the series is not overtly nationalistic in content, it nevertheless clearly reflects Canadian values and attitudes; like Don Shebib's celebrated film *Goin' Down the Road*, the program "holds a mirror to the environment in which it was produced."[7] That it does this "without necessarily [overtly] reflecting a 'Canadian identity' to Canadians" does not make it any less a product of a Canadian sensibility. As such, the show combines Canada's celebrated excellence in documentary realism with a sense of grassroots authenticity common to many of the culture's other expressions of identity.[8]

The air of authenticity that is the hallmark of the *Degrassi* series is the product not only of its content but also of its approach and production values, which lack the slick polish of American television series. In the words of one fan, "It was cheesy, badly acted, cheaply produced. Yet it remains one of our country's most successful television programs. Perhaps the reason for this is that unlike [*Beverly Hills 90210*], *Degrassi* was real."[9] Certainly, as the critics noted, the show "portrays real-life situations ... in an open gutsy manner" with "scripts [that] ... have been praised for their psychological accuracy and dialogue that rings true."[10] In place of professional actors, *Degrassi Junior High* and *Degrassi High* featured ordinary kids, whose instructions were "to act natural, to just be themselves."[11] The kids were normal looking young people, without slick professional wardrobe or makeup; indeed, they were encouraged to choose their own clothes and hair styles for the show. As a fan unkindly put it, "The kids had zits. They wore embarrassing clothes. They were unathletic." But all of this was forgivable, because "they were played by actual teenagers instead of thirty year olds with plastic surgery." The same theme is replayed by yet another fan, who declares in mock suprise, "Instead of being played by models (like *90210*) the kids are played by ... kids."[12]

The performers added to the authenticity of the show in more than appearance, contributing as well to the development of story ideas and scripts, to the issues that were explored on the show, to the reactions and concerns of the characters they played, and to the depth of the dilemmas, many of which were drawn from the kids' lived and observed experiences. In another context, series co-creator Kit Hood has described his goal of making "a TV show for young people, treating 'real' issues ... designed and developed by its young audience," calling the idea "one of my favourite concepts."[13] The *Degrassi* series came close to this ideal, dealing with sensitive issues "in a realistic manner. It's not sugar-coated, and can be shocking sometimes."[14]

Topics covered on the show ranged from adolescent concerns about "fitting in" (as in "The Big Dance," when Voula defies her father in order to attend a school dance, or in "Smokescreen," when Rick attempts to curry favour with Caitlin by joining the school's anti-pollution committee) to more challenging issues of teen pregnancy, abortion, AIDS, homosexuality, drug use, family violence, cancer and the death of a parent. All of the issues are realistically treated, and the long-lasting impact of each is dramatized. As one fan observed, "Characters suffer consequences for actions, and problems are not always neatly resolved by the final frame."[15] For example, in "It's Late," Spike discovers she is pregnant and is later barred from attending school; when Caitlin decides to make her situation into a cause, the two fall out ("Censored"); Spike's struggles with pregnancy and with becoming a mother while still a child herself are realistically portrayed for the remainder of the two series; when Erica later becomes pregnant and opts for an abortion, she and her sister are accosted by protestors at the clinic ("A New Start"), and Heather suffers from long-term emotional distress as a result ("Natural Attraction"). In "Just Friends," L.D. is diagnosed with leukemia and has to undergo chemotherapy, which causes her to lose her hair; Dwayne learns in "Bad Blood" that he has been infected with HIV; in "Showtime," Claude commits suicide at school, and his body is discovered by Snake, who is left shaken and traumatized; Shane's drug use at a concert leads to an accident that leaves him permanently disabled ("Taking Off," "Pa-arty," "Bye Bye Junior High" and "It Creeps"); Wheels's parents are killed by a drunk driver ("Can't Live With 'Em"), sending him into a tailspin of irresponsible behaviour and eventually leading to his own drunk-driving accident that claims the life of a toddler, seriously injures Lucy and lands him in jail *(School's Out)*.

Most important of all, from the point of view of the show's realistic approach, the tragedies and lapses in judgement dramatized on the program are those of the central characters rather than of peripheral figures introduced for only a single episode; just as in life, not every adventure ends happily. As one critic points out, "Writer Yan Moore and director Kit Hood never flinch ... *Degrassi* is a tough, compelling slice of life."[16] For example, Rick is revealed to suffer routine abuse at the hands of his father, and is sent to live with an older brother ("The Cover Up"); Joey is kept back a grade at school ("Pass Tense"); Melanie discovers Kathleen's eating disorder when she reads her friend's diary ("Food for Thought"), and later blurts out this and other secrets at a group sleep-over ("All-Nighter"); Snake's admired older brother is revealed to be gay and is rejected by his parents ("He Ain't Heavy"); Wheels is thrown out of the house by his grandmother ("A Tangled Web"), and is later caught stealing from Joey's mother ("Home Sweet Home"). In all cases, the impact of their choices and action stays with the characters for the duration of the series, to resurface in later episodes.

The show's authentic documentary-style representation of the "lived narratives and experiences"[17] of its teenaged subjects heightens audience involvement and identification with the characters, as many fans readily note: "The characters are a lot like my friends were in junior high ... The show gives teenagers something and someone to relate to." Another declares, "I will never forget the other school I went to on the weekends, and the fun times I shared along with millions of other people. I hold those moments closer to my heart than my time in high school. Even though they weren't real, they felt real. Thanks, *Degrassi*."[18] Director Kit Hood provides the following example of the show's impact on its teenaged audience, some of whom

> would actually make major decisions based on our show … It was encouraging to read how we touched their lives. For that reason we tried to cover as many issues as possible. One letter was from a boy who wanted to kill himself but the episode where Claude commits suicide motivated him to seek help. He realized that he was angry with other people and was seeking a way to end his frustration.[19]

Another fan observes that "this show made you think, not just enjoy. You loved and hated characters. Cried when they cried, laughed when they laughed … *Degrassi* [is] real life!"[20] It very well might be: though the storylines and characters are fictional (or fictionalized), the events and actions are highly realistic, complex and morally shaded.

Indeed, moral complexity is another important feature of the show; dilemmas are not easily resolved and conflicting perspectives are given weight. For example, in "Everybody Wants Something," Liz's pro-life stand prompts her to leave anti-abortion propaganda in Erica's locker; however, before we have a chance to judge her too harshly, it is revealed that Liz's mother nearly had an abortion when pregnant with Liz. In "The Whole Truth," Liz opposes animal testing and encourages Caitlin to join her in a campaign to ban the practice, but when Kathleen points out its role in medical research, Caitlin is torn between her activist impulses and her awareness that her epilepsy is controlled thanks to drugs developed through animal testing. In "All in a Good Cause," Caitlin joins Claude in spraying anti-nuclear graffiti on a local factory; when they are caught, Claude runs away, leaving Caitlin behind to be arrested. These and other dilemmas have no simple solution: as in life, there are few black-and-white issues and no easy answers.

Through its compelling drama, the *Degrassi* series portrayed a clear moral centredness without becoming preachy or heavy-handed. Years after its production, Kit Hood insists that "the message of *Degrassi* and the need for morality has not changed. The issues are still highly relevant." When he watches reruns, it prompts "a new appreciation. I realize that the data is still valid today, and the [dramatic and moral impact] has not lost its punch." Hood has also emphasized the creators' desire to "keep the show honest" so that it did not "reach the point where the viewers could predict that show's formula and outcomes."[21]

The air of authenticity that distinguishes the *Degrassi* experience places it firmly within the Canadian tradition of documentary realism. However, that fact alone is not enough to explain how the series encodes its strong sense of Canadian difference. For example, there is little apart from its realistic style to mark the series as distinctively Canadian. Though its Toronto locations are recognizable to anyone familiar with the city, there are no overt references to locale in the program nor are there any other explicit indications of its Canadian origins. And yet, as the *Toronto Star*'s Greg Quill insists, "it looks and sounds like us"[22] — in other words, like something other than the dominant discourse of American programming. But in what sense, exactly, can it be said that the *Degrassi* series is authentically Canadian, and in what sense can it teach us what such authenticity means? The answer to these questions lies not only in Canada's long-standing documentary film tradition but also in our pervasive pattern of resistance to American cultural domination. What follows is a brief exploration of how the two are conjoined in a text like *Degrassi*.

RESISTING AMERICAN CULTURE

The tradition of Canadian documentary realism that is so visible in the style and technique of *Degrassi* took shape, like many other expressions of Canadianness, explicitly as a response to "the increasing influx of American influence from their easily accessible popular culture."[23] Few countries in the world have remained unmarked by American globalization, but Canada's situation is more precarious than most due to the combination of its geographic proximity to the American cultural powerhouse and its smaller population and economic clout. Unlike other countries, most of the public discourse to which Canadians are exposed comes from a different culture, and a different *kind* of culture:

> Canada, unlike virtually any other country in the world, has a cultural transmission system that is almost entirely in the hands of a foreign power. Most Canadian children pass into adulthood without, for example, ever seeing a Canadian feature-length film ... They see American commercials and read American advertising.[24]

The potentially overwhelming impact of American media on Canadian culture was formally acknowledged in the 1951 *Report of the Royal Commission on National Development in the Arts, Letters and Sciences,* led by Vincent Massey. While recognizing that television would "almost certainly exercise a profound influence" over Canadian culture in the future, the report flagged film as "not only the most potent but also the most alien of the influences shaping our Canadian life" and expressed concern that, since "most movies come from Hollywood … Hollywood refashions us in its own image."[25] By the 1980s, not much had changed and American domination of the media was if anything "an even more significant issue"[26] than it had been in 1951, partly because of the influence of television. Writing in 1982, Pierre Berton observed that "if Canadians continue to hold the belief that there is no such thing as a national identity — and who can deny that many hold it? — it is because [Hollywood] movies have frequently blurred, distorted, and hidden that identity under a celluloid mountain of misconceptions."[27] What is needed, he suggested, is a storytelling tradition of our own.

At the beginning, reports Martin Knelman, no one was certain "just exactly what an indigenous Canadian film culture might consist of," except that it would have to have "something to do with an alternative style — with the freedom to be North American without being quite so fiercely and aggressively, well, American."[28] What *was* certain, as Massey and his colleagues realized, is that a small country "on the rim of another country many times more populous and of far greater economic strength … [whose] invasion by film, radio, and periodical is formidable,"[29] needs strategies that will define and preserve its sense of cultural distinctiveness. Such a culture will typically create for itself a cultural "anti-language" of resistance and difference, which, as Norman Fairclough explains, provides "conscious alternatives to the dominant or established discourse types."[30]

The "anti-language" of Canadian film turned out to be a form already evident in other areas of cultural production, particularly Canadian literature, which itself already exhibited "a drive for documentary realism [as a] defining characteristic."[31] Not surprisingly, then, the thrust of Canadian filmmaking also became documentary in shape, a focus intensified by the fact that "feature films in particular were acknowledged vehicles of widespread indoctrination of American ideological perspectives."[32] The National Film Board, established in 1939 to "interpret Canada to Canadians and other Nations,"[33] became noted for, among other things, its pioneering developments in social documentary, documentary drama and direct cinema, and its influence has been both pervasive and long lasting. As Knelman notes, "For decades Canadian filmmaking was largely a matter of documentaries in the National Film Board style."[34] The Canadian Film Development Corporation, created by an Act of Parliament in 1967, although targeting the feature film industry, was similarly intended "to unify the country through the telling of its stories, and to establish a creative identity"[35] of our own.

The documentary impulse of Canadian film is, then, part of just such a cultural "anti-language," a conscious alternative to the overwhelming pressure of American media domination, which had formed an "economic and cultural stranglehold on the Canadian movie theatres that affected the viewing practices of Canadian movie-goers."[36] The result of such cultural inundation has been a rhetoric of identity that has always been marked by a pattern of resistance to American cultural influences and a concomitant insistence on difference. Indeed, some have claimed that Canadian identity exists *only* as a kind of anti-Americanism;[37] more perceptive observers have recognized the necessity, even inevitability, of such expressions of difference, particularly for a marginalized culture faced with maintaining a strong and necessary sense of "us" amid the prevailing influence of "them." As cultural theorist John Fiske explains, "All social allegiances have not only a sense of *with whom* but also of *against whom*: indeed, I would argue that the sense of oppositionality, the sense of difference, is more determinant [of identity] than [is a sense] of similarity."[38]

Given that we are "so endlessly bombarded by American culture and American images and American dreams and American everything,"[39] it's not surprising that much of our identity discourse is spent on distinguishing ourselves from the United States. As Pierre Berton's well-known formulation would have it, "We know who we are *not* even if we aren't quite sure who we are; we are not American." Such emphasis on difference serves two functions: first, it is an authentication of our own unique cultural identity and, second, it is a reminder of the culture's marginalized position in the shadow of a larger, more economically powerful and culturally extroverted nation, a position we can never take for granted. As Berton explains, "We admire Americans, but it's a bit of a love-hate relationship. We don't like cosying up too closely" — mostly because "we are in danger of being swamped by [them]."[40]

Exactly how does documentary realism function as a "conscious alternative" to American discourse forms and, in this case, to American television programming? Judith A. Rolls and Carol Corbin provide a clue in their study of the culture of Cape Breton Island, wherein they note that the "authentic and the 'real' of any culture" is its "truly people-generated quality ... [that] has in its makeup a certain resistance to commodification and quantification."[41] The realistic approach taken by the *Degrassi* series lends it a truly "people-generated" authenticity that is unlike comparable American vehicles. Its narrative form is also important, since, as Eric Watts notes, "narrative [is] as an important form of rhetorical agency ... storytelling entails a depiction of the manner in which persons make sense of their lives as historical and cultural events."[42]

Significantly, the most frequent comparison invoked for the *Degrassi* series is *Beverly Hills 90210*, a slick Hollywood-style production entirely unlike *Degrassi* in sensibility. Kit Hood explains the difference in cultural terms: "I truly hate it when people compare *90210* to *Degrassi*. We had entirely different concepts and appealed to different audiences ... Toronto is not Hollywood, we do not have the same mentality or resources."[43] Although Hood does not seem to feel it necessary to spell out the implications of this comparison, they are not difficult to uncover. For Canadians, Martin Knelman explains, "Hollywood symbolizes ... false values," a place "you had to stay away from if you wanted to maintain your integrity and purity of heart."[44] Most important, its products lack the "people-generated" authenticity of an artifact like *Degrassi*, since "it was the place people went when they wanted to pretend to be someone else, and a place from which they would eventually return when they were ready to be themselves again."

It is not only Canadians for whom Hollywood represents "a new category in human emptiness."[45] In his classic treatment of American popular media, Daniel Boorstin describes a "new kind of synthetic novelty which has flooded our experience," which he labels the "pseudo-event." There is nothing authentic in the artificial world of these pseudo-events, in which "synthesized images take the place of external standards." Unfortunately, they have become ubiquitous in American media; indeed, according to Boorstin's analysis, "the making of the illusions which flood our experience has become the business of America"[46] and, in particular, the business of Hollywood. These manufactured, counterfeit images bear little relationship to underlying cultural experience, which they have effectively displaced; instead, they are products of mass-communication technologies and defined by cleverly contrived marketing campaigns. In the world of "pseudo-events," genuine experience has been replaced by synthetic images; genuine grassroots "folk" culture has been replaced by "mass" culture; and authentic cultural heroes have been replaced by celebrities. Boorstin explains the distinction:

> The folk expressed itself. Its products are still gathered by scholars, antiquarians, and patriots; it was a voice. Its characteristic products were the spoken word, the gesture, the song: folklore, folk dance, folk song. But the mass, in our world of mass media and mass circulation, is the target and not the arrow. It is the ear and not the voice. The mass is what others aim to reach — by print, photograph, image, and sound. While the folk created heroes, the mass can only look and listen for them ... The mass lives in the very different fantasy world of pseudo-events.[47]

Boorstin equates the Hollywood "star" system with this same decline in authentic culture: "'Stars' were the celebrities of the entertainment world [and] as a species of celebrities, stars, too, were spawned in the world of pseudo-events."[48] The nature of celebrity, he explains, can best be understood in contrast with the figure of the cultural hero; the distinction between them lies in the relationship of each to underlying cultural values. Whereas the hero embodies the culture's values and is a manifestation of the "people-generated" culture to which Carol Corbin and Judith Rolls refer, the celebrity is a media creation with no connection to underlying culture, which, far from embodying cultural values, actually masks an absence of values. As Boorstin points out, the true figure of folk culture stands in contrast to the homogenizing effects of mass culture, or may even function as an expression of resistance to those effects.

In spite of Kit Hood's avowed dislike of the comparison between *Degrassi* and *90210*, the invocation of Hollywood values does serve to intensify the sense of *Degrassi*'s authenticity and realism; it also points to a commonplace prized in the language of Canadian cultural resistance, whereby "the only way to fight American values was to make them appear vulgar and vaguely comic."[49] Hollywood values are those of slick salesmanship and crass commercialism, the values of "the mass," who live in the world of pseudo-events, and the best way to resist them is to ridicule them. Pierre Berton explains: "It goes like this: Americans are good at blowing their own horn, but Americans are vulgar; therefore, blowing your own horn is vulgar. Thus advertising is vulgar, the hard sell is 'sharp,' show business is crass."[50]

When understood against the context of Boorstin's analysis, the resistance to American popular culture implicitly encoded in the *Degrassi* experience is brought into sharp focus. While the *Degrassi* kids are not quite cultural "heroes" in the sense that Boorstin uses the term, they are nevertheless portrayed and perceived as genuine expressions of a "folk" — real kids who look "like people [you] might have gone to school with,"[51] and the show's "people-generated" scripts and storylines, along with documentary-style production values, serve as a repudiation of slick Hollywood concoctions. These gestures are in themselves acts of resistance, and this spirit of resistance to American-style "pseudo-event" values carries through the entire approach to the show. For example, there were no "stars" on *Degrassi*; instead, as Hood recalls, he, Linda and Yan "would frequently meet to discuss how we could try to spread out the best roles. We did not want to create a 'star system' and knew it was important to keep [all] the other characters alive and busy."[52] This insistence appears again in a separate interview: "*Degrassi* was always a small show … we never referred to the actors as stars; it was a team effort."[53]

As well, Hood explicitly characterizes the difference between *Degrassi* and Aaron Spelling's *Beverly Hills 90210* in exactly the terms that Boorstin uses to distinguish cultural authenticity from the "synthethized images" of American mass culture: the difference is attributed to the latter's emphasis on marketing — the same "vulgar" values Berton describes as characterizing the American mindset. "Aaron Spelling knew how to market *90210*," Hood admits. By contrast, "Linda and I were not experienced in marketing."[54]

Although it is both explicitly and implicitly associated with Canadian resistance to American values, the authentic quality of *Degrassi* has appeal for more than its Canadian audience. American and Canadian fans alike compare *Degrassi* favourably with American programming aimed at a similar audience, with a clear preference for the more realistic over the escapist fare produced by Hollywood; one fan rejects "the imbecilic trash with canned laughter so common on American TV" in favour of the more "realistic look at teenage issues" offered by *Degrassi*, deeming the show "outstanding."[55] A young teacher from Syracuse, New York, uses the program in his classes "to involve [his] students and create meaningful discussions. It has never failed." He praises the fact that "the actors look and sound like real young adults, instead of the young-looking 20-year-olds you find in series of the same kind made in the U.S.," and, like many other fans, he emphasizes "the affection and interest that the long-gone series can still generate."[56] Yet another fan declares that "it's absolutely laughable to think that *90210* once claimed to be 'realistic!' But it *did* … *Degrassi*'s kids look like KIDS … *90210*'s 'kids' not only look like actors, most of them looked like twentysomethings."[57] One fan, who hosts a Web site devoted to the show, typifies the preference of fans for the realistic, documentary approach of *Degrassi*:

> It was a Canadian produced television series about REAL high school life. *Degrassi* was not like those fake American teen shows like*: Saved by the Bell, California Dreams, Hang Time* (and on a side note, who made up those crappy titles?) … *Degrassi* was about real life and all the fun that goes along with it: suicide, pregnancy, cool high school bands, eating disorders, bullies, pornography, getting beaten by your bearded boyfriend, getting the courage to dump that same bearded boyfriend, hitchhiking, booze, fake ID's, and the most important of all: the art of 'buying everything in the drugstore so you can blend a package of condoms into the purchase'… And those were just some of the topics that *Degrassi* covered in its many years of television goodness.[58]

Professional critics, like the *Toronto Star*'s Greg Quill, cite similar comparisons in their attempt to capture the appeal of *Degrassi*, which he declares to be "as different from the kind of homogenized, sanctified, purified family fare from American networks as a Ferrari is from a Buick."[59]

Given the prominent place of themes of cultural resistance in the rhetoric of Canadian identity, the appeal of *Degrassi* to Canadian fans is easily explained; what may be more difficult to understand is what it offers its American fans, who "have become so accustomed to … illusions that we mistake them for reality" and who therefore "demand them."[60] Perhaps the answer can be found in discussions of another "authentic" Canadian cultural artifact of quite a different kind. Ronald Caplan, editor of the award-winning *Cape Breton's Magazine* and himself an expatriate American, describes the impulse that prompts people to seek "a touchstone" for reclaiming a sense of centredness and authenticity amid the flood of unreal events and images that have displaced genuine cultural experience. They are seeking, Caplan says,

> some reminder, if not of their own former lives at least of their own capacities … They are looking for something they might, if pressed, call "the authentic" … for qualities they hope are still within themselves, for something of which they are still capable, regardless of where they now live or how they live out their lives.[61]

As will be immediately obvious from this discussion, Caplan might well have been talking about the comparison between the authenticity of the *Degrassi* series and the "imbecilic" pseudo-events depicted in American prime time. Indeed, Martin Knelman goes so far as to suggest that the answer lies in "what English Canada at its best represents to the rest of the world if not to itself: America without the power and the problems, America the way it used to be before it lost its innocence."[62] *Degrassi* appeals, then, because it provides its American viewers with the possibility of reclaiming that lost authenticity.

★

I began this discussion by observing that a culture's public discourses, including its film and television narratives, participate in the "common-sense" assumptions of that culture, reflecting that culture's understanding of itself and its relationship to the rest of the world. Its dramatizations embody the culture's "unquestioned beliefs," creating embedded arguments that invite our willing participation and suspension of disbelief, as we anticipate what is needed and fill in with our own awareness what has been left unstated.[63] This combination of the anticipatory and participatory helps to account for the dynamics of identity in this discourse: it is anticipatory because it fulfills through its form our unspoken, unrecognized, "common-sense" expectations, reflecting us back to ourselves; it is participatory because it functions as an enthymeme that requires us to supply those very common-sense assumptions in order to make sense of the world it depicts. Speaking at a benefit for the Canadian Centre for Advanced Film Studies in 1987, actor Christopher Plummer addressed exactly these issues, observing that part of the function of indigenous film and television programming is to "help us rediscover ourselves and prove that we do have something to say — that we're interesting *because* we're so damn complicated. That dilemma of us is funny, it's touching, and it's worth holding on to. It's part of what makes us different, unique — us."[64]

Degrassi Junior High and *Degrassi High* capture that uniqueness and, as indelibly Canadian artifacts, invite us to see the world from a Canadian point of view, a perspective that implicitly rejects the dominant North American discourse types. Its blending of documentary realism with elements of grassroots authenticity places it solidly within a recognizably Canadian filmmaking tradition. But there is more to its rhetorical significance than its "cheesy, badly acted, cheaply produced" appearance, and the choices made by the creators of the show are not simply a product of limited resources; instead, the look and feel of the show is a reflection of something deeper, of cultural values that resist "what playwright John Gray calls 'the American hallucination in Canada.'"[65]

Documentary realism is a choice, and as such it is also a repudiation of American-style production values, of American-style "mass" culture, of slick marketing and polished appearance. *Degrassi* is a genuine artifact of Canadian culture precisely because of its implicit resistance to the overwhelming influence of American media. It shows us ourselves, "the way we express ourselves and how we express ourselves, through everything we do," and that, says Mary Walsh, "*is* our culture."[66] Knelman recounts that when the Canadian Film Development Corporation became Telefilm Canada, it was headed by Peter Pearson, who was

> determined to find a group of younger, unknown people who ... would have the energy to make indigenous Canadian films for TV — films that would work on the country's own terms rather than imitate American movies and American TV shows. To a remarkable extent, Pearson succeeded. Along came a whole pack of young unknowns who brought forth such ventures as *The Kids of Degrassi Street* ... TV series that usually had American co-production money and American distribution deals, but still managed to seem distinctly Canadian in style and content.[67]

The remarkable success of *Degrassi Junior High*, its forerunner *The Kids of Degrassi Street* and its sequels *Degrassi High* and *School's Out* demonstrate that there is room for another cultural voice on the North American continent, a voice with a distinct sound all its own and one that provides an alternative to the shallow dreams of Hollywood. Perhaps, as Pierre Berton foresaw, "the task of making films about Canada has been left at last to the people best able to make them — ourselves."[68]

NOTES

1. Chaim H. Perelman and L. Olbrechts-Tyteca, *The New Rhetoric: A Treatise on Argumentation*, trans. John Wilkinson and Purcell Weaver (Notre Dame: University of Notre Dame Press, 1971), 20–21.

2. Aristotle, *The Rhetoric and Poetics*, trans. W. Rhys Roberts, ed. Friedrich Solmsen (New York: The Modern Library, 1954), 1395a.

3. Perelman and Olbrechts-Tyteca, *The New Rhetoric*, 99; Norman Fairclough, *Language and Power* (New York: Longman, 1989), 83.

4. Edwin Black, "The Second Persona," *Quarterly Journal of Speech* 56 (June 1972), 172.

5. "Award-Winning *Degrassi Junior High* and *Degrassi High* Come to Showcase Television" (September 1, 1997). Retrieved August 23, 2003, from http://news.de-grassi.ca/article; and Natalie Earl, "Interview with Kit Hood." Retrieved September 7, 2003 from www.degrassi.ca/Interviews.

6. Steve Lutwin from Syracuse, New York. Fan review. Posted 18 July 2000. Retrieved on May 5, 2003, from www.amazon.com.

7. Jennifer VanderBurgh, "'Identity' Crisis in Canadian Film," *Queen's University Film Studies* (1996). Retrieved May 5, 2003, from www.film.queensu.ca/Critical/VanderBurgh.html.

8. For discussions of other "authentic" Canadian discourses, see Jennifer MacLennan and John Moffatt, "An Island View of the World: Canadian Community as Insularity in the Popular Writing of Stompin' Tom Connors," in Conny Steenman-Marcusse, ed., *The Rhetoric of Canadian Writing* (Amsterdam: Rodopi Press, 2002) and Jennifer MacLennan and John Moffatt, "Reclaiming 'Authenticity': *Cape Breton's Magazine* and the Commodification of Insularity," in Sherry Devereaux Ferguson and Leslie Regan Shade, eds., *Civic Discourse and Cultural Politics in Canada: A Cacophony of Voices* (Westport, CT: Greenwood Press, 2002).

9. John Hansen, "Canadian Content, Part I: *Degrassi Junior High*," edited by Mark Polger. Retrieved October 13, 2003, from www.degrassi.ca/dl/ESSAYS.

10. "Award-Winning *Degrassi Junior High* and …," as per note 5.

11. Earl, "Interview with Kit Hood."

12. Hansen, "Canadian Content, Part I"; and Jennifer Davis, Fan review. Retrieved May 5, 2003, from www.amazon.com.

13. Earl, "Interview with Kit Hood."

14. Jay Itchon from Michigan. Fan review. Posted 16 June 2000. Retrieved May 5, 2003, from www.amazon.com.

15. Lutwin. Fan review.

16. "Award-Winning *Degrassi Junior High* and ...," as per note 5.

17. Eric King Watts, "'Voice' and 'Voicelessness' in Rhetorical Studies," *Quarterly Journal of Speech* 87 (May 2001), 183.

18. Leah from Dallas, Texas. Fan review. Posted 17 July 2002; and Pat McCurry from Wilton, NH. Fan review. Posted 31 July 2000. Bot retrieved May 3, 2003, from www.amazon.com.

19. Earl, "Interview with Kit Hood."

20. Beth from Bloomington, Minnesota. Fan review. Posted 1 September 2000. Retrieved May 3, 2003, from www.amazon.com.

21. Earl, "Interview with Kit Hood."

22. "Award-Winning *Degrassi Junior High* and ...," as per note 5.

23. VanderBurgh, "'Identity' Crisis in Canadian Film."

24. David V.J. Bell, "The Sociocultural Milieu of Canadian Politics: Political Culture in Canada," in Michael S. Whittington and Glen Williams, eds., *Canadian Politics in the Eighties* (Toronto: ITP Nelson, 1983), 168.

25. Vincent Massey et. al., *Report of the Royal Commission on National Development in the Arts, Letters and Sciences* (Ottawa, ON: King's Printer, 1951), 50.

26. VanderBurgh, "'Identity' Crisis in Canadian Film."

27. Pierre Berton, *Hollywood's Canada: The Americanization of Our National Image* (Toronto: McClelland and Stewart, 1975), 12.

28. Martin Knelman, *Home Movies: Tales from the Canadian Film World* (Toronto: Key Porter Books, 1987), 148.

29. Massey et. al., *Report of the Royal Commission on National Development ...*, 11, 18.

30. Fairclough, *Language and Power*, 91.

31. Stan McMullin, "A Matter of Attitude: The Subversive Margin in Canada." Retrieved May 5, 2003, from www.gu.edu.au/centre/cmp/6_1_07.html.

32. VanderBurgh, "'Identity' Crisis in Canadian Film."

33. Peter Morris, "National Film Board," in *The Canadian Encyclopedia* (Edmonton, AB: Hurtig, 1985), 1194.

34. Knelman, *Home Movies*, 3.

35. VanderBurgh, "'Identity' Crisis in Canadian Film."

36. Ibid.

37. Theodore Plantinga, "Anti-Americanism and Canadian Identity," *Myodicy* 3 (April 1997). Retrieved May 5, 2003, from www.redeemer.on.ca/~tplanti/m/MAM. HTM; and Jack L. Granatstein, *Yankee Go Home? Canadians and Anti-Americanism*

(Toronto: HarperCollins, 1996).

38. John Fiske, *Understanding Popular Culture* (London: Methuen, 1989), 24.

39. Mary Walsh, "A Hymn to Canada," 8 December 1993 Spry Lecture, transcript (Toronto: CBC Radioworks, 1993), 6.

40. Pierre Berton, *Why We Act Like Canadians*, 2d ed. (Toronto: McClelland and Stewart, 1987), 72, 5, 71.

41. Carol Corbin and Judith A. Rolls, "Introduction," in Carol Corbin and Judith A. Rolls, eds., *The Centre of the World at the Edge of a Continent* (Sydney, NS: UCCB Press, 1996), 13.

42. Watts, "'Voice' and 'Voicelessness' in Rhetorical Studies," 183.

43. Earl, "Interview with Kit Hood."

44. Knelman, *Home Movies*, 2.

45. Daniel J. Boorstin, *The Image: A Guide to Pseudo-Events in America* (New York: Vintage Books, 1992), 49.

46. Ibid., 9, 192, 5.

47. Ibid., 56.

48. Ibid.

49. Berton, *Why We Act Like Canadians*, 70.

50. Ibid., 71.

51. "*Degrassi vs 90210.*" *Angelfire* Fan Web Site. Retrieved October 13, 2003, from www.angelfire.com/80s/ degrassicanada/90210.html.

52. Kit Hood, interview by Mark Polger. Retrieved June 27, 2003, from www.degrassi.ca/Interviews/ kit-hood-interview.htm.

53. Earl, "Interview with Kit Hood."

54. Hood, interview by Mark Polger.

55. Alexander Janums from Kingston, New York. Fan review. Posted 6 December 2001. Retrieved May 3, 2003, from www.amazon.com.

56. Lutwin. Fan review.

57. "*Degrassi vs 90210.*" *Angelfire* Fan Web Site.

58. A.J., "Welcome to My Little Side of the *Degrassi* Universe." Retrieved August 23, 2003, from www.geocities.com/morbidaj/degrassi.htm.

59. "Award-Winning *Degrassi Junior High* and …," as per note 5.

60. Boorstin, *The Image*, 6.

61. Ronald Caplan, ed., *Down North: The Book of Cape Breton's Magazine* (Wreck Cove, NS: Breton Books, 1991), viii.

62. Knelman, *Home Movies,* 149–150.

63. Perelman and Olbrechts-Tyteca, *The New Rhetoric*, 20–21.

64. Christopher Plummer, speech presented at the Benefit for the Canadian Centre for Advanced Film Studies, 1 February 1987. Quoted in Knelman, *Home Movies*, 21.

65. Quoted in Knelman, *Home Movies*, 1.

66. Walsh, "A Hymn to Canada," 9.

67. Knelman, *Home Movies*, 152–153.

68. Berton, *Hollywood's Canada*, 18.

"THAT WHITE GIRL FROM THAT SHOW":
RACE AND ETHNICITY WITHIN CANADIAN YOUTH CULTURES

Michele Byers &
Rebecca J. Haines

A CONVERSATION

INTRODUCTIONS

MICHELE: I have been thinking about *Degrassi* for a long time now. And for the most part, my thoughts have been on the ways in which *Degrassi* challenged existing ideas about adolescence (and adolescents) and what could be shown on television. Recently, I wrote an article describing *Degrassi* as a multicultural context.[1] My argument was that because of the way the show was organized, especially because of its racially diverse ensemble cast, it managed to create story arcs that featured complex questions about race and ethnicity without tying them to "guest stars" who appeared one day and were gone the next. I was particularly interested in the cross-racial relationship that developed between Michelle and BLT, and with the issues of race and class that came up in the friendship of Yick and Arthur. But there are a lot of other issues to tackle with regard to the way race and ethnicity were made such integral parts of *Degrassi*.

I had the occasion to think a little bit more critically about these things in relation not only to the old but also to the new *Degrassi* series for a paper I presented at a conference not long ago. The paper, which is about what it means (and who gets) to be "authentically" Canadian and which is influenced by the work of Himani Bannerji,[2] made me think through what multiculturalism and diversity actually mean in Canada, especially since they are so much a part of the political language endorsed by our nation state. As we become increasingly comfortable with the language of multi-culturalism, and with attributing it uncritically to media products, it becomes harder for us to take a step back so we can see what is really going on in our country. If we are not careful, we participate in the way this language obscures the fact that Canada continues to privilege whiteness, Christianity, English-speakers and people of European descent.

I grew up in Montreal in the 1970s and 1980s, just a couple of years ahead of the kids of *Degrassi*. I went to a public urban high school that had quite a lot of racial and ethnic difference in terms of its students. My school was like *Degrassi* in many ways, the characters on the show looked like people I knew and we did the same kinds of things and got into the same kinds of trouble. Growing up in Quebec, language was the primary difference, but other questions of difference were part of my experience of everyday life as well. As a little kid, I had a number of friends who were adopted and grew up in multiracial families, and that was my first experience with racial difference. But certainly, as a white kid, I did not think much about privilege and racism.

I remember girls I knew who only dated Black men, but without thinking about the objectification of racial difference. One of them had to leave home when she became pregnant because she was afraid of what her father would do when she gave birth to a biracial child. I had a boyfriend who emulated the rockabilly style of the Vietnamese boys he hung out with. I remember being told by a friend to "be careful" on my way to a dance at another high school because some of the Black girls might try to beat us up. A Greek friend of mine in high school was told by his mother that she would not give him a wedding present if he married his girlfriend who was Italian and Portuguese. The same girl lost another boyfriend for the same reason, he was a Moroccan Jew and his parents did not approve of interfaith dating. As a Jew myself, I found it fascinating that I would have been a more appropriate girlfriend, even though I lived a totally secular life and his girlfriend, while living with her Jewish stepfather, attended synagogue and weekly Shabbat dinners. And I myself had the experience of being told that I couldn't be Jewish because of the way I "looked." At the same time, as I got older, I became increasingly frustrated by the fact that I passed so easily as a non-Jew. When I think back to high school, I remember that there was also a lot of self-segregation that went on, and we see this less on "diverse" ensemble shows like *Degrassi*. Where does *Degrassi* fit with my memories?

In this chapter, I discuss some of these issues — and others — with former *Degrassi* actress Rebecca Haines, who played the character Kathleen on *Degrassi Junior High* and *Degrassi High*. We are both scholars who have spent time thinking and writing about Canadian youth culture, and this conversation gives us an opportunity to discuss *Degrassi* from a theoretical space that is conditioned by our own experiences of growing up in a country where difference is anything but invisible.

REBECCA: The experience of acting on the *Degrassi* series during my teenage years has undeniably shaped both the person I am today and the work I have chosen to do as an academic researcher. When Michele and I first met to discuss her proposal for this book, I learned that we shared several common research interests with regards to youth and popular culture, including mass media depictions of racial and ethnic identities in the Canadian context. I was especially interested in that fact that she had written on the cross-racial relationship between the characters BLT and Michelle, as I had also done some previous graduate work on teenage mothers of multiracial children, their experiences with everyday racisms and the potential implications for the racial identity of their young children in the future.[3]

As a white woman, I have been thinking about issues of racial identity for a long time. Long before I had the academic vocabulary to analyze and theorize my experiences, I had the practical instruction on the workings of racism through growing up in the context of a working-class community and social circle where "white" people were the minority. Like Michele, I was a teenager in the 1980s, but lived in a low-income neighbourhood in downtown Toronto. Growing up, the majority of my close relationships were with friends that were Black and of Caribbean heritage. My own immediate family is of British and Irish descent, racially homogenous and predominantly Anglo-Christian. However, in addition to the strong influence of my cross-racial peer group and friendships, the main values that shaped my identity are rooted in my upbringing as a child of a struggling single-parent and in experiencing many of the so-called risk factors related to growing up in a socio-economically disadvantaged setting.

When I entered university in Montreal in the early 1990s, I experienced a profound sense of "otherness" and an inability to relate to this new social context of student life at an elite academic school. Despite having been on a major Canadian television series for most of my teen years, the social and economic circumstances of my family and upbringing were decidedly less than "privileged." It was at this time that I began to explore some of my experiences around racial identity as an adolescent and young adult, which culminated in the essay I wrote, "Becoming an 'Invisible Minority': Reflections of a White, Working-class Woman Entering Academia."[4] My evolving class awareness and academic understanding of the intersection of race, class and gender privileges strongly directed my studies and research, providing me with the tools not only to articulate my feelings of being disconnected from academia but also to express how young people experience the process of racial identity within the context of close cross-racial friendships and participation in interracial youth cultures.

At the time, research that addressed questions of race and ethnicity within Canadian youth cultures was basically non-existent. Moreover, there was literally no writing on the influence of rap music and hip-hop culture in Canada's urban contexts, despite a growing academic attention to the genre in the United States. Influenced by the long tradition of work on the racial politics of adolescent style subcultures that emerged from the Birmingham Centre for Contemporary Cultural Studies in Britain,[5] I became interested in how Canadian youth engage with hip hop in order to articulate their own understandings of racial identity.[6] Although the research landscape has shifted considerably in the past decade due to the explosion of hip hop into mainstream youth and commercial cultures, I am still struck by the polarization of "race" in popular cultural products geared towards young people, especially on North American television.

Because I have been so focused on the role of music-based popular cultures, it was not until I began to read some of Michele's work and to dialogue with her on these issues that I realized how "progressive" the *Degrassi* series was in its handling of race and ethnicity in the lives of adolescents. I hope that my contribution to this conversation provides some useful insights from the perspective of someone who has lived out these issues both on and off-screen, and as an academic who is interested in youth cultures. However, I would be remiss if I did not add that my contribution to this volume is also framed by a desire to show people what I have been up to since the series ended. People are always asking me what I am doing now, and why I decided not to act or pursue a career in television. Although working on a PhD may not be quite as exciting as being a TV star, I feel that the work that I am doing is motivated by the approach to telling the stories of teenagers that I learned while on *Degrassi*, in that it prioritizes the views and needs of adolescents and employs a youth-centred orientation to research.

THE CONVERSATION: *DEGRASSI* ON RACE AND ETHNICITY

MICHELE: One of the storylines that continues to captivate me is the cross-racial relationship between Michelle and BLT. You have suggested really interesting issues about this story arc, some of which I've been thinking about as well. For instance, how does *Degrassi* relate or measure up to other examples of cross-racial couples portrayed in the media? Does *Degrassi* offer us a radically different image of these issues than other texts? What might this text have looked like if it had focused on a Black woman and a white man?

REBECCA: My interest in deconstructing this particular storyline stems mainly from my personal experience of growing up in a neighbourhood, peer group and social network where cross-racial friendships and romantic relationships were not just common but the *norm* among my girlfriends who were Black, Asian and white. In this context, the issues I encountered in cross-racial relationships were very different from the issues depicted in the Michelle–BLT storyline as there were a myriad of ways in which race, identity and difference were negotiated, played with and redefined within my particular group of friends, the complexities of which I think are not easily captured on television or film. These redefinitions of racial identity have been central to shaping who I am today, and they form the basis of what I've been trying to research, theorize and work through in my "adult" life after television and in my academic work on Canadian youth cultures since my role on *Degrassi* ended.

First off, I have to say that looking back on this particular storyline, I think it was a bold move for the series to take on the topic of adolescent cross-racial romance in the Canadian context. In doing so, the message to the viewing public was in effect one of "Look, there are racist attitudes that exist here too — this is not just an American issue." I think the point you raise about the Black male–white female dyad is an important one though, because in this sense the show's approach was not radically different from the typical approach to cross-racial couples seen in popular film and television. In a way, this storyline could have been even more thought-provoking had it flipped the race and gender issues or problematized racial or ethnic differences in another way. For example, what if there had been a relationship between Susie and Arthur? What if Yick's parents had objected to him dating Melanie, or another character who was not Asian? The Black male–white female relationship has always received a lot of attention in North American popular culture, and in my opinion it is a narrative that is usually fraught with stereotypes based on white fears about Black male sexuality. That being said, while depictions of white male–Black female relationships have been less prominent, stereotypical portrayals of Black female sexuality have also been very visible within popular culture.

To be blunt, when the theme of white parents being threatened by their daughter's choice of a Black male partner is constantly replayed in media imagery, I think it actually reinforces rather than usurps people's racist attitudes towards cross-racial couples. Ultimately, I think it results in the perception that cross-racial relationships are "risky" and will end poorly, inevitably leading to rejection by friends, family and society. Viewers may in fact come away with the message that these relationships will not succeed in the long run and that people are better off "sticking with their own kind." Moreover, I think the way that storylines are resolved often portray the white characters as the "heroes" or the tragic victims. When we see the story from the perspective of the white partner only, when the conflict centres on her/his sacrifices and defiance of her/his family, the Black partner is then reduced to the object of racist objections rather than being a subject that must also navigate these complexities in relation to her/his own set of interpersonal relationships, family and community.

MICHELE: That brings me to another really important part of this story arc, the relationship the characters have with their parents. In my work, I have written about the interesting fact that Michelle's parents are shown to be racist and how Michelle actively rebels against them. But Rebecca, you have raised an interesting question: Why does it always seem to be the white parents who are racist? Or is it always white parents? I will throw into the pot two counter-examples: one from *Beverly Hills 90210* and one from *Sex and the City.* In the last season of *90210*, the storyline followed the inter-racial romance of Janet (Lindsay price, who is Asian American) and Steve (Ian Ziering, who is white), a romance which ended with them marrying and having a child. Both sets of parents, though Janet's Asian parents in particular, were resistant to the idea of their children entering an interracial marriage. In the third season of *Sex and the City*, Samantha (Kim Cattrall) briefly dated an African-American man (Chivon/Asio Highsmith), taking great pleasure in her ability to infiltrate his world. His sister Adina (Sundra Oakley), however, saw Samantha as a white woman appropriating both her brother and Black culture. Although Samantha resisted what she saw as Adina's refusal of cultural "fusion," Chivon ultimately made it clear that blood was thicker than water and ended the relationship.

What do these storylines mean? One of the fascinating parts of the *Degrassi* episode happens when Michelle's mother suggests that, although she is not racist, she is worried about the trouble that Michelle and BLT will face since they do not share the same culture. Michelle responds that he's Canadian, just like she is. But is he? Is he just Canadian? Is he just Black? Is Michelle just white?

REBECCA: You know, I think it is really significant that in stories such as these the Black character's family and entire social network is absent from the narrative, as if to say that all you need to know about them is that they are not white and therefore the family is racially "different." Michelle's mother voices her concern about so-called cultural differences, but we as viewers are not really clued in to what these might entail. Implicit in Michelle's debate with her parents is an essentialist notion that white Canadian and Black Canadian families are very much culturally different, but we're not given enough information to understand how or why this may or may not be true. What is missing is a more nuanced picture of what it means to *both* Michelle and BLT to be a white or Black "Canadian" and how this is negoti-ated within the context of their intimate relationship and also among their other friendships at *Degrassi*. Furthermore, because we don't see the Thomas family either supporting or rejecting their son's choice of a white partner, you get the sense that BLT does not have the same level of parental involve-ment in comparison to Michelle's concerned and overprotective white par-ents. When the voices of the Black parents are absent from the storyline, are we then left to assume that his parents have no concerns or opinions about their son's choice of a white partner?

A few years ago I did see an example of this type of characterization through the portrayal of a young adult cross-racial relationship on the short-lived CBC series *Drop the Beat*, which I fondly refer to as a hip-hop version of *Degrassi*. I think in many ways this series was groundbreaking, mainly because for the first time in Canadian television there was a series that was centred exclusively on the lives of two Black teens, their struggles with racism, their relationships and their aspirations in the music business. They were not the token visible minorities in an ensemble cast or the secondary characters that came around to teach viewers a lesson when there was a storyline on racism; rather, their lives *were* the story, period. In one episode, the main character, Dennis, becomes involved in a relationship with a white female, Kat, who works with him at the local college radio station. The hassles that he goes through when this is discovered by his friends and family are shown through his eyes — his mom gives him flack, he is labelled a sell-out by some of his boys, and he has to deal with his discomfort about "going public" with his white girlfriend for fear of the repercussions this will have on his reputation in the hip-hop community. For me, this was a more complex portrayal of the traditional cross-racial relationship story as told from the "other's" side. It was the first time I've seen this on Canadian television outside of the American examples you've raised and also the youth-oriented feature films *Black & White* (2000) and *Save the Last Dance* (2001*)*, which I think also did a nice job of providing a more balanced portrayal of a cross-racial romance plot than what we typically see in Hollywood films.

MICHELE: I have to ask about the way the public reacted to this cross-racial couple. Of course, as Canadians, we have a tendency to assume that such images would cause no reaction, because we like to think of ourselves as completely open-minded and tolerant, certainly not racist. Is this, in fact, the case?

REBECCA: My memory is a bit fuzzy on this point, but I remember hearing something at the time with regards to some negative reactions to the Michelle–BLT pairing on the part of viewers. If I recall correctly, it was somewhat surprising that many of the objections to this story came not from a "white" perspective but from some Black viewers who felt that, by spotlighting a Black male–white female couple, the show was reinforcing some broader cultural notion that "Black men prefer to date white women" and thereby unconsciously devaluing Black couples in general and Black women in particular. Although this was obviously not the intent of the show, I think this line of argument really caught people off guard at the time; I think the assumption was that the storyline would raise objections from white viewers rather than the other way around.

Before we had this discussion, I read your comments on the resolution of this story arc in your conference paper in which you question the politics around the fact that when Michelle and BLT's relationship ends, his next girlfriend, Cindy, is Black. It's interesting to me that you picked up on this "switch," because the race dimensions of BLT's choice of a new girlfriend are not overtly problematized in the context of the story. Michelle seems upset that BLT has moved on to a new relationship when she has not, and the story positions BLT's taking up with Cindy as based on the fact that they are both "jocks" and involved in school athletics. Again, it begs the question whether or not this plot resolution leaves viewers with the impression that young people are better off making the choice not to date cross-racially. I am sure this was not the conscious intent behind this narrative choice, which I imagine was based more on the need to show a "positive" example of a young Black couple, reflecting the critical feedback that was received on this storyline.

MICHELE: Difficulties because of race are not confined to the heterosexual couple; another interesting story arc from *Degrassi* follows the friendship between Yick, an Asian-Canadian refugee, and Arthur, a middle-class Jewish kid. Yick is novel, in that he is a rarity in North American programming where Asian youth are largely absent as characters. But having a character who is a refugee is also quite unusual on television. How are the class implications of Yick's character related to questions of racialization and representation on television? What does it mean to be racialized outside of the Black/white binary?

REBECCA: I am glad you raise this because I feel really strongly that having Yick Yu as a central character in the series is one of the ways in which *Degrassi* was exceptional as compared with other teen-oriented shows. Yick is a fully developed character who brings more to the plot line than being "a token Asian" or a stereotype of someone whose family are "New Canadians." The Arthur–Yick friendship is an excellent example of how *Degrassi* was able to capture the commonalities of the adolescent experience, addressing issues of race and ethnicity outside the romantic–sexual relationship or the Black–white dyad. What I like about the way in which this friendship is shown to viewers is, in some ways, the opposite of what I highlight in my critique of the Michelle–BLT relationship. In this case, the portrayal does not problematize the characters' different racial, ethnic or religious backgrounds, nor is it an issue that seems to get in the way of their friendship. Along these lines, the boys are shown as more similar than they are different, as two somewhat "nerdy" and awkward kids struggling with typical pre-adolescent dilemmas — cheating on tests, concerns about wet dreams and asking girls out. Later on in the series, there is an issue of class rather than race or ethnicity that upsets the friendship and threatens to divide the two. After Arthur's mother wins the lottery, he spends the summer travelling in Europe before returning to school, and this causes some static between himself and Yick, who perceives his friend as acting "rich" and stuck-up. And as is often the case in high school, over the course of the series the two drift apart as Yick becomes a bit "cooler" than Arthur, taking up smoking, getting his ear pierced and hanging out with more popular boys like Luke and Joey.

This reflects quite accurately, I think, what was common for many of us who grew up in neighbourhoods and attended schools where difference was the norm. That is, that having friendships that span these differences is, in fact, a normal and, for the most part, an uneventful occurrence in the lives of many teens. I myself had a similar social context in junior high at Winchester Public School in downtown Toronto. The school's catchment spanned the working-class areas of St. Jamestown, Cabbagetown and Regent Park. In grade seven I was one of only a few white Canadian kids in the class, and my clique of best girlfriends were Filipina, Chinese and Korean. In our little preadolescent world we were not yet navigating the terrain of racialized identity because our primary concerns were clothes, popularity and "who was going around with whom." I was never conscious of being a "white minority" until looking back at the class photo some years later. The school photographer had sat me, the singular female who was blonde and pale, directly in the centre of the photograph. An aesthetic choice perhaps, but one that I believe was obviously race conscious on his part. I do not think it was until we reached high school and later adolescence that issues of race and ethnicity came to the forefront and that our choice of bestfriends, cliques and boyfriends became imbued with more meaning than simply who was cool and who was not.

I know you have also written at length on the episode where Yick feels pressured to fabricate a family artifact and history, not wanting his classmates or his bestfriend to know his family were refugees from Vietnam. It is interesting to me that it is through the context of his friendship with Arthur that Yick makes the decision to come forward with this story, sharing his past in a class presentation. Once this episode is complete, Yick's past is now behind him and the two proceed with their friendship as before, as if that part of his experience has magically disappeared. There may have indeed been a place for the show to address anti-immigrant sentiment and racism from a young person's viewpoint, perhaps in the form of having another character arrive at *Degrassi* as a newer immigrant, or looking a bit more at the struggles between second-generation Canadian kids and first-generation parents. These points aside, I don't think this analysis takes away from the fact, as you said before, that Yick was one of the only refugees and perhaps the only Asian leading character that we've seen in a major Canadian television production.

MICHELE: As you note, the other major ethnic group represented on *Degrassi* is Greek, and I went to a high school with quite a lot of Greek students. It is interesting that a lot of the representations of Canadian Greekness on *Degrassi* are so familiar not only to me, but to others as well, as we can see by the popularity of the film *My Big Fat Greek Wedding* (2002), which employs a lot of the same cultural stereotypes, especially about "old-world" parents and their inability to understand North American culture and values. Himani Bannerji makes an interesting argument that because Canada prides itself on allowing ethnic diversity, it can attribute all kinds of things to ethnic "others."[7] To give an example, there is a scene in which Michelle, Lucy, Alexa and L.D. are sitting in the cafeteria talking about BLT. Lucy challenges Alexa's racist statement that BLT is a good athlete and dancer because he's Black. Alexa says that her parents would die if she dated someone who was not white, that they do not even want her to date Simon because he is not Greek, and that they think they are still back in their little Greek village. L.D. and Lucy say that her parents are racist, and even though Michelle's mother is also racist, there is this strange feeling in this scene that Alexa's parents, who are not "real" Canadians, are the racist ones. By displacing racism onto ethnic "otherness," we can distance ourselves from it.

What do you think about *Degrassi* in relation to other Canadian shows in terms of how it dealt with these issues? Was *Degrassi* unique, or was it articulating something that is part of what we might think of as "the cultural mythology of Canada"? And that being said, is the way Canadian television depicts issues around racialization and ethnicity fundamentally different from the way these issues are treated on American television?

REBECCA: For me, when you engage with the question of whether or not Canadians are somehow more diversity oriented or "less racist" than Americans, it can work to obscure responsibility for addressing racism and discrimination as it exists in our society, and racism is most certainly present in our society's popular culture and the media. To be fair, *Degrassi* was a show centred on some of the most universal coming-of-age struggles that make up what it means to be an adolescent in North America. I do not think it was ever a show that purported to be "about" racial and/or ethnic identity in any substantive way, as compared with, say, my previous example of *Drop the Beat*, which was explicitly (but not exclusively) about race and the Black adolescent experience in an urban Canadian context. However, I think the series was extremely valuable in the way that it continually challenged the notion of what were "appropriate" topics to address on a program aimed at youth (i.e., AIDS, abortion, dating violence). As well, through presenting these issues exclusively from an adolescent's point of view, the show had the capacity to appeal to teenagers not only in Canada but also in many other countries.

You know, since the series has ended, I have been approached by people that recognize me as Kathleen almost everywhere I have travelled, and here in Toronto by tourists from countries all over the world. It raises some questions for me about the fifty or so countries to which the series has been sold and its syndication internationally. What picture of "Canadian" life do international viewers come away with after watching *Degrassi*? Are the narratives, the settings and the characters distinguishable from British or American dramas aimed at youth? As a whole, I think the composition of the cast provided a fairly accurate representation of the racial and ethnic mix that was prevalent in Toronto's downtown, working-class neighbourhoods in the late eighties. I do not know if viewers from other places see the show and believe that all Canadian cities and neighbourhoods are as "multicultural" and diverse as the cast appeared on *Degrassi*.

As a whole, I think where both Canadian and American popular television and film are lacking is in their depictions of multiracial families and people, in terms of representations of people negotiating racial differences as a part of their everyday lives. I have seen a few recent examples of Canadian films where this has been done quite well in terms of the sibling relationship, notably Clement Virgo's feature *Love Come Down* (2000) and my former *Degrassi* colleague Anais Granofsky's film *On Their Knees* (2003). In both these films, racial differences between the two main characters are woven into the narratives, which centre on difficult family dynamics and the sibling relationship. The effect for me is that racial difference in families is somehow presented as naturalized rather than as pathologized. I can't say for certain whether these films are part of a broader "Canadian" as opposed to American cinematic sensibility, but I have not seen a comparable form of subtlety in Hollywood-genre films that deal with multiracial families and relationships, especially those geared towards adolescents. Admittedly, my approach to this issue has been influenced by my personal feelings of frustration, having been negotiating these issues for most of my teenage years and adult life. There are many of us that live in families and intimate relationships that cross and combine racial differences, and yet I feel that our stories are still not very well represented in the broader Canadian culture.

MICHELE: Given the issues we've been discussing, do you think that the media have a chance in trying to give us a view of relationships among families, lovers, friends and colleagues that cross racial, ethnic, religious, national and class lines?

REBECCA: I think we are now seeing a broader range of narratives around race and ethnicity produced by this generation of cultural producers and there are increased possibilities for counter-narratives of identity concerning youth. The recent British film *Bend It Like Beckham* (2003) is a great example of this in my view. But for the most part these stories remain on the margins of popular culture. What I would like to see in regards to Canadian popular or youth culture are more examples and explorations of what it means to the current generation of adolescents to be "Canadian" and how the complexities of race, ethnicity and nation are renegotiated by youth in everyday life. In my own life and experiences, I have encountered so many people who have found spaces that allow them to rework the discourses handed down to them from parents, schooling and the broader culture. I know that personally, questioning my own identity and interrogating white privilege has become a lifelong project, and it would be truly interesting to see more examples of this incorporated into mainstream media and culture. That, in my eyes, would be more interesting than the traditions of tokenism and simplistic portrayals of racial archetypes that we see so often in North American media. I'm not quite sure if there's a place for that yet, but I'm hopeful.

RACE AND ETHNICITY OFF-CAMERA

MICHELE: What about the episode where Kathleen raps? Can you speak here to what you have described to me as "the gap between your character as a white, middle-class teen and your own experiences around race and class off-screen"?

REBECCA: This story is just a little anecdote about how my onscreen and off-camera adolescent years were really miles apart. As I mentioned before, I grew up in a low-income community and in a school and neighbourhood context that was racially diverse. In the late eighties and early nineties, it was the hip-hop culture of rap and reggae music that was dominant among my group of friends, and the Toronto "scene" I became involved with during high school was, loosely speaking, a Black/Caribbean youth culture.

As you may recall, late in *Degrassi High* there was an episode where Lucy and the twins were filming a video greeting at Degrassi for L.D.'s six-teenth birthday — her character at the time was in remission from leukemia and she was off on some kind of round-the-world sailing expedition with her widowed father. Part of the montage of birthday greetings called for a "birthday rap" to be presented by some of the cast members. As a teenager I was really into writing poetry and hip-hop lyrics, but I had absolutely no "flow" or rapping talent. One of the extras and I sat down before the scene and wrote the rap, which wasn't really very good. Then I somehow managed to con my way into the filming of the scene, dressed in my prissy Kathleen clothes, rapping alongside the black characters BLT, Bronco and Scooter, despite the fact that Kathleen did not hang out with those guys and was definitely *not* a character you would picture as a "rapper." I remember being so proud of the whole thing at the time, and every now and then someone will say to me, "Hey, I saw that show where Kathleen was rapping — you were horrible."

MICHELE: You have mentioned that there have been a few occasions when you have attended "Black" events in the Toronto club scene and were referred to as "that white girl from *that show*." This is a really complex statement; what does it say about you, your body and the different ways you are read depending on where you are and who is doing the reading? You also pointed to these questions: *Which* white girl are you, when the show is predominantly white? And how is your race related to your position as a celebrity, as someone who is on TV?

REBECCA: I raise this example, first because it's one of the funnier stories I have about the experience of being recognized from *Degrassi* in public, and second because it pretty much encapsulates my experience of race and identity in terms of what you might call my cultural choices as a white person who has spent the majority of my teens and twenties within relationships and social contexts that are majority-Black. As someone who has spent a lot of time thinking and writing about race, this example is interesting to me because it's an obvious reminder that within certain settings my whiteness is perhaps *more* visible to other people than my status as a former television actress or minor Canadian celebrity. Yet, as you've also noted, this statement assumes that I am the only white girl on or from the show, almost reversing the racist colloquial "they all look alike," sort of in the form of "those white girls from *Degrassi* — they all look alike to me!" And this was not only said to me but also to a Black friend of mine who knows me on and off-screen. An acquaintance approached this person and said, "I always see *that white girl* from the show when I'm out." So I think what people are getting at when they say this type of thing is that I am that white girl who goes to certain clubs or parties, the one who appears where you might not expect her to because of how I appeared on television. Being known as the white girl from *Degrassi* doesn't really bother me, though — there are, after all, worse things to be known as!

MICHELE: Another interesting issue that you have raised is about the off-screen context of the series' production. What were the issues around racialization and ethnicity that happened off-screen? Can you speak to the story you told me about noticing that the extras were being grouped racially?

REBECCA: As I mentioned before, there are many different ways in which race and ethnicity are "played" with and negotiated within the context of intimate relationships, things that are too nuanced to capture onscreen, and issues I believe individuals have to "live out" in everyday life in order to fully understand all of the dynamics involved. Sometimes I think this is a generational issue. I look at the "mix" of different people that I have been close to in my lifetime and compare that with my parents' generation; mine is really an entirely different experience of race and identity which has occurred because I am the product of a more diverse and urban social context. In terms of the composition of the cast and background extras that were part of the show, I think the mix of kids selected was a fairly accurate representation of the groups of teens you would have found in many urban Canadian high schools at the time. Given the fact that we were a diverse community of young people thrown together in the context of a working relationship, not entirely different from a "real-life" high-school setting, I do not recall that issues of race and ethnicity were overtly problematic, but these issues were still present in our interactions with each other behind the scenes and in the context of our off-screen socializing.

One example that I remember well involves something I noticed while doing work as a background extra during an episode of *Degrassi High*. This particular scene was a typical *Degrassi* opening set-up — a wide, moving shot of the school entranceway, with lots of background action and many extras. As is customary, the second or third assistant director (AD) was responsible for grouping and positioning the "background," giving us starting positions and actions around the major players in the scene. After observing a few of the different set-ups for various shots in the scene, on this particular day I noticed that the AD was positioning and grouping extras based on same-race pairings. I was probably the only person who noticed this, because, as I mentioned previously, I was hyperconscious about racial differences as a teenager. When I asked this person about why they were grouping the extras in this way, he said, "Well look at the cast cafeteria at lunch break, that's how people sit together and socialize." While this might have been true at times, I argued that as a cast we were in fact much more "integrated" off-screen although, there were some "cliques" among us based on musical preference, style or even neighbourhood. I also argued that whatever the social reality was off-screen, it should be the goal of the show to promote and depict integration onscreen. It wasn't a full-blown argument, but after I pointed out this fact to him I noticed that the AD no longer made the same types of groupings among the extras in the following scenes.

However, I want to add an important addendum to this example, by stating that in no way was the off-screen atmosphere of the show informed by any kind of racial hierarchy or incidents of discrimination. In fact, at one point in the show I remember that there was an extra who was let go after referring to another cast member using a derogatory racial slur. Although it was not spelled out for us at the time, I think the fact that this person was dismissed made it clear to us as young cast members that this type of behaviour would not be tolerated.

Another more personal example from my own life that I can use to demonstrate my experiences with racial essentialism relates to how a few of my close friends off-screen have used the racial/ethnic representations from *Degrassi* as "joke material." When I was recognized as "Kathleen" at the university I attended, an Asian male friend of mine would joke that he was "Yick Yu" and begin chanting "Out of the way with Stephanie Kay!" just like the character had done on the *Degrassi Junior High* episode "Revolution." Another play on this theme happened to me just a few months ago. I was out for dinner in suburban Toronto with a male friend of mine, who is African Canadian, and a young girl came up to our table and asked me if I was Kathleen. As she proceeded with the standard fan question "Do you still keep in touch with anyone from the show?" I pointed to my companion and said, "Well this is BLT — don't you recognize him?" "Really? You are?" she said, clearly too excited to pause and realize that although Black and male, this person looked NOTHING like Dayo Ade, the actor who played BLT. An inappropriate joke to some, maybe (and perhaps unfair to this young woman on my part, to use her admiration for the show in this way) but something my close friend and I found very funny. I want to add that I think this type of play on racial essentialism is something that can only occur when two people have established terms of trust within the context of a close friendship. It is something that has always been present for me, and more often than not I am the butt of jokes among my friends that play on stereotypes about "white people."

By relaying these examples, I am definitely not trying to imply that this type of behaviour is a form of anti-racism in any way. I merely want to point out that the ways in which we live out race and ethnicity in our daily lives can be complex and is constantly being renegotiated as we grow older and learn, as described by an acquaintance of mine, "age-appropriate" racial behaviours. The question of how cross-racial relationships and experiences around racial differences shift as young people move from adolescence to adulthood has been the focus of the academic work I have done on cross-racial youth cultures, hip-hop culture in Montreal and young mothers of multiracial children in downtown Toronto.[8]

Working in Canadian Popular and Youth Cultures

MICHELE: Since you stopped being an active part of the creation of Canadian popular culture, you have been working on and thinking about it in other ways. Could you speak some more about the research you've been doing on youth cultures? How does your celebrity affect the way that you are received by both your academic peer group and the young people you are studying?

REBECCA: It is not lost on me that after being a part of Canadian popular/youth cultures as a teenager I then chose to focus my research on youth cultures in Canada. For me, the process of doing an academic research project is really not so far from producing a television show or film; it is just another way to document a particular aspect of the world you find interesting. As I mention above, my interest in focusing on the cross-racial aspects of music-based youth cultures such as hip hop was obviously motivated by my own experience of adolescence and was heavily influenced by Hebdige's seminal text *Subculture: The Meaning of Style* and the work of the Birmingham Centre for Contemporary Cultural Studies on the racial dynamics of youth cultures and politics.[9] At the time, in the mid-nineties, there was very little academic theory and research work on rap music and hip-hop culture coming out of the United States and practically none on Canadian youth cultures. In addition to locating rap music as an expression of identity politics among Canadian youth, I interviewed young people from different racial backgrounds involved with the production of hip-hop music about how they negotiated issues of racial identity, cultural appropriation and the experience of everyday racisms within the context of the hip-hop music scene and within their broader communities.

Following this, I took this analysis a bit further to look at how adolescent mothers negotiate issues of difference and identity when they have a partner from a different racial background and the implications their experiences in cross-racial relationships might have on their parenting of a multiracial child. In Canada, there has been very little research on the ethnoracial characteristics of young mothers, or the situations of minority or immigrant youth who become pregnant. Although absence of race from the research agenda is in some ways preferable to the highly visible role that racial stereotyping has played within past discourses about young mothers in the United States, the comparative nature of research on adolescent pregnancy which emphasizes, and in doing so often pathologizes, differences between racial groups has failed to consider the possibility of racial diversity *within* young families. In pursuing these types of projects, I was trying to argue for an approach to research on youth cultures that challenges the traditional assumption that young people of different backgrounds belong to separate and homogeneous categories. While it is important not to neglect where the structures of racism in society can cause their paths to *diverge*, I've tried to argue that we must also look seriously at what happens when the lives of youth of different races *converge*.

In my current project on young women and smoking, I've moved away from a central focus on race and ethnicity, but these aspects are still a part of my analysis of young women's tobacco use within a youth cultural framework. I want to look critically at how young women interpret broader popular cultural representations of tobacco use and the gendered messages about feminine beauty, sexuality and body image that these entail. Again, I've had my own experience with smoking as a teen and it is something I've struggled with for most of my adult life, so I also bring the "insider" perspective to this work. In a way, I guess you could say that my experience with *Degrassi* has had a lasting impact on my perspective and on my approach to my academic work, which prioritizes the experiences, views and needs of young people, in particular teen girls and young women.

What has been absolutely invaluable to me personally is how the visibility of my role on the *Degrassi* series and the popularity of the show in Canada have opened doors for me professionally that would otherwise have been closed or more than likely slammed in my face! I know that my portrayal of Kathleen has been like a calling card for me in that sense, one that I have not been afraid to use if I feel it will give me an extra edge over the competition. Yet in some ways, I think that growing up on television and now being an "Ex-*Degrassi* Kid" is similar to being the child of a wealthy or famous Canadian — everybody knows you, but there's still a certain pressure to achieve something worthwhile on your own terms. Now that some ten or so years have passed since I was on television, being recognized publicly is not something that is constantly with me, but the *Degrassi* thing has a tendency to show up at the oddest times and places in the academic world. For example, when I presented my first paper at a major national conference I was introduced to the audience by the session chair as a former *Degrassi* actress, which only added to the pressure I was already feeling about being a new and relatively young researcher in this context.

These sorts of things happen to me frequently, and I am not sure whether the celebrity status enhances or diminishes my credibility within academic circles. At the same time, I've also had ethical concerns about how the "recognizability factor" influences my qualitative fieldwork and research interviews with young people. Although it has been a definite asset to me in gaining entry to certain settings, I have also had to be careful not to let this exert undue influence within the research process. For example, a few years ago when I spent the summer doing fieldwork at a group home for pregnant teenagers, one of the young participants in this study explained my presence there to a newcomer by saying, "Oh, she's not pregnant, she's from *Degrassi*," and the fact that I was there as a researcher was just glossed over. So I think I have had to work at striking a balance between using my former status as a way to break the ice in a new research setting and also making sure that it doesn't distract too much from the research process.

MICHELE: How does it feel to move, as you yourself put it, "from child actress to child and youth advocate?"

REBECCA: The line "child actress to child and youth advocate" is something that I included in my application to graduate school and I think it nicely frames the work I have been doing in child and adolescent mental health, and the work I hope to do as an academic. It's interesting to me that I find myself working in this area, given where I started. When I was younger I did very well in school, and it was my late mother's aspiration for a time that I become a pediatrician. Through my experience with acting I quickly became sidetracked from this goal during high school; I eventually applied to medical school, but was rejected, twice. It turned out to be a type of blessing in disguise, because I ended up working in a pediatric health-care setting and have been able to parlay my experiences into an academic and research career focused on helping children and youth. Putting the needs of children first, being able to see the world from their point of view was something my mother excelled at in her job as a medical social worker, dealing with extremely challenging family scenarios on a daily basis. As an older adult, she had an instant rapport with teens, managing that tricky terrain between "mother" and "buddy," authority figure and confidante. I would like to think that I have inherited these qualities, and I hope that some of this legacy informs the work that I do now.

FROM THE OLD TO THE NEW

MICHELE: Have you been watching *Degrassi: The Next Generation*? If you have, how do you think it fits into the questions of racialization and ethnicity that we have been discussing?

REBECCA: I am embarrassed to admit that I have only seen a few episodes so far and while they were not storylines that addressed race explicitly, there seems to be a similar attention to diversity among the main characters, teachers and background extras that make up the student body of *The Next Generation*. As an aside, from what I have seen of the character Liberty (who is Black), I am reminded of my character Kathleen. She's portrayed as the same type of uptight, overachieving control freak that tends to get under everyone's skin, although she's not quite "the Wicked Witch of *Degrassi*," as they used to refer to my character.

An episode I caught recently in reruns focused on the romantic relationship between Ashley (who is white) and Jimmy (who is Black), although the issue in this case was not about race but about a young woman experimenting with different styles and social cliques, making a move from a trendy-type popular girl to a goth. What I liked most about the episode was that Ashley challenged Jimmy for not fully accepting her stylistic change, and ultimately deciding to end the relationship because she felt it was limiting her ability to express herself and was a subtle act of control on the part of her boyfriend. In what I think is the trademark *Degrassi* style, this episode was able to articulate an important message about gender, adolescent identity and self-esteem with none of the typical and hackneyed clichés that can be so prevalent in shows geared towards teenagers.

MICHELE: Any other comments on the differences between the new series and the old?

REBECCA: Part of what I have noticed about *The Next Generation* is that this group of young actors as well as the overall look and feel of this new version of the show appear a bit more sophisticated or even "middle class" than the previous series. I think that from *Kids of Degrassi Street* through to *Degrassi High*, there was very much a sense that the show reflected a kind of hodge-podge group of working-class and first-generation Canadian kids, all of us wearing decidedly "untrendy" clothes, little screen makeup and most of the time not looking very "cool." I think this homegrown feel was part of the appeal of the show and a main reason why so many people related to the series. As a cast we looked, spoke and dressed like everyday kids, like we had just walked off a downtown east-end street and onto a film set. From what I've seen of *The Next Generation,* I think there is more attention to the importance of the style culture, fashion and consumerism, and the kids seem to be a much more "put together" bunch than we were at the time. I mean, I could be way off on this point, and maybe I am really just jealous that these kids have better clothes than we did! But seriously, from the handful of episodes I have seen, the characters in this version do appear to be more "mature" and style conscious than in the previous series, which I think is a natural and logical progression, rather than trying to recreate the visual style of past shows. I think it is also an accurate reflection of how adolescence in North America is changing. Young people are now much more media savvy, have greater access to technology and live in a world that is already quite different from the one that we experienced as teenagers in the late 1980s.

MICHELE: Any final thoughts?

REBECCA: I don't think anyone would dispute the fact that the show has done much towards the goal of increasing mainstream media images that are representative of Canadian teens from a range of ethnic and racial backgrounds. In this sense, I think *Degrassi* remains unique within the teen drama genre in North American popular television.

I'd like to conclude my contribution to this discussion by reiterating that I am very proud to have been a part of the *Degrassi* series and to have the opportunity to use my experience on the show as a springboard for a research career on youth and youth cultures. I think one of the things the show was always praised for was the fact that there was limited adult intervention in the plot lines when it came to the characters addressing serious issues. It was very much not the typical sitcom or after-school special model of "adult intervenes to save the day." What I think was perhaps one of the most valuable messages from the show was that young people turned to each other for support and advice and helped each other struggle with whatever dilemma it happened to be. This is what made the show unique and truly "teen centred" in my view. I also think the fact that we as teens and cast members had a chance to provide our own input on some of the issues and give our feedback on whether or not certain scenarios "rang true" from our age-based viewpoint really contributed to this aspect and helped to create an approach to complex issues that was balanced and unbiased, and ultimately left it up to the viewers to form their own opinions. The approach that prioritizes the views of young people guides my work and research strategies with teens. Without a doubt, I know this approach was inspired by the opportunity I had as a teenager to participate in a television project that put the voices of teens first.

NOTES

1. Michele Byers, "Race In/Out of the Classroom: *Degrassi (Junior) High* as Multicultural Context," in Camille A. Nelson and Charmaine A. Nelson, eds., *Racism, Eh? A Critical Inter-Disciplinary Anthology of Race and Racism in Canada* (Concord, ON: Captus Press, 2004), 298–315.

2. Michele Byers, "Canadianizing Canada in the Age of Globalization," paper presented at the Congress of the Social Sciences and Humanities, Dalhousie University, Halifax, NS, June 2003; Himani Bannerji, *The Dark Side of Nation: Essays on Multiculturalism, Nationalism and Gender* (Toronto: Canadian Scholars' Press, 1994).

3. Rebecca J. Haines, "Beaders and Baby-Fathers — Racial and Sexual Stereotypes in the Lives of Adolescent Mothers of Multiracial Children," paper presented at Colorlines in the Twenty-first Century: Multiracialism in a Racially Divided World, Roosevelt University, Chicago, Illinois, September 1998.

4. Rebecca J. Haines, "Becoming an 'Invisible Minority': Reflections of a White, Working-class Woman Entering Academia," paper presented at the Working-Class Academics Conference, University of Wisconsin-Green Bay, Green Bay, Wisconsin, June 1996.

5. See, for example, Dick Hebdige, *Subculture: The Meaning of Style* (London: Routledge, 1979); Roger Hewitt, *White Talk-Black Talk: Inter-racial Friendship and Communication amongst Adolescents* (Cambridge, UK: Cambridge University Press, 1986); and Simon Jones, *Black Culture, White Youth* (London: Macmillan Press, 1988).

6. Rebecca J. Haines, "'Break North': Rap Music and Hip-Hop Culture in Canada," in H. Troper and M. Weinfeld, eds., *Ethnicity and Public Policy in Canada* (Toronto: University of Toronto Press, 1999).

7. Bannerji, *The Dark Side of Nation.*

8. Rebecca J. Haines, "'Telling Them Both Sides': Issues of Race and Identity for Young Mothers of Multiracial Children" (MA thesis, York University, 1997); and Haines, "'Break North.'"

9. Hebidge, *Subculture.* "The 'official' beginning of cultural studies in Britain came … with the founding, by [Richard] Hoggart, of the Birmingham Centre for Contemporary Cultural Studies in 1964. In the early years, the [centre's] approach to culture was more or less evenly divided between history, philosophy, sociology, and literary criticism; however, after 1968 its focus became increasingly sociological, following the replacement of Hoggart as director by Stuart Hall. It was during this period that critics affiliated with the Birmingham Centre did the work for which it continues to be best known: studies of neglected aspects of contemporary culture, with an emphasis on popular materials and, above all, the defining rituals of subcultures. During this same period, members of the [centre] adopted continental theoretical materials, especially the work of Marxist thinkers like the members of the Frankfurt School, Antonio Gramsci, and Louis Althusser." Joseph Childers and Gary Hentzi, eds., *The Columbia Dictionary of Modern Literary and Cultural Criticism* (New York: Columbia University Press, 1995), 65.

HAVE TIMES CHANGED?
GIRL POWER AND THIRD-WAVE FEMINISM ON DEGRASSI

Michele Byers

GIRL POWER IS AN AWKWARD CONCEPT that is frequently wielded in discussions of girls and popular culture. Though the term itself may seem rather transparent — giving, or appearing to give, girls power — it actually has a broad and slippery usage. Some people connect girl power to the American girls' movement, others with the early 1990s riot grrrl punk rock subculture, and still others with third-wave feminism. These branches on the girl power tree are distinct from one another. The girls' movement is an adult vision of who girls should be and how they should be politically rooted in second-wave politics.[1] Riot grrrls, as Marion Leonard observes, is "a reclamation of the word 'girl' and a representation of it as a wholly positive term";[2] the name, Jessica Rosenberg and Gitana Garofalo add, "was chosen to reflect the perceived passivity of 'girl.'"[3] The third wave is a more staunchly political movement that grew out of second-wave feminism, but it insists on its own diversified identity and activism. Despite their differences, these two groups share a desire to make girls strong and visible.

The purpose of this chapter is to examine the successful *Degrassi* television franchise in relation to changing discourses about girls and feminism. The most familiar face of girl power is linked to the mass media. Since the mid-1980s, with the slowly increasing recognition of girls as a powerful consumer market, media executives have drawn on the political language of second-wave feminism, adding a sanitized version of the punk liberationist style and attitude of riot grrrrl, to create the new language of girl power. A major critique of girl power is that all it offers girls are routes to empowerment based on consumption, but this ignores the complex processes and pleasures involved in popular culture and the active capacity of girls as its producers and interpreters.[4] Pleasure is very important, and it was the pleasurable recognition of powerful young women in the original *Degrassi Junior High* and *Degrassi High* (referred to as *Degrassi Classic* or *DC*) that drew me to the series when I was in high school in the 1980s. When the new series, *Degrassi: The Next Generation* (*TNG*), began airing in 2001, I was curious to see if, and how, its vision of empowered girlhood differed from that of *DC*. In the following pages I examine both the linguistic (using explicitly feminist language) and more generally narrative (stories that centre on female empowerment) strategies *Degrassi* has employed over the last two decades to get its message across.

In May of 2002, I delivered a paper that discussed whether articulating feminist discourses on television might help create spaces for young women to imagine themselves as active, feminist subjects.[5] Examining how feminism and anti-sexism were integrated into the *DC* series, I argued that television is not only a vehicle for the co-optation of resistant discourses, it can also make them active parts of its discursive structure.[6] Making feminism part of television's discursive reality can help "give voice to [the] marginal and submerged voices," and can become "part of the discursive strategies young women use to negotiate their identities."[7] If, as Himani Bannerji argues, "words… express our socio-political understandings, because they are more than just words,"[8] then using words like "feminism" and "sexism" may help to create feminist spaces in television. This is not straightforward; television and our relationship to it is open, contingent, shifting and often both ambivalent and ambiguous, much like our relationship to feminism. The 2002 paper addressed a series of questions about language that continue to interest me. Part of that interest involves questioning what happens when there is a shift in the way that feminist language and narratives are presented on television. Thus, the importance of not simply focusing on the presence of feminism as a word but focusing on the presence of broadly defined feminist discourses or ideologies, whether explicitly named as such or not, within the television narrative. *Degrassi* is a uniquely suited text to study in this regard because of its commitment to presenting empowering narratives about youth, and also because its two main incarnations are separated by almost a decade, a decade during which many changes occurred in televised representations of girls and empowerment.

Feminism and girl power are certainly terms that are connected to one another. Cultural critics like Elyce Rae Helford find the 1990s awash with televisual representations of powerful young womanhood, although, as she remarks, these are "contradictory and sometimes even reactionary."[9] Jennifer Bavidge suggests that this period is not unique but grows naturally out of a long history, reaching back into the nineteenth century, of popular cultural artifacts that debate the limits of girlhood.[10] Sarah Projansky and Leah Vande Berg, drawing on Bonnie Dow's formulation of "prime-time feminism," suggest that television since the 1980s "has made particular aspects of feminism ubiquitous." The authors point out a contradiction visible in many television texts: feminist goals are endorsed, but at the same time there is a suggestion that feminist activism is no longer needed because those goals have been achieved.[11] While the *Degrassi* series is not among the television shows these authors examine — they primarily focus on American series like *Buffy, Sabrina, Dawson's Creek* and *Xena* — the way they articulate the relationship between girl power and second-wave feminism is instructive. *DC* was produced during the early period of "prime-time feminism" when discourses about gender, power and equality had entered common language and popular culture. *TNG*, produced a decade later, uses explicitly feminist language less often, a legitimate choice given that this language is less accepted in the mainstream today. However, the new series is staunchly feminist in its presentation of images of empowerment and in its narrative choices in story arcs that deal with issues like date rape and abortion.

Both "feminism" and "girl power" are ideologically laden terms that are ambivalently produced; they can seem like universal projects, while actually articulating only the possibility of empowerment of certain girls and women. Neither term is wholly positive or unified; both are ambivalent and contested, disseminated and received differently at different times and in different spaces. Girl power and feminism are not equivalent terms either. The girl who is put into the discourse through the word feminist is not necessarily the same girl who would be put there through the term girl power. The young woman who calls herself a feminist today might not mean the same thing as the young woman who called herself a feminist in the 1970s. Although the discourses of second-wave feminism, the third wave, riot grrrl and girl power share similar aims, the languages they employ constitute girls and young women differently.

I do not, however, mean to suggest that one is inherently better than the other, nor do I believe that girl power is equivalent to what is often called post-feminism. What these terms represent is a shift in the public discourses through which ideas about female empowerment are articulated in the public sphere. Attaching the label post-feminist to articulations of female empowerment that fail to conform to second-wave ideals reveals a power struggle: whose way of imagining the emancipation of girls and women is "right"? While the perceived refusal of young women to use the term feminist is problematic, icons of mainstream girl power are not inauthentic nor do they trick girls into heterosexuality, anorexic-thinking, domesticity or passivity.[12] Girls are not cultural dupes and they are not a transparent demographic cohort.[13] The disparagement of girls and girl cultures represents a backlash against a youthful cohort's resistance to sliding into the space bequeathed to them by second-wave feminism. It is important to ask, If girls live feminist lives, does it matter what they call themselves? And it is just as important to ask, If girls refuse to call themselves feminists and yet embody feminist principles in their everyday lives, what is it that they are rejecting? The *Degrassi* series offers an important ground upon which to begin to ask these questions.

Changing Times: Narrating Feminist Issues on Degrassi

Television is constantly shifting as it relates the changing contexts and regimes of truth and power. The images and stories about being a girl produced on *DC* have long been applauded for their realism, especially when dealing with difficult and often highly gendered issues. *TNG* deals with similar issues, but begins from a position where gender equality and emancipation are more likely to be assumed, and where explicitly political language is seen as less useful. The different linguistic and narrative structures employed by *TNG* coincide with Projansky and Vande Berg's suggestion that television today presents much of the political work of feminism as having been completed. We can see this in several ways. First, in the fact that the characters on *DC* are much more likely to call themselves feminists and to name their experiences as sexist than the girls who populate *TNG*. Second, *TNG*'s narratives intimate that the feminist work that still needs to be done is of an individual rather than communal nature. On *DC* the female characters are more likely to band together in the pursuit of goals that they identify as explicitly feminist: creating a feminist film, fighting to keep a pregnant teen in school, arguing for abortion rights in class or demanding equality for girls' sports. On *TNG*, feminist issues are more likely to be tackled in interpersonal space: arguing with your best friend about abortion rights, yelling at a boy who is fatphobic and so on. Attempts to engage in collective action, for instance Emma's fight to show that cheerleading is sexist, do not elicit the same reaction as Lucy's fight for equal rights for the girls' volleyball team did on *DC*. Lucy enlists many other girls in her struggle and, although they ultimately fail to change the entrenched sexism of their school administration, their fight is presented as just. Emma's is presented more ambivalently; her best friend Manny wants to be a cheerleader and does not support Emma's efforts. In the end, it is Emma who must learn a lesson of tolerance.

Third, many *TNG* stories are articulated in an ambivalent space between activism and "increasing girls' self-esteem and personal empowerment without 'sacrificing' preoccupations with beauty, boys and consumerism."[14] Both generations of *Degrassi* discuss boys and beauty, but *TNG* presents us with young performers who fit much more neatly into what we expect TV actors to look like. Their higher class status also means that products and fashion are much more centrally displayed as part of feminine and youth identities than they were in *DC*. Fourth, the focus on individual achievement has the potential to divert attention from the realities of continued, systematic gender inequality. The question of how girlhood is linked with other aspects of identity continues to be only very rarely explored.

There is also considerable continuity between *DC* and *TNG*. The series share many similar story arcs about girls and girl cultures. An examination of *DC* and *TNG* reveals that both deal with such issues as puberty, activism, sexism, body image, eating disorders, girlfriend abuse, pregnancy and abortion, condoms, sexual abuse, school politics, and drugs and alcohol. The way these issues are taken up is somewhat different because the context of their production is different. As both the executive producer (Linda Schuyler) and head writer (Yan Moore) have pointed out: "times have changed," although Schuyler also points out that many adolescent rites-of-passage have not.[15] But what does this mean in relation to questions of gender, feminism and empowerment? Examining examples from each series in some depth may offer some clues.

Both series have developed story arcs that deal with body image and eating disorders. On *DC*, already-thin Kathleen develops an eating disorder (bulimia). On *TNG*, Toby, slightly chubby and self-consciousness, develops eating disorder "symptoms" in his quest to increase his popularity by joining the wrestling team. I say symptoms because Toby is only bulimic for a few days, after which he seems to return to a healthy relationship with his body and food. Shifting the focus of the eating disorder narrative from a female to a male character recognizes that eating disorders among young men, and pressures on them around body issues, are on the rise. But Toby's is a flirtation, whereas Kathleen's eating disorder is presented as systemic. In an interview, Yan Moore mentioned that another eating disorder narrative will be developed in the future, which suggests that the eating disorder theme has not been adequately addressed to date on *TNG*. The new story arc, Moore obliges, will likely focus on a female character and will be more fully integrated into the series' structure, rather than being the focus of a single episode.[16]

Other story arcs also raise the issue of body image and gender. On *DC*, Alexa tries to lose weight because she believes that is what her boyfriend Simon (a model) wants her to do. On *TNG*, Terri is embarrassed when her friends discover that she is a plus-size model. The story arcs are similar in that both girls overcome their concerns about their weight through the intervention of their friends, and it is also worth noting that both actors who portray these roles are heavier than most young women who appear on television today, though this is truer for Alexa. In both cases, the girls begin to worry about their bodies because of boys. But in Alexa's case, Simon, with seeming sincerity, insists that he is unconcerned about her weight, whereas a classmate (Mohammed) harasses Terri when he discovers her after-school career. Further, although Alexa is not thin she has a boyfriend, whereas Terri is usually single. When Terri finally does begin dating in season three, her boyfriend is abusive, beating her so severely that she ends up in the hospital; this also stands in contrast to Alexa's healthier relationship with Simon.

The resolution of Alexa's and Terri's story arcs are quite different. Alexa tells Simon he has no right to tell her how she should look as long as she is happy with herself, and he agrees. Terri gets back at her harasser, who works at an ice cream stand, by telling him: "Hey! Most girls on the planet look like this so get used to it. I made five hundred dollars today as a plus-size model. Yeah. Plus-size. How much did you make ice-cream boy?" Terri uses Mohammed's lack of class privilege as a way of equalizing herself. It is not clear that Terri feels better about herself or that she believes it is acceptable for her not to be thin, nor is it made clear whether Mohammed has learned anything. Instead, Terri tries to lessen her feelings of fat oppression by identifying Mohammed's class oppression. It is worth noting that Mohammed is not a central character, and it is easier to attribute negative attitudes to him than to Simon, who is a core cast member.

Pregnancy and abortion are the subjects of multiple story arcs on *DC*. Over the course of the series three characters become pregnant, two have abortions and one has and keeps her child. These narratives focus on questions of knowledge and power in teenagers' sexual decision making around such issues as having sex, contraception and how to deal with unplanned pregnancies. These storylines follow the characters as they make choices and deal with the consequences of those choices. The story arcs about teenagers and sex are produced in a feminist framework that sees sexual knowledge as central to female empowerment, that recognizes self-determination about one's own body as an inherent right, and that places questions of "choice" in the foreground. Spike, who becomes pregnant at fourteen, considers abortion and adoption, but ultimately decides against both. Erica chooses abortion despite her religious beliefs and the strong opposition of her twin sister; she also struggles with the harassment of an anti-abortion classmate. Tessa chooses to have an abortion when she becomes pregnant by a boy who is also dating someone else. Ultimately, each of these young women have to make choices that "work" for their particular situation; none of them feel that they must comply with the wishes of parents, friends or the boys with whom they've conceived.

On *TNG*, pregnancy and abortion are first raised in relation to the now adult Spike, the character who became pregnant on *DC* and whose daughter, Emma, is a core character on *TNG*. In the episode "White Wedding," Spike discovers she has accidentally become pregnant again, this time by her fiancé, another *DC* alum, Snake, who is a teacher at the Degrassi Community School that Emma attends. When Emma discovers that her mother is pregnant and is considering having an abortion she is furious. Her immediate response is to insist that by considering an abortion her mother devalues her — Emma's — life, because Spike could have terminated her pregnancy when she was pregnant with Emma. Interestingly, this is precisely the argument Spike's best friend Liz uses as an excuse for her torment of Erica on *DC*. Like Emma, Liz links someone else's choice — Erica's — to her conception and birth. For Liz, it is as if refusing choice to someone else will make her own mother's reality less real; for Emma, it is as if refusing choice to her mother will erase the fact that Spike had contemplated an abortion fourteen years earlier. On *DC*, Spike is sympathetic to her friend (Liz), but she refuses to take an actively anti-abortion stance. Instead, she argues that she had the right to make the choice that was right for her, and others should be allowed to do the same. This is certainly a pro-choice position and one that is repeated in *TNG*.

Emma insists that Spike tell Snake that she is pregnant before she makes any decision about terminating the pregnancy. When she becomes concerned that her mother will not reveal her pregnancy to Snake, Emma intervenes and tells him herself. Emma's argument, that Snake as the father has a right to know and a right to share in the decision-making process about the fetus in her mother's womb, is ultimately about her bid to keep her mother from having an abortion. Emma assumes that while she may not have the power to control her mother, Snake does. Spike, when confronted by Emma, makes an argument about her right as a woman to control her own body; but Emma's voice and "black and white view of the world" (in Yan Moore's terms) may ultimately be what capture the viewer.[17] This is very different from the multi-layered discussion of abortion that takes place on *DC*, where anti-abortion and pro-choice positions were both represented, but in staunchly political language that reflected the anger and violence that surround this issue.

The second abortion story arc featured on *TNG* brings political language more clearly to the fore and, importantly, makes a young woman, rather than her mother, the centre of the narrative. Manny becomes pregnant after having sex with Craig. Craig, recently orphaned, sees this as an opportunity to create a new family and pleads with Manny to keep the baby and marry him. But Manny draws strength from the support she gets from Spike and, surprisingly, from her own mother. In fact, the longest holdout is Emma, who violently resists Manny's desire to have an abortion. That is, until the crucial showdown when Craig tries to insist that his desire for a baby trumps Manny's desire to have an abortion. Emma reminds Craig that the choice, in the end, is Manny's. When he insists "But it's my baby," she counters immediately with "In Manny's body, what about her?" While Emma strongly articulates her opposition to Manny's desire to have an abortion, she continues to argue that it is Manny's — not her own or Craig's or Manny's mother's — right to choose. The episode ends with

Manny and her mother talking to a counsellor at a clinic; Manny's last words are "I'll be okay."

Linda Schuyler, Stephen Stohn and Yan Moore continue to take a no-holds-barred approach to creating youth-oriented television in Canada. They acknowledge that they are guided by their context of production, which means that issues that were central to *DC* might not be raised in the new series or might be raised in new ways. Yet issues that are or could not be dealt with on television in the 1980s — issues like homosexuality, date rape and the adoption of abandoned Chinese girls, all of which are important to feminism and anti-sexism — are being incorporated into the new series, often in feminist ways. Abortion is a controversial issue and on American television, which makes up the vast majority of series that air in Canada and abroad, it is rarely raised, particularly not by mainstream networks (public or private) or in youth programming. When abortion issues do make it to the small screen, the crisis turns out to be a false alarm or characters choose not to have abortions, have spontaneous miscarriages, are wracked with guilt or are severely punished for their choices. Telling stories about abortion that present a full range of arguments rooted in the feminist conception of reproductive choice for women, including young women, is clearly a narrative — and a feminist — device that has remained central to *TNG*.

Just a Girl? The Girls of Degrassi, 1987–2004

Many of *DC*'s archetypal images of girlhood are carried over into *TNG*, including "body image girls" (Terri *(TNG)* / Alexa *(DC))*, "fun, young girls" (Manny, pre-season three *(TNG)* / Melanie *(DC))*, "cool girls" (Ellie *(TNG)* / Spike, Liz *(DC))*, "annoying good girls" (Liberty *(TNG)* / Kathleen, Michelle *(DC))* and "go-along-with-it girls" (Hazel *(TNG)* / Diana, the twins *(DC))*. I would note that while I am designating these characters by trait, I do not mean to imply that they are one-dimensional. All the characters are complex and these traits simply reflect those that seem most central to the way each character is defined. The characters that I am most interested in here, however, can be characterized as "feminist girls" (Ashley, Emma *(TNG)* / Lucy, L.D. *(DC))*, "activist girls" (Emma *(TNG)* / Caitlin, Voula *(DC))*, and "sexy or "hot" girls" (Paige, Manny, season three on *(TNG)* / Stephanie, Tessa *(DC))*. These characters, while similar, reflect the times in which they were created.

Yan Moore, describing Caitlin and Emma, says:

Emma, we have got a lot of Caitlin in her, but ... she's not totally Caitlin. Miriam brings a different persona to it, slightly more determination, more brains, more nerves ... Emma is the product of a spunky mom who has made a go of it without a man, and Caitlin was the product of a major yuppie household ... it was such a different place from where Emma comes from.[18]

Emma and Caitlin are activists who write about and fight for social issues that concern them. On *TNG*, when Mr. Raditch (the principal on both *DC* and *TNG*) gives Emma the choice to keep quiet about her opposition to genetically modified (GM) foods or be suspended, she takes the suspension and continues to protest. Emma tells a reporter for the school paper: "It's about freedom of speech. It's about my right to protest." When Mr. Raditch asks that she apologize on the morning broadcast of the school television station or face suspension, she goes on camera and announces, "I can't apologize for wanting to be heard ... The point is I have a right to express my opinions, and you have a right to be informed. If fighting for that will get me a week's suspension ... I can live with that." Although Mr. Raditch suspends Emma, she still gives her speech and we see a shot of her stepfather Snake smiling his support for her position.

On *DC*, Caitlin fights to keep a pregnant Spike from being forced to leave Degrassi Junior High. Caitlin learns that issues are not clear-cut when she is confronted by Spike who feels Caitlin has exploited and used her for her own ends. Despite the fact that Caitlin receives enormous praise from her peers, she learns that the consequences of her actions are not clear-cut either.[19] In contrast, Emma's experience of activism is presented as much more straightforward, a question of freedom of expression and unequal power relations between students and school administrators. Where Caitlin faces opposition along a number of axes, including from her peers, the opposition Emma faces is more simply portrayed as bureaucratic and unreasonable. Yet, Yan Moore is right to point out that the language through which Emma is written is smarter, more determined, nervier, and that it is her drive and willingness to face the consequences of her actions that are highlighted. Though the consequences are lessened by the support she receives from friends and family — itself a lesson for young people and their parents — what is contiguous between the two series is the way they show activism as a normal, positive avenue through which young women can express themselves. Emma's narrative is more likely to elicit a unified response in the viewer. Caitlin's story is more ambivalent, in that the audience may sympathize with Spike and view Caitlin's actions as problematic. The choice to focus on GM foods is topical, but it is an issue that audiences are more likely to agree on than, say, animal testing, itself a theme used on *DC*, where opposition to animal cruelty is presented against the benefits such testing may have for people suffering from a variety of illnesses.[20]

How feminism and feminist girls are represented is more complicated than the way activist girls are represented. Many episodes of *DC* contain language and story arcs that are explicitly feminist, though my reading of the political significance of these episodes may be at least partly attributable to my own desire to read feminism into these shows.[21] The people involved with the production of the series do not remember feminism being as pervasive a part of the show as I do. But the highly identifiable use of feminist language suggests that this was a more common and everyday experience in the 1980s when *DC* was being made. That is, using words like "feminism" and "sexism" were less likely to come under the critical scrutiny that they might today. For instance, in "Consequences," L.D. challenges Joey and his friends when she hears them comparing women in a magazine to the girls in their school: "You're disgusting! Rating girls is sexist, and so are those pictures. You're making women into sex objects." When L.D. decides to complain to the principal about the pictures hanging in Joey's locker, Alexa suggests she is making too much of what are *just* pictures. L.D. responds, "No. It's how people look at women. It's important. If we don't battle sexism, who will?" The episode is full of political language that easily slides off the tongues of the series' young actors.

Examples of this type abound on *DC* — from Lucy's refusal to shoot a music video for her friends' band because she thinks it is sexist (in "Breaking Up Is Hard To Do"), to her decision to make a feminist horror film as a class project. In that episode ("It Creeps") Lucy explains that she and her friends want to make the film because they are "tired of women being portrayed as victims all the time." To which Mr. Walfish, the English teacher, responds: "A feminist slasher film … I love it." Having won support for her project from Mr. Walfish, Lucy and her friends look for actors. They choose Caitlin as their heroine because "she's done plays, and she's a feminist." When Caitlin refuses the part, Lucy appeals to her feminist sensibilities and wins her over. In her attempt to enlist Joey, Snake and Wheels, she has this exchange with Joey:

Joey: A feminist horror movie, why?

Lucy: Because a lot of horror films are sexist.

In the end, everyone gathers in Mr. Walfish's class and enthusiastically cheers Lucy's feminist film project.

In another *DC* episode, "Body Politics," the girls' volleyball team's practice time is given to the more successful boys' basketball team. The girls discuss their unequal treatment; Lucy describes the school's attitude as sexist and plans a revolt. But when she realizes that the cute boy who asked her to the dance is the captain of the basketball team, Lucy has to choose between keeping the boy interested and speaking her mind. During the episode she discusses her dilemma in a video letter she is making for her friend L.D., musing on her conflicting desires to be liked and to be heard. While Lucy tries to keep quiet, she eventually chooses to speak up for her rights and for those of the other members of the school's girls' teams:

> Wait a minute, excuse me. Obviously people are more interested in boys' sports, you guys get more promotion than we do. And you have the complete support of the sports department, while we have to beg just to get a new net. And so what if the boys' team has a better chance at winning? This is high school not the pro leagues. I thought sports was about participating, and exercising, and having fun. And I think it is irresponsible for a school to uphold traditions that are out-of date and prejudiced. We're tired of being treated as second-class citizens in our own school.

Lucy gets a lot of applause, and a broken date for the dance. Although she wins a vote at the student level, the principal overturns the vote. She tells L.D., "I keep telling myself I should be proud for standing up for what I believe in. And I guess I am. But L.D. ... I really wanted to go to that stupid dance."[22] Many episodes from *DC* draw explicitly on feminist language to make their point, yet they also show the ambivalence many young women feel between their desire to act politically and their fear that this will rob them of the conventional pleasures of heteronormative girlhood they also desire. This is far less visible on *TNG*, although the narrative in which Jimmy tries to control Ashley raises these questions ("Dressed in Black," see below), if more obliquely than *DC*. Lucy and L.D. are often the focus of narratives about feminism and sexism, but many other female characters also participate in and speak to feminist visions of girlhood.

Although *TNG* does deal with issues in a feminist manner, it is less likely to name them in an explicit way, and its characters are less likely to call themselves feminists. Two episodes that are concerned with feminist issues and/or sexism on *TNG* are "Wannabe" and "Dressed in Black." In the former, Emma is dismayed when her bestfriend Manny decides she wants to become a cheerleader. Despite Manny's obvious enthusiasm, Emma is disappointed with her friend's desire to hang out with the older, popular girls:

Emma: It's like we're travelling back in time, cheerleading is so over.

Manny: What? Cheerleading is huge, more popular then ever.

Emma: So are a lot of things that that are just sexist and wrong.

Manny: How can it be sexist if there are guys?

Emma: I bet the guys won't be wearing tight sweaters and miniskirts.

Manny finally gives up and agrees not to try out for the "spirit squad." But Paige and Hazel continue to recruit her, hoping to keep Emma from writing an anti-cheerleading editorial for the school paper. Mocking Emma's attitudes, Paige says, "But I guess we shouldn't be rating boys, perfect little Emma would say it's sexist." "Just like cheerleading," Hazel responds on cue. Feeling neglected, Emma writes a scathing editorial, commenting that "the spirit squad's only spirit is the spirit of sexism." In the end, Manny stands up to Paige, Emma admits she was wrong, and she and Manny make up. Manny decides, with Emma's support, to audition for the spirit squad. Sexism is raised here, but Emma's original question about the objectification of cheerleaders, even as female athletes, is never fully addressed. What we get instead is a clearer sense of narrative closure; the episode ends not in a space of ambiguity (Lucy's space), but in the more conventional homeostatic space of narrative resolution where order is restored.

In "Dressed in Black," Ashley struggles to decide whether she should remain true to her desire to be different, articulated by her adoption of a quasi-goth style, or to return to the more "normal" style that her on-again, off-again boyfriend Jimmy prefers. The episode opens with Ashley putting on eye makeup at her locker. Jimmy comes up and shows Ashley her yearbook picture from the previous year, when, as Ashley suggests, it looked like her mother picked out her clothes. While they are standing there, three boys walk by and make fun of Ashley, referring to her as a "freak show." While Jimmy apologizes to her, he is clearly uncomfortable. Later, in Ashley and

Jimmy's English class, they are given the assignment of playing out a short scene from Shakespeare's *The Taming of the Shrew* in a version that "rings true" for them. Ashley is partnered up with Craig with whom she discusses the play:

Ashley: I can't believe we have to do this comedy. It's so —

Craig: Sexist, outdated, unfunny?

They decide to play the scene "for what's really going on." While Jimmy and Hazel go for a humorous if sexist interpretation incorporating a football player and a cheerleader, Ashley and Craig come up with a different version, based on their earlier discussion of the characters:

Ashley: … the way Petruchio wants to change Kate, isn't it out of love?

Craig: That's what he claims. So?

Ashley: So, and we're making him into a villain, what if we're wrong?

Craig: Ash, the guy's a sexist pig, and abusive.

Ashley: I know, I read the play, but —

Craig: But nothing, even if he wasn't he'd still be a jerk.

Ashley: Why?

Craig: Because, if he really loved Kate, he wouldn't want to change her, he'd love her for who she is.

When Ashley and Craig finally bring their scene to the stage, they reimagine it as a scene between a wife and her battering husband. The episode explicitly links Jimmy's desire to control Ashley's "look" to Petruchio's attempt to control Kate, especially since Ashley wears a wig and no make-up and so strongly resembles the version of herself that Jimmy wants her to reclaim (or wants to reclaim for her).[23] An interesting aspect of this interpretation is that it is a male character who takes a strong feminist position and who verbally identifies sexism and women's oppression. Putting these words in Craig's mouth is a positive move because it makes the battle against sexism one that can be owned by both sexes. The danger, however, is that his voice will overshadow Ashley's, but this is remedied at the end of the episode when Craig encourages Ashley to be the one to speak. Responding to Ms. Kwan's question about their interpretation of the scene, but looking directly at Jimmy, Ashley says: "It's about breaking a person, their spirit.

Taming a person and making them into someone that they're not, making them into a lesser version of themselves." While Ashley wavered, and her friend Ellie suggested that Ashley — like Kate — looked tamed when she abandoned her style for someone else's, Ashley, in the end, decides it is better to be her own woman.

A feminist position is also strongly articulated in the two-part episode "Shout," in which Paige is raped. While Paige worries that she may be responsible for the rape, her friends insist that she is not. Hazel tells her: "Paige, honey, if you said no … that's rape." And later:

Hazel: What Dean did was illegal, you know that, right?

Paige: Yeah, and what about what I did?

Hazel: You didn't do anything.

Paige: So I didn't dress like a slut? I didn't drink? I didn't come on to him in front of the whole party?

Hazel: Paige —

Paige: I guess I didn't ask him to go upstairs either.

Hazel: You said "No."

Paige: It doesn't matter.

Hazel: It does matter.

In a style very much in keeping with many emerging forms of feminism, Paige is empowered to confront her rapist by taking control of cultural production. She sings a song about date rape, when her band, PMS, plays at a local competition; Dean, the rapist, is present. In "How Soon Is Now," the third episode of this story arc, Paige decides to press charges against Dean. She tells him: "I have one thing to say to you Dean. Get ready, because I am coming after you this time … For real." She then tells her counsellor: "I want to scare him Ms. Sauve, so bad, that he never thinks of doing this to someone else." This is an important moment; Paige links her desire for self-empowerment to a collective project.

The date-rape story arc continues in the two-part episode that opened the fourth season. As the date of her trial approaches, Paige has second thoughts about going through with her charges. Her anxiety is further heightened when she runs into Dean while visiting her brother; both are first-year students at the local university. The vision of Dean being free to enjoy university, while she continues to have unresolved issues stemming from the rape, gives Paige the motivation she needs to proceed with the trial. Unfortunately, Paige loses and Dean goes free without having to pay any visible price for the rape. This treatment, while perhaps unsatisfying for some viewers, is realistic; many rapists do go unpunished. Paige remains angry, and at a university party, she takes her boyfriend's car and crashes it into Dean's sports car. By taking responsibility for her actions, recognizing the enduring pain of the rape and understanding that the justice system is not always fair but that prosecuting rapists is still necessary, Paige is able to come to terms with her experiences without making those experiences disappear or resolving them unrealistically.

★

At the start of this chapter I posed the questions, If girls live feminist lives, does it matter if they call themselves feminists? If girls refuse to call themselves feminists and yet embody feminist principles in their everyday lives, what is it that they are rejecting? Words like "feminism," "feminist," "sexism," "pro-choice" and girls as "second-class citizens" are more visible and audible on *DC* than on *TNG*, reflecting their different contexts of production. The 1980s, when *DC* was made, was a period in which these words and the politics that they were understood to embody were cultural narratives that filtered into public life, including television, through common ways of sense making. *TNG* retains some of this language and, more importantly, similar feelings about women's rights, expressing them through its engagement with a variety of girl-centred issues from a clearly feminist perspective. The loss of the explicitly political language might suggest that young viewers reject the label feminist, that because they are no longer afforded the opportunity of hearing this political language in play, they now view the emancipatory potential of girlhood as an individual, rather than a collective, feminist struggle or political project. Yet the great popularity *TNG* has achieved in many countries suggests that the refusal of this language has not caused the audience to run away from the feminist treatment of political issues that are central to the lives of girls and women: body image, reproductive choice, activism, self-esteem and girlfriend abuse, for example.

DC anticipated the emergence of third-wave feminism as a visible, if never unified, social collective, constructing characters who are actively critical of entrenched structures of oppression and actively fight for gender emancipation. Emma, Ashley, Terri, Paige, Hazel, Ellie and Manny are a new generation, growing up in a period where feminism is less likely to be explicitly named within the mainstream cultural narratives of girl or youth culture. If feminism is now less likely to be explicitly articulated, but we, like Bannerji, believe that words and naming are part of an important ideological project, than not naming feminism in moments when it is present is problematic.[24] Does this makes *TNG* post-feminist, in the sense that it uses common-sense notions of gender-equality but does not connect them to explicit feminist political positions? I am not so sure. *TNG* is clearly not post-feminist in the sense of using feminist language and ideologies to subvert feminist goals. The girls of *TNG* actively articulate feminist positions and engage in feminist cultural production. Although they do not necessarily name their project as feminist, it clearly is and, as such, it offers a good model for its young viewers. At the same time, feminists of all stripes must ask what kind of work needs to be done to make our politics and political languages more open and interesting to girls and young women.

The absence of the words "feminism" and "feminist" may create a missed opportunity for *TNG* to show its viewers what young, engaged, named feminism can look like. But by foregrounding feminist positions on important social and political issues, *TNG* still helps bring feminism out of the strange and shadowy margins and into everyday life, and it is clear that female empowerment and equality are central concerns of the series. *TNG* exists at the ambivalent intersection between generations and languages of feminism and girl power. With its fourth season firmly under its belt, I eagerly await the possibilities it may hold for empowering girls and young women, curious about what new stories it will tell and how it will tell them. At the same time, *DC* continues to attract audiences in syndication, who revel in its kitsch value, but also in the sense of authenticity it offers. The political language so visible in *DC* clearly continues to be part of that authenticity.

NOTES

1. Jennifer Baumgardner and Amy Richards, *Manifesta: Young Women, Feminism, and the Future* (New York: Farrar, Strauss and Giroux, 2000).

2. Marion Leonard, "'Rebel Girl, You Are the Queen of My World' Feminism, 'Subculture' and Grrrl Power," in Sheila Whiteley, ed., *Sexing the Groove: Popular Music and Gender* (New York: Routledge, 1997), 232.

3. Jessica Rosenberg and Gitana Garofalo, "Riot Grrrl: Revolutions from Within," *Signs* 23, no. 3 (1998), 809.

4. Catherine Driscoll, *Girls: Feminine Adolescence in Popular Culture and Cultural Theory* (New York: Columbia University Press, 2002), 269.

5. Michele Byers, "Girls into Feminists: The Possibilities of Television Discourse," paper presented at the Congress of the Social Sciences and Humanities, Canadian Association of Sociology and Anthropology, Toronto, ON, May 2002.

6. Robert H. Deming, "*Kate & Allie*: 'New Women' and the Audience's Television Archives," in Lynn Spigel and Denise Mann, eds., *Private Screenings: Television and the Female Consumer* (Minneapolis: University of Minnesota Press, 1992), 206–207. Herman Gray makes a similar argument in relation to studying televised images of "blackness" in *Watching Race* (Minneapolis: University of Minnesota Press, 1995).

7. Jana Sawicki, *Disciplining Foucault: Feminism, Power, and the Body* (New York: Routledge, 1991), 28.

8. Himani Bannerji, *The Dark Side of Nation: Essays on Multiculturalism, Nationalism and Gender* (Toronto: Canadian Scholar's Press, 1994), 41.

9. Elyce Rae Helford, "Introduction," in Elyce Rae Helford, ed., *Fantasy Girls: Gender in the Universe of Science Fiction and Fantasy Television* (Lanham, MD: Rowman and Littlefield, 2000), 1–9.

10. Jennifer Bavidge, "Chosen Ones: Reading the Contemporary Teen Heroine," in Glyn Davis and Kay Dickinson, *Teen TV: Genre, Consumption and Identity* (London: The British Film Institute, 2004), 41–53.

11. Sarah Projansky and Lean R. Vande Berg, "Sabrina, the Teenage …?: Girls, Witches, Mortals, and the Limitations of Prime-Time Feminism," in Helford, ed., *Fantasy Girls*, 13-40.

12. Cynthia Fuchs, "Too Much of Something Is Bad Enough: Success and Excess in *Spice World*," in Frances Gateward and Murray Pomerance, eds., *Sugar, Spice, and Everything Nice: Cinemas of Girlhood* (Detroit, MI: Wayne State University Press, 2002), 346–347.

13. Driscoll, *Girls*, 268.

14. Elyce Rae Helford, "Feminism, Queer Studies, and the Sexual Politics of *Xena: Warrior Princess,*" in Helford, ed., *Fantasy Girls,* 137.

15. Schuyler and Moore, interviews.

16. Moore interview.

17. Moore interview.

18. Ibid.

19. While Caitlin forcefully argues the obligations of the free press, both Mr. Raditch, who insists that the press must present a balanced view of events, and Spike, who wonders why Caitlin never even talked to her about her feelings, offer opposing positions to her own. As Spike puts it, "I don't need little miss perfect making me her cause of the week."

20. This theme has been used extensively in youth-oriented TV and film.

21. In their 2004 volume *Teen TV,* Davis and Dickinson argue, "Often shows like *Buffy the Vampire Slayer* are valorized precisely for their nourishment of our particular adult needs, like the desire for mainstream feminist discourse — and this is no bad thing" (5).

22. And she does get to go, with the much more sympathetic class president, Bronco.

23. A more explicitly feminist rethinking of the play is the very enjoyable 1999 film, *10 Things I Hate about You.*

24. Bannerji, *The Dark Side of Nation.*

GETTING IT WRONG AND RIGHT:
REPRESENTING AIDS ON *BEVERLY HILLS 90210*
AND *DEGRASSI HIGH*

Kylo-Patrick R. Hart

WHEN I BEGAN MY career as an academic researcher, one of the first conference papers I presented addressed the representation of AIDS on the Fox television series *Beverly Hills 90210*, which occurred at the start of that show's seventh season in the fall of 1996. When I first learned that *90210* was planning to represent AIDS as an important social concern of young people, I was very optimistic. Because the show had a solid reputation for dealing honestly and candidly with contemporary aspects of young adult life that other programs tended not to address, I expected that its writers would create an AIDS storyline that would be of relevance to its primary viewers. I was seriously disappointed. Rather than offering an innovative representation of AIDS that would motivate young adults to internalize the risks of HIV/AIDS and to engage in safe-sex practices, *90210* approached the topic in much the same way as so many other programs had since the discovery of HIV/AIDS a decade earlier: by introducing a gay white male as its central character with AIDS and killing him off quickly (in this case, after just three weeks) to restore the natural order of things in the story world.

To my dismay, the representation of AIDS on *Beverly Hills 90210* seemed more like something right out of the mid-1980s, rather than the mid-1990s, and I was baffled by the programming decision. Well into the second decade of AIDS by that point, it seemed suspicious to me that the show's writers did not offer an alternative representation of the pandemic, especially at a time when AIDS had become a leading cause of death among young Americans of all sexual orientations. To see if others felt the same way, I conducted a series of focus groups with regular *90210* viewers at the University of Michigan, shortly after the AIDS episodes aired. I found that my impressions were widely shared by others. Participants explained that featuring a gay white male with AIDS worked against the goal of showing that this is a disease that anyone can contract. They commented that "The stereotyping of the gay guy with AIDS didn't really show us the reality of AIDS today" and "[He] was the stereotypical gay man with AIDS; it didn't 'hit home' that hard."[1]

The *90210* AIDS storyline solidly reinforced the social construction of AIDS in the minds of viewers as a "gay disease." At the same time, it ignored the changing demographics of the AIDS pandemic by failing to create a storyline that would be of greater interest and relevance to the show's primary viewers. Following the focus groups, I began searching for a more appropriate representation of AIDS on television that was directed towards young adult viewers. And then I found one. Several years before the *90210* episodes aired, the series *Degrassi High* had offered a much more effective AIDS storyline. Using relevant concepts pertaining to media representation, social constructionism and social psychology, this chapter compares and contrasts these two representations of AIDS to demonstrate why *Beverly Hills 90210* "got it wrong" and *Degrassi High*, for the most part, "got it right."

GETTING IT (MOSTLY) WRONG ON BEVERLY HILLS 90210

The AIDS storyline on *Beverly Hills 90210* aired in three consecutive episodes during September 1996, when character Kelly Taylor (Jennie Garth) began working at an AIDS hospice in order to earn an academic credit. There, she met an aspiring gay magician named Jimmy (Michael Stoyanov), who was dying from AIDS.

During the first episode, "A Mate for Life," Kelly and Jimmy begin interacting and conversing as friends. This peaceful co-existence is relatively short-lived, however. Early in the second episode, "Disappearing Act" (a clever magic-show reference that actually refers to the way Kelly vanishes from Jimmy's life once she believes his illness has posed a threat to her well-being), Kelly gets some of Jimmy's blood on her hands after he cuts himself while chopping vegetables. Despite the reality that she has no cuts or other open wounds on her hands, and that Jimmy assures her that the odds of contracting AIDS that way are perhaps one in a billion, Kelly rushes home to wash her hands and share AIDS facts and statistics with her roommates, incessantly. Shortly thereafter, she awakens from a nightmare in which her arms and chest are, just a day later, covered with KS lesions.[2] In the days following her having come into contact with Jimmy's infected blood, Kelly avoids further interpersonal communication with him, making excuses about how busy she is when he telephones for an explanation. It is only after Kelly's doctor confirms that unbroken skin acts as a barrier to HIV transmission and the results of an HIV test reveal that Kelly has not contracted AIDS as a result of her own personal sexual history, that Kelly renews her friendship with Jimmy. As she does so — and even though he looks entirely healthy and possesses a great deal of energy — Jimmy informs Kelly that the end is near.

Jimmy was right. In the third and final episode, "Pledging My Love," Kelly learns that Jimmy has become quite ill overnight and will not live to see another day. She rushes to his bedside to say her final farewells. The AIDS storyline concludes with Kelly crying, holding a picture of Jimmy and being comforted by her half-brother David (Brian Austin Green), as they stand together on a deck overlooking the ocean. Neither Jimmy nor the risks of HIV/AIDS was mentioned again in the weeks that followed.

As previously stated, by jumping on the prime-time bandwagon and telling the story of AIDS using a gay white male character, *Beverly Hills 90210* did its viewers a serious disservice for several reasons. For starters, by focusing primarily on the "gay Jimmy" plot developments, the AIDS storyline did nothing — with the exception of briefly raising the issue that Kelly could possibly have contracted HIV as a result of her promiscuous sexual past — to challenge or undermine the stereotypical social construction of AIDS as a "gay disease" or, more crudely stated, as "a gay plague," "the price paid for anal intercourse" and "a disease that turns fruits into vegetables."[3] As such, it dangerously reinforced the harmful notion that Americans fit into two broad categories in relation to HIV/AIDS: "us" versus "them." In this usage, the "us" refers to members of the so-called general population, containing "innocent" individuals threatened not by their own risky behaviours but rather by members in the "other" category. The "them" refers to the so-called guilty villains in the AIDS crisis, such as gay men and intravenous drug injectors, who threaten the well-being of "innocent" others and are perceived as undeserving of compassion and sympathy because they are viewed as a threat to members of the general population.[4]

In addition, by failing to adequately explore the risks of heterosexual behaviour, this representation dangerously reinforced patriarchal gender roles by simultaneously perpetuating heterosexism, which has been defined as the "ideological system that denies, denigrates, and stigmatizes any non-heterosexual form of behavior, identity, relationship, or community."[5] The decision to feature a white male character with AIDS was also problematic because the majority of AIDS representations on U.S. television up to that time had already featured white males rather than non-white males or females of various races and ethnicities.

There are additional shortcomings in the *90210* representation of AIDS. A significant one is that the show's competing storylines, which were interwoven into the main storyline over its three-week run, sent conflicting messages about the need for safe-sex practices. One of these competing storylines featured Brandon Walsh (Jason Priestley) sleeping with a young woman he had just met, in her hotel room, without any evidence (such as condoms or condom wrappers) to suggest that they even thought about, let alone practised, safe sex. Another competing storyline featured Valerie Malone (Tiffany-Amber Thiessen) having increasingly kinky sex with her married male accountant; the scene in which she confronts the man with news that she believes she is pregnant strongly suggests that safe-sex practices were not priorities in their encounters either. A mixed message is communicated loudly and clearly in these episodes: "gay men must either avoid unprotected casual sex with others or die, whereas non-gay individuals can cavort sexually with various others to their hearts' content, without protection, and without significant negative consequences."[6] Unfortunately, these competing storylines compromised the potential effectiveness of the main storyline because they failed to communicate a coherent message about the need for all young people, regardless of sexual orientation, to engage responsibly in sexual activities.

Perhaps the greatest shortcoming in the *90210* episodes, however, has to do with the lack of homophily between its AIDS character and the show's primary viewers. In this case, homophily (a term borrowed from diffusion theory) is defined as the degree to which the AIDS character is similar to the show's primary viewers in noteworthy ways — for example, similarities in gender or in sexual orientation.[7] According to research findings in the fields

of social psychology and media studies, the greater the homophily that exists between the central AIDS characters in a television program or movie
and the viewers, the greater the chance that the medium will be regarded as
credible by the viewers and the greater the chance that the viewers will be
personally influenced by it.[8] At the time the AIDS storyline aired, the primary viewers of *90210* were heterosexual women between the ages of eighteen and thirty-four; the show was also quite popular with teenage girls.[9]
Why, then, did the writers and producers of *90210* choose to create an AIDS
storyline featuring a gay male as the primary AIDS character rather than a
heterosexual female? This is an especially important question given the fact
that, by the time these episodes aired, instances of heterosexual transmission
of HIV/AIDS had increased dramatically, with new cases of HIV infection
occurring more frequently among women than among men.[10]

The preceding discussion is not intended to imply that the representation of AIDS on *Beverly Hills 90210* was without merit. The series did, for
example, portray Jimmy as a strong, masculine and well-adjusted gay male
character, rather than as a weak and effeminate stereotype. In addition, it
provided some factual information about HIV/AIDS in the characters' dialogue and identified the importance of HIV testing and safe-sex practices.
Aside from these attributes, however, the representation gave inadequate
information to its audience and failed to motivate young people to internalize the risks of HIV/AIDS and to engage in safe-sex practices. A common
obstacle for AIDS prevention efforts in the United States has, to date, been
"the tendency to dismiss it as a disease of 'the other'"[11] — that is, those
whose sexual orientation is not heterosexual — and the representation of
AIDS on *90210* did little to alter this perception in the eyes of its primary
viewers. Numerous studies have found that as long as individuals in specific demographic groups continue to believe (erroneously) that members of
their group are not really at risk of contracting HIV/AIDS, they are unlikely
to engage in safe sex themselves.[12]

GETTING IT (MOSTLY) RIGHT ON DEGRASSI HIGH

Like *Beverly Hills 90210*, the television series *Degrassi High* has been highly
regarded for the way it has dealt honestly and effectively with a range of
controversial issues of importance to young adults. This is certainly true
in the case of the show's representation of AIDS, which aired during the

1990–91 television season on the CBC and PBS as part of the second (and final) season of *Degrassi High*. Since this was five years earlier than the representation of AIDS on *Beverly Hills 90210*, it is a shame that the *90210* writers did not take a lesson in effective AIDS storytelling from the writers of *Degrassi High*.

In contrast to *90210*, *Degrassi High* featured a heterosexual male character, one of the regular characters on the show, who becomes infected with HIV. The AIDS storyline began in the first two episodes and concluded in the final episode of the 1990–91 season. In the first episode, "Bad Blood, Part One," Dwayne (Darrin Brown), one of the school's bullies, brags to his fellow bullies Nick (George Chaker) and Tabi (Michele Johnson-Murray) about the girl he dated over the summer. When they express doubts that such an attractive individual would actually go out with someone like Dwayne, Dwayne emphasizes that not only did she date him but she also had sex with him. Minutes later, as these three characters enter their special education classroom, they learn that Joey Jeremiah (Pat Mastroianni) — Dwayne's enemy from junior high school — has failed some classes and, as a result, will be joining them this year in special ed. Joey asks Dwayne to let bygones be bygones, but it is clear that their contentious relationship will continue. In class, the students learn that, as part of a new sexual awareness program, speakers will be visiting the class to talk about AIDS. Dwayne and Nick insist that they have already heard enough about AIDS, especially because it is only of concern to gay men, intravenous drug injectors and hemophiliacs. Their teacher is appalled by their outdated understanding of the realities of the AIDS pandemic. Dwayne soon learns that she is right, when he arrives home and returns a telephone call to the young woman he slept with. She tells him that both she and her former boyfriend have tested positive for HIV and that Dwayne should get tested immediately.

The second episode, "Bad Blood, Part Two," begins with Dwayne in his doctor's office, having blood drawn for his HIV test. The doctor informs him that he is certainly part of a high-risk category for AIDS, because the person he slept with has tested positive for HIV and they did not use a condom during sex. Days later, two men with AIDS talk to the special education students about the realities of the pandemic. They provide information about the ways that people can and cannot contract HIV/AIDS and explain how friends and loved ones may react negatively once they learn that someone is HIV positive. Dwayne asks how they deal with the fact that they are going to die. In response, both men explain that AIDS is more like a chronic illness that you have to deal with for the rest of your life rather than a death sentence. As the students exit the classroom, several remark to each other how they expected these men with AIDS to be emaciated and sick-looking; instead, it was impossible for them to tell, just by looking at them, that they had AIDS. After school, Dwayne returns to his doctor's office and learns that he is HIV positive; the doctor informs him that he must do everything in his power to stay healthy.

The next day at school, Joey runs into Dwayne in the restroom. It is clear that Dwayne is in a bad mood, and their verbal argument quickly escalates into a fistfight. Moments later, Dwayne catches a glimpse of his bleeding nose in the mirror and declares that he does not want to fight anymore. Joey calls him a wimp and a chicken because Dwayne seems to be afraid of a little blood. "Do you want this on you?" Dwayne asks Joey, motioning to the blood that is running down his face. "What if I had AIDS?" Dwayne adds. Joey responds that, if Dwayne has AIDS, he will be the guy laughing at Dwayne's funeral. "You think it's a joke? You think I'd joke if I had it?" Dwayne says, punching and kicking a stall door in frustration. Dwayne continues: "I didn't do anything wrong — I was just careless, that's all. And now I'm gonna die." Dwayne begins to sob uncontrollably and orders Joey to leave. Later, Dwayne approaches Joey with a large sum of money (that Joey felt was owed to him, after Dwayne foiled one of Joey's money-making schemes to walk nude through the school cafeteria for cash), hands it to him and tells Joey to keep quiet about the information he learned in the restroom.

The third and final episode, "One Last Dance," aired nearly three months later at the end of the season (and of the series). Dwayne arrives at school and learns from Nick and Tabi that someone at Degrassi has AIDS, but nobody knows who it is. Once again, Dwayne encounters Joey in the restroom and he immediately accuses Joey of starting the rumour. Joey insists that he has not told anyone. Later that day, in the special education classroom, Nick insists that he will bash the guy with AIDS when he learns who it is. His classmate Joanne (Krista Houston) asks him why he believes it is a guy. Nick insists that AIDS is the "gay plague"; Joanne counters by telling him to wake up, because AIDS is not just a gay problem. Joanne points out that her mother works with AIDS patients and explains that you cannot contract it from casual contact or kissing. Listening closely, Dwayne asks how Nick and Tabi can be so certain that it is not one of them, or even himself. Nick responds that although Dwayne is "weird," he certainly isn't "a queer"; Tabi adds that Dwayne cannot possibly have AIDS. "Not yet," Dwayne replies, "but I'm HIV positive. And I got it from a chick. How do you like that?"

Following this exchange, neither Nick nor Tabi — Dwayne's two closest friends at Degrassi High School — want anything to do with him. All of the students then learn that Degrassi High will be closing in June, and that they will be sent to other high schools in the area to complete their education. As a result, the last dance of the school year takes on added significance. Dwayne insists that he plans to attend, which makes his fellow classmates uneasy. Tabi asks Joanne how dangerous it is to be around Dwayne; Joanne responds that AIDS is transmitted through bodily fluids so, unless Tabi has been sleeping with Dwayne, she is not at any risk. Joanne suggests Tabi talk to him, shake his hand, hug him. "I know I sound like a pamphlet," Joanne says in anger, "it's just I get so mad at how people with AIDS get treated by people like you!" The night of the dance, Dwayne approaches the school building alone, wearing a suit and tie. As he enters the gymnasium, everyone stops interacting and stares at him; he seeks refuge in the restroom. Again, Joey enters and engages in a conversation with Dwayne, who explains that Degrassi was his school, too, so he wanted to be part of the final event. Joey tells him he has as much right to be at the dance as anyone else; Dwayne straightens his tie, fixes his hair and returns to the dance. Nick bolts out of the gym when Dwayne reappears and urges Tabi to leave with him. Instead, Tabi approaches Dwayne, places a hand on his shoulder and asks him to dance. The series concludes with images of them on the dance floor, surrounded by other students.

By featuring a heterosexual male character, who became infected with HIV from a heterosexual female, at the centre of its HIV/AIDS storyline, *Degrassi High* took an important representational step towards undermining the conceptualization of AIDS as a gay disease. This approach was especially noteworthy in an era when instances of new HIV and AIDS cases among heterosexuals of various demographic categories continued to increase, whereas instances of new cases among gay men had begun to level off. In addition, although the two people with AIDS who addressed the special education class about the realities of the pandemic were men, there was nothing explicit in the script to suggest that they were gay men rather than heterosexual men. As such, the representation of AIDS on *Degrassi High* effectively spread vital social information about HIV/AIDS to the many members of the "general population" who inaccurately believed that they are somehow shielded from infection with HIV/AIDS by virtue of their non-gay social identities.[13]

Unlike *90210*, the AIDS storyline on *Degrassi High* was accompanied by related storylines that effectively reinforced the safe-sex message. It was Sexual Awareness Month at Degrassi when Dwayne learned that he was HIV positive; as a result, it seemed logical, and less forced, when the show incorporated facts about HIV/AIDS as part of the larger narrative and brought speakers in to address the students. In addition, when condom machines were placed in the boys' and girls' restrooms at Degrassi (as well as in every other school in the city), Dwayne and his friends first thought they were a big joke: they pried one open and used the condoms as water balloons to assault Joey and his friends. This development made Dwayne's lack of condom use seem all the more tragic when he learned that his health had been compromised.

Finally, the representation of AIDS on *Degrassi High* featured a great deal of homophily between its central characters in the AIDS storyline and the show's primary viewers. Because this show featured heterosexual young people contracting HIV through heterosexual sex, it likely resonated quite substantially with its primarily young heterosexual viewers and expanded the social construction of AIDS as a disease that can infect individuals of various sexual orientations, not just gay men or intravenous drug users. In addition, it challenged the widely held misperception that, even though HIV/AIDS can be transmitted readily through heterosexual intercourse, young heterosexuals are somehow "protected" or "shielded" from the realities of the AIDS pandemic because they view themselves as being inherently different from gay men, the type of individuals who have been overrepresented as people with AIDS in U.S. television programs and movies.[14] In other words, this representation made impressive strides towards undermining the erroneous perception that AIDS is a disease of "the other" rather than of "the self."

Despite the fact that the representation of AIDS on *Degrassi High* did so many things effectively, there are nevertheless a few shortcomings. Most notably, the show selected Dwayne, the bully, as the character who contracted HIV; at one point in the storyline, Dwayne explained to Joey, "I used to like it when people were afraid of me, but this is different." Unfortunately, some viewers may perceive this storyline as being constructed in such a way as to imply that HIV/AIDS is the deserved punishment for Dwayne, who chose to violate academic social and moral norms by tormenting so many other students around him. In addition, and in a related way, this representation of AIDS reinforced socially constructed distinctions between "innocent victims" and "guilty villains" when both Dwayne, as well as the girl he slept with, insisted that they did not "deserve" AIDS because they were not "bad people." Finally, by featuring four white people (three males and one female) as the individuals infected with HIV/AIDS, this representation did little to disseminate important social information that people of colour are also at risk of contracting HIV/AIDS and that they are often infected at more extreme rates than whites.[15]

THE NEED TO GET IT RIGHT

Although neither show was without shortcomings, the representation of HIV/AIDS on *Degrassi High* was far more effective than on *Beverly Hills 90210*. In the majority of televised representations of AIDS in the United States during the early years of the AIDS pandemic, gay men, who were already stigmatized as being "deviant," were further stigmatized as being "lethally contagious" and were represented as significant health threats to "innocent" individuals in the "general population."[16] The representation of AIDS on *90210* simply contributed to this representational trend. In contrast, the AIDS storyline on *Degrassi High* offered an early example of a television program that strived intentionally to break the erroneous, socially harmful representational link between gay men and AIDS. By effectively representing a wider range of individuals who are at risk of HIV/AIDS infection and transmission, it was as a breakthrough in the social reconstruction of the AIDS pandemic.

From 1985 to the present, television programs have devoted a good deal of attention to representations of adult men and women with HIV/AIDS. Topics have included homophobic heterosexuals who discover they are personally infected with HIV/AIDS (e.g., *Hotel*, 1986); lawsuits against companies that discriminate against people with HIV/AIDS (e.g., *L.A. Law*, 1991; *The Practice*, 2000); assisting people with AIDS to end their lives (e.g., *Law and Order*, 1990; *New York Undercover*, 1996); women becoming infected with HIV by bisexual men (e.g., *Midnight Caller*, 1988); doctors refusing to provide medical assistance to people with AIDS (e.g., *L.A. Law,* 1990); and doctors becoming exposed to infected blood (e.g., *St. Elsewhere,* 1987). Character types have ranged from fashion designers (e.g., *Designing Women,* 1987), artists (e.g., *Doogie Howser, M.D.,* 1989), medical professionals (e.g., *St. Elsewhere,* 1986; *Doctor, Doctor,* 1990; *ER,* 1996) and pregnant women with HIV/AIDS (e.g., *Chicago Hope,* 1998) to HIV-positive murderers (e.g., *Chicago Hope,* 1999) and drag queens with AIDS (e.g., *Chicago Hope,* 1996; *Sisters,* 1996).

In contrast, representations of teenagers with HIV/AIDS in television programs have been much fewer in number, and most have occurred in one-shot episodes that simply introduce a new teen character with HIV or AIDS, explore some aspect of that character's experience in relation to the actions and interactions of one or more regular characters, and then never refer to, nor incorporate, that HIV/AIDS character again after the individual episode comes to an end. Such an approach has been prevalent in the majority of U.S. television shows that represented teenagers with HIV/AIDS during the mid-1980s to the mid-1990s. Take for example, the 1988 episode of *21 Jump Street* in which Detective Hanson (Johnny Depp) acts as a bodyguard to an HIV-positive gay teen who is hassled at the different schools he is forced to attend because of his medical condition; or the 1995 episode of *ER* when Dr. Ross (George Clooney) provides assistance and compassion to a homeless teenager with AIDS; or the 1995 episode of *Party of Five* when Julia (Neve Campbell) discovers that her friend Danny is HIV positive. Media critic Steven Capsuto has criticized such approaches as being "'message' scripts," according to which a safe-sex message is superficially communicated and then life goes on as before.[17] The primary shortcoming of these approaches is that younger viewers are insufficiently motivated to care about the HIV/AIDS characters that are so briefly introduced. Nor are young viewers motivated to internalize the risks of HIV/AIDS or engage in safe-sex practices. In comparison, AIDS storylines that directly affect central characters that viewers already know and love or that continue over several episodes during the same season, tend to motivate viewers and better educate them.[18]

After 1995, teenagers with HIV/AIDS disappeared almost entirely from U.S. television programs. Most likely, as scholar Gabriele Griffin has argued, this was a result of the shifting perception of HIV/AIDS as a condition that one "lives with" rather than "dies from."[19] Although drug combination "cocktails" are not cures for HIV/AIDS, they were certainly presented that way, especially during the period from 1996 to 1998, and that perception remains widespread today.[20] Accordingly, the writers and producers of television programs most likely felt that audience members were no longer interested in hearing about HIV/AIDS, that there was no remaining urgency to spread HIV/AIDS prevention messages or that the most interesting ways of telling the story of AIDS on television had already been presented. As such, although it aired nearly a decade and a half ago, the AIDS storyline from *Degrassi High* remains one of the most outstanding representations of HIV/AIDS that has been created to date. It is perhaps rivalled only by the representation of HIV/AIDS on the dramatic series *Life Goes On* (1989–93), which introduced HIV-positive teen Jesse (Chad Lowe), who was Becca's (Kellie Martin) love interest during the show's final two seasons. Although Becca and Jesse broke up at one point, they ultimately reunited and were married. From a representational standpoint, the advantage that this latter series enjoyed, as compared with *Degrassi High*, was that it featured an attractive, likeable individual — rather than the disliked school bully — as its central character with HIV.

Despite recent trends in television programming, the need for effective representations of teenagers with HIV/AIDS has never been greater. Rather than being eradicated, HIV has continued to mutate and become more resilient. By the turn of the century, it was infecting approximately 16,000 new individuals around the world every day, with U.S. adolescents composing an increasingly sizable high-risk group for contracting and transmitting HIV/AIDS.[21] Many teenagers today do not seem to be especially concerned about the possibility of contracting HIV/AIDS from casual sexual encounters; this perception is strengthened by findings of a 2004 study by researchers at Arizona State University, who discovered that approximately 75 percent of students who engaged in casual sex during spring break never, or only rarely, used condoms.[22] The current dearth of televisual representations of adolescents with HIV/AIDS contributes substantially to this unfortunate state of affairs by concealing, with remarkably few exceptions, the potential effects of casual sexual experimentation in the age of AIDS from today's young audience members.

NOTES

1. Kylo-Patrick Hart, "Representation of AIDS on *Beverly Hills 90210:* Theoretical Concerns and Focus Group Findings," paper presented at the Far West Popular Culture Association Conference, Las Vegas, Nevada, February 1, 1997.

2. Kaposi Sarcoma (KS) is a rare form of skin cancer that commonly afflicts individuals who are affected with HIV/AIDS. KS lesions are the purple blotches that frequently cover the bodies of individuals in the advanced stages of AIDS.

3. Paula Treichler, "AIDS, Homophobia, and Biomedical Discourse: An Epidemic of Signification," in Douglas Crimp, ed., *AIDS: Cultural Analysis, Cultural Activism* (Cambridge, MA: The MIT Press, 1988), 32–33.

4. James Croteau and Susanne Morgan, "Combating Homophobia in AIDS Education," *Journal of Counseling & Development* 68 (1989), 87; Larry Gross, "What is Wrong With This Picture? Lesbian Women and Gay Men on Television," in R. Jeffrey Ringer, ed., *Queer Words, Queer Images: Communication and the Construction of Homosexuality* (New York: New York University Press, 1994), 147.

5. Gregory Herek, "The Social Context of Hate Crimes: Notes on Cultural Heterosexism," in Gregory Herek and Kevin Berrill, eds., *Hate Crimes: Confronting Violence Against Lesbians and Gay Men* (Newbury Park, CA: Sage Publications, 1992), 89.

6. Kylo-Patrick Hart, "Retrograde Representation," *The Journal of Men's Studies* 7 (1999), 206.

7. Everett Rogers and Corinne Shefner-Rogers, "Diffusion of Innovations and HIV/AIDS Prevention Research," in William N. Elwood, ed., *Power in the Blood: A Handbook on AIDS, Politics, and Communication* (Mahwah, NJ: Lawrence Erlbaum Associates, 1999), 412.

8. Ibid., 412.

9. Brett Garwood, telephone interview by author, 15 November 1996.

10. Centers for Disease Control and Prevention, *HIV/AIDS Surveillance Report, Year-End 1996* (Atlanta: CDC, 1997), 4.

11. Emile Netzhammer and Scott Shamp, "Guilt By Association: Homosexuality and AIDS on Prime-Time Television," in Ringer, ed., *Queer Words, Queer Images*, 98.

12. Kylo-Patrick Hart, *The AIDS Movie: Representing a Pandemic in Film and Television* (New York: The Haworth Press, 2000), 64.

13. Ibid., 60.

14. Kevin Clark, "Pink Water: The Archetype of Blood and the Pool of Infinite Contagion," in Elwood, ed., *Power in the Blood*, 9.

15. Cheryl Zupan, "Clinton Declares AIDS Emergency for Minorities," *Between the Lines*, 26 November 1998, 13.

16. Steve Cadwell, "Twice Removed: The Stigma Suffered By Gay Men With AIDS," *Smith College Studies in Social Work* 61, (1991), 237.

17. Steven Capsuto, *Alternate Channels: The Uncensored Story of Gay and Lesbian Images on Radio and Television* (New York: Ballantine Books, 2000), 218.

18. Richard Perloff, *Persuading People to Have Safer Sex: Applications of Social Science to the AIDS Crisis* (Mahwah, NJ: Lawrence Erlbaum Associates, 2001), 83.

19. Gabriele Griffin, *Representations of HIV and AIDS: Visibility Blue/s* (New York: Manchester University Press, 2000), 8.

20. Laurie Garrett, "The Virus at the End of the World," *Esquire*, March 1999, 104.

21. David Wheeler, "As AIDS Continues to Spread, Some Scientists are Pessimistic about Developing a Vaccine," *The Chronicle of Higher Education*, 26 March 1999, A21.

22. Lisa Jones, "Girls (and Guys) Gone Wild," *Men's Health*, May 2004, 50.

Swamp Sex Robots: Narratives of Male Pubescence and Viewer (Mis)Identification

Ryan Robert Mitchell

I BEGAN JUNIOR HIGH shortly before *Degrassi Junior High* went on the air (1987), and I graduated high school shortly after the *Degrassi* movie *School's Out* (1992) was shown. In many ways, I went through my teen years with the *Degrassi* characters as cohorts. Now mind you, many of my experiences did not overlap with those of the characters from the series — I never had the opportunity, for example, to jump off bridges while tripping on acid like Shane did nor did I have a "ride" as cool as Clutch's — but there was still some uncanny connection to these Canadian fictional teens who were struggling through the same "teen years" that I was. I didn't quite use the *Degrassi* series as a guidebook, but I did feel a connection to the show. It was refreshing for once to watch a "teen" program that wasn't cheapened by a laugh track.

I don't think I was alone, either. The majority of the people I knew in both junior high and high school were *Degrassi* fanatics, and nearly every one of them had a favourite character they would champion. For example, my younger brother's favourite was the relatively obscure character Alex Yankou. Without a doubt my favourite was the sinister and miserable Kathleen who made the teen years all that much harder on those around her. I always thought Kathleen to be the Nelly Olson character from *Little*

House on the Prairie reincarnated as a severely repressed Canadian teen; and, for some reason, I appreciated her constant acts of emotional sadism on the long-suffering and sweet Melanie.

Now, my brother is not neurotic in exactly the same way that Alex was, and I can't claim to have half the problems Kathleen did, but this raises an interesting question: Why do we identify with characters that are different than us, or why do we identify with fictional characters at all?

What I'd like to do in this chapter is discuss how viewers identify with a work of fiction and why the *Degrassi* series was so successful in creating different kinds of viewer identification. I would also like to discuss the inverse to this process, where we as viewers guard against a writer's overture that is intended to get us to identify with her/his narrative. I believe we do this through a dual process of ironic distancing and the reinscription of the narrative. I will demonstrate this through an exploration of the male pubescent narrative arcs of *Degrassi* that featured Arthur K.

VIEWER (MIS)IDENTITY AT THIRTEEN

One of the greatest verbal exchanges ever in Canadian television history (at least since *Wayne and Schuster* went off the air) took place during the "The Best Laid Plans" episode of *Degrassi Junior High*. Yick, who has just stolen a porno video titled *Swamp Sex Robots* from his older brother, shows the verboten videotape case to his best friend Arthur. Confused by the title, Arthur asks, "What exactly do Swamp Sex Robots do?" To which Yick replies, "I don't know, but I hear it's so hot it'll fry your eyeballs."

When this episode first aired, I was a very naive thirteen year old who had not seen "real" pornography before, so I couldn't help but share in Arthur's confusion. What the hell *did* "Swamp Sex Robots" do? After watching the episode, I remember rolling over in my head the semantic meaning of "Swamp Sex Robots." That double adjective really had my mind and imagination working overtime. Was the porno concerned more with "swamp sex," with "robots" being peripheral or was it a "sex robots" skin flick set in a "swamp"? If you try to combine each of these three variables and then think it over long enough, you can come up with, how should I say, "creative" scenarios, trust me. Although the dirtiest and most "creative" scenarios involving swamp, sex and robots will invariably come from the mind of a sexually clueless and naive thirteen-year-old male.

Being thirteen, I was a part of the perfect demographic of this show when it first aired. I began junior high at the same time as Arthur, Yick and the rest of the "younger" cast members. I could not help but feel a bit of identification with the characters; or rather, I could not help but feel that I was *supposed* to identify with the characters. The writers and producers constructed the *Degrassi* series to perform a didactic purpose that allowed the adolescent viewers to see themselves reflected onscreen. Mind you, not every thirteen and fourteen year old falls off bridges or is accosted by B-level soap stars, but I felt like the *Degrassi* series did not totally alienate pubescent viewers in the way that other heavy-handed teen programs did.

Though the series was shot in the Canadian metropolis of Toronto, the chosen locations and settings were decidedly un-urban and anonymous. You got the sense that the *Degrassi* universe was a practical stand-in for any Canadian location replete with quaint and anonymous strip malls, ubiquitous Shoppers Drug Marts and other suburban settings that nearly any bored Canadian adolescent is familiar with. The whole *Degrassi* series, beginning with *The Kids of Degrassi Street*, was shot with a foot-traffic ethic where action was confined to only a few locations all seemingly within relative proximity. Watching the series, I often found myself drawing up a mental map of the neighbourhood as the characters travelled through it. Whereas most programs that only use a limited amount of set-ups and locations feel claustrophobic, the *Degrassi* series invited identification with its "space."

Beyond the use of space, another area that immediately allowed me to connect or identify with the series was the casting and the use of not-especially-attractive untrained actors as the principle leads. To actually see acne on teenagers for the first time on TV was at first jarring but also strangely comforting. I could relate to kids with crooked teeth and bad hair, but I was never sure how I was supposed to identify with the sulky-millionaire-playboy Dylan character (played by fake teen Luke Perry) and his receding hairline on *Beverly Hills 90210*. For this reason, the series felt really comfortable. (I have to say that I did feel disappointed when *Degrassi: The Next Generation* decided to employ a "prettier" cast of professionals.)

When watching *Degrassi*, I didn't feel totally cheated the way I often did when watching other, mostly American, television programs aimed at teens. One only has to look at, say, ABC's very transparent and slick *After School Specials* to see a format aimed at adolescents that, in the opinion of this lifelong TV addict, really did not work. Overly earnest yet histrionic at the same time, the *After School Specials* on ABC were the perfect fodder on which jaded and irascible adolescents could train their ironic eyes. You knew you were going to be cheated when you sat down to watch them and I would like to think this was the reason why they were so popular. I cannot imagine most kids being gullible enough to take the narratives at face value. I mean, I do not think I knew a single (pre)teen who did not laugh uproariously when a young Helen Hunt in the subtle and ambiguously titled *Angel Dust* (1981) snorted PCP and then famously jumped out a window, or when a drunk Chachi (Scott Baio) killed his brother with an oar in a tragic canoeing accident in the subtle and ambiguously titled *Stoned* (1980). The bald faced anti-drug narratives and "very special episodes" of the "Just Say No" and subsequent "War on Drugs" eras of television churned out a generation of youth who were mistrustful of what adults thought was best for them, no matter what the message was.

At the same time, the *Degrassi* series was different from the irresponsible teen trash of the then wildly and inexplicably popular *Saved by the Bell* or *Beverly Hills 90210* series. That's not to say, however, that the sometimes didactic writing always succeeded. I'm thinking, for example, of when the series tried too hard to equally appeal to the kids and get a message across. What immediately comes to mind is the *Degrassi Junior High* episode that tried to bring attention to air pollution being caused by the emissions of a local factory via Rick and Caitlin's rap, which was broadcast over the school's PA system for the enlightenment of the student body (and those watching at home). In instances like this, it was obvious that you were *supposed* to identify with the message or characters. I believe that using such a heavy-handed approach to persuade viewers to identify with the narrative actually inhibits any sense of identification that viewers might generate on their own. For the most part, however, *Degrassi* won viewer identification without trying too hard or being too heavy handed.

Degrassi was the first series to explore the "real" issues of teens in a near *cinéma-vérité* approach. That is, the series followed a near-documentary approach in the daily lives of each of the characters, following a structure that was polyphonic where characters would be traded in and out of narrative focus. Outside of a few central incidents, like the burning down of the first school, there was no real major story arc but rather a persistent fictional world where characters progressed on the arcs within their own self-contained narratives. It should also be remembered that the *Degrassi* series began in the latter part of the eighties, an abysmal decade for teen programming. For the most part, teen programming was relegated to the "sitcom ghetto" with practically no dramas devoted to "real teens." I do not think many teens, for example, were able to identify with Ricky Schroeder's "Richie Rich" character who had a life-size model train running through his mansion in *Silver Spoons*, or the equally contemptible Gary Coleman vehicle of *Diff'rent Strokes*, which had the fully grown Coleman frozen at adolescence for the series' entire eight-year run. I remember being taken aback by *Degrassi's* approach, after being simultaneously pandered to and patronized by television programs my whole life.

Narrating Puberty and Teen Angst

One aspect of the *Degrassi* narratives, of which the "Swamp Sex Robots" episode is a perfect example, that comes close to being real is the focus placed on the characters' experiences of puberty. Or rather, how a certain set of characters experienced puberty. The older *Degrassi* cohort (Joey, Wheels, Stephanie Kaye and others), on the one hand, seemingly passed through puberty easily, reaping the benefits of the new hormones coursing through their nubile bodies. A testament to this are the plot lines that involve the "older" kids scheming about how they are "going to get it on." The younger cohort (Arthur, Yick, Melanie, Kathleen, Caitlin and others), on the other hand, are the perpetual wallflowers of the series whose encounters with dating and sexual developments are largely negative. Going through puberty for this younger group meant training bras, acne, hairy armpits and failed romantic attempts or encounters. This didn't change much throughout the series either. As far as I know, Caitlin was the only member of the original "younger" cohort fortunate enough to lose her virginity by the series' end.

Then there's Arthur K. Poor Arthur Kobalowsky, the failed hero of the "Swamp Sex Robots" episode. His character bore the brunt of every problem associated with puberty and almost served as a pubescent "scapegoat" through which I could project all my early teen angst. Perhaps because of his innocuous and non-threatening appearance and demeanour, the *Degrassi* writers chose him to be the pubescent "everyman." I would argue that you see Arthur's character as a type of narrative device through which the mysteries of puberty are demystified for the adolescent male (and possibly female) viewer. Outside of the one plot line about Melanie's budding breasts and the blatant product placements for Tampax and Clear-Tech in the later *Degrassi High* episodes, there wasn't a pubescent female "everywoman" that dealt with female puberty or sexuality. But for boys, every embarrassing aspect of both puberty and burgeoning sexuality were laid out in Arthur K's character.

The best place to begin is the "The Best Laid Plans" episode from the first season of *Degrassi Junior High*. Besides having the best and most aptly named episode title in the *Degrassi* catalogue, "The Best Laid Plans" exemplifies the difference between the series' two age cohorts and their different relationship to puberty/sexuality. Arthur Kobalowsky's "secret" and precociously trashy sister Stephanie Kaye (who goes to great lengths to distance herself from her brother and their ethnicity and has changed her name as a way of doing this), has planned a date with Wheels. Through a series of misunderstandings and goading by their respective friends, Stephanie and Wheels tentatively make an appointment to "do it" at Stephanie's house. Wheels even plans ahead and buys condoms for the occasion, but he first gets chewed out by the woman working behind the counter at the Shoppers Drug Mart. The younger group — Yick, Arthur and Alex — have very different "solo" plans. As explained earlier, Yick has stolen the *Swamp Sex Robots* video from his older brother and the boys plan on enjoying the movie together at Arthur's house while his mother is at work. Can they all pull it off? Will Steph and Wheels engage in pubescent sex? Will the boys discover the mysteries of "Swamp Sex Robots"? These are the questions the viewers wait to have answered.

Of course, the answer is no for both sets of kids and for the voyeuristic viewers. What was great about this episode was the "evildoing" perpetuated by the young teenagers. Of course, immature teen sex is wrong to responsible parents everywhere, let alone to TV censors. So is watching a porno flick before age eighteen. But just like any good "heist" or "caper" film, the viewers' identification is clearly located with the evildoers. Maybe we respect their resourcefulness in the execution of their plans, or maybe we really want to see another person's evildoing pay off. At any rate, if we root for Mr. Pink in *Reservoir Dogs*, then we can root for the boys getting in some quality porno viewing time.

It didn't really work out for Mr. Pink and it never worked out for evildoing kids on network television, or public television for that matter. Stephanie's mother comes home early and is, of course, revealed to be the busybody who chewed out Wheels at Shoppers Drug Mart. Stephanie Kaye is caught by her mother in one of her, as Alexa so succinctly put it, "woman of the night" outfits. Lastly, and most regrettably, Alex Yankou, in his great way, ruins everything for the boys when he shows up at Arthur's doorstep and loudly blabs "You got the porno!?" within earshot of Arthur's mother, putting the kibosh on the boys' porno viewing plans.

In another narrative arc, the occurrence of wet dreams is explored. In the episode "Great Expectations," Arthur confides in his best buddy Yick that he's been having dreams. These are not the normal kind, but as Arthur explains, "Strange dreams ... the kind you know ... when you sorta leak." Because of his nightly leaking and strange dreams, Arthur diagnoses himself as a "sex maniac." I remember that when I first saw this episode, with the wisdom of an additional year added to my life, I thought that based on the type of "action" Arthur liked in his porno, his diagnosis was probably correct. The content of the dreams are left as an "off-camera monster" and are never described, but Arthur's disturbed reaction to them means that they must have been really goofy and lascivious rather than enjoyable.

"Great Expectations," of course, served the didactic purpose of illustrating that Arthur was not a "sex maniac" and that his nightly leaking and strange dreams were something boys everywhere experience. Fair enough. Where things went strange, at least in my reading of the episode, was in the writers' "solution" for both Arthur's leaking and his identity problem.

When the episode opens, everyone has their big 1980s "ghetto blasters" and transistor radios tuned to the radio program *Talking Sex with Dr. Sally*, a fictionalized stand-in for Canada's great sex information program *Sex with Sue Johanson*. Arthur is fretting about his problem and is not comfortable with his new vision of himself as a sex maniac. Arthur and Yick then decide that this radio program — which is suddenly wildly popular this one week in the series' five-year history — might be the answer to Arthur's problem. Here's where the narrative, or at least my reading of it, moves into interesting territory. The boys both know how popular the program is and, in an act of exhibitionism, decide to broadcast Arthur's problem on the air waves by calling Dr. Sally. So not only is Arthur a "sex maniac" with wild dreams, he is also an exhibitionist. But Arthur doesn't ask Dr. Sally the question, Yick does. On top of this, many of their friends are regular listeners to the radio show. In a separate shot, we see Melanie and the girls listening in, and their reaction to Yick's question gives the impression that they suspect who is making the call.

This is the type of gossip that my favourite character Kathleen revelled in, so it was a bit disappointing that they did not dramatize the fallout of the Yick/Arthur phone call because nothing happens at all. The episode ends with Dr. Sally telling Yick/Arthur that he is not a sex maniac, that what he's going through is perfectly normal. In a way, Arthur is "cured" of his "sex maniac" status, which was only based on his reaction to his leaky and strange dreams, but what about his exhibitionism and the "soft" exhibitionism of people who use programs like Dr. Sally's to confess their sexual issues? Not that such things should be cured, but it would have been interesting to see Kathleen's reactionary response to Arthur's "problems" dramatized. In what I found to be an unsatisfactory and abrupt ending to this episode, the viewer is left to create his/her own resolution and interpret the motives/reactions of the characters.

Entry into high school was rough for Arthur. Formerly a major character in *Degrassi Junior High*, by the time *Degrassi High* started, he seemed to have been demoted to a hall walker. He did have a couple of moments in the later series, with the best one happening early in the first season. The episode "Dream On" dramatizes Arthur's fantasies and dreams about the "way-out-of-his-league" Caitlin, and the way these fantasies affect his friendship with her. Now before you get all excited, these dreams were not the kind that … you know … leaked. The actual dream content, despite being filmed with a soft focus lens, is extremely chaste involving candlelit dinners, romance and the great Alex Yankou as a waiter pouring a soft drink into champagne glasses. Well, they weren't entirely chaste … In one dream, both of her ex-boyfriends, Joey and Claude, are tied-up (!) as Arthur and Caitlin enjoy a romantic interlude. Maybe he really is a sex maniac! But Arthur's dreams are always interrupted before anything leaky can happen, at least that the audience can see.

★

I think it's impossible, or even irrelevant, to discuss the intention of the series' creators. I think that I've shown, through my own interpretation, that ultimately it's the viewer who constructs the intentionality of the narrative. But then again, it'd be difficult to discuss the intentionality of my own "coming of age" narrative because I am sure how I interpret and re-member it was equally influenced by watching television events as by "real-life" events. My reading of Arthur K's character undeniably reveals more about my own than his. That I am still mystified by what those "Swamp Sex Robots" got up to after all these years is an affirmation of my fondness for and attachment to the program.

"Everybody Wants Something":
Drugs, Sex and Money in Canadian and American Teen Programming

Bettina Spencer

Degrassi High DEBUTED AT THE END of the 1980s and ran until the beginning of the 1990s. In both Canada and the United States, the changes taking place in society were reflected in politics, fashion, music and, especially, television programming. Amidst the dominating swell of glossy teen comedies that served as a form of escapism and distraction from the conflicts of the times, *Degrassi High* provided a pragmatic view of everyday life that candidly addressed issues relevant to North American teenagers. By comparing *Degrassi High* to its U.S. television counterparts *Saved by the Bell* and *Beverly Hills 90210*, this chapter illustrates how television programming in Canada and the U.S. either served as a buffer to the reality of the new decade or straightforwardly addressed emerging developments in teenage drug use, sexual activity and relationships to money.

YEARS OF TRANSITION

The year 1990 was a one of transition for Canada and the United States alike. Fashion, music and television reflected the optimism of a new decade. The fall of the Berlin Wall in 1989, the Gulf War in 1991 and the end of apartheid in South Africa in 1993 were indications that the world was rapidly changing. Whereas some people embraced the new era with hopes that the economic and political strife of the 1980s was now firmly in the past and a thing to be forgotten, others looked at the 1990s as a chance to confront and rectify the damage that had previously been incurred. Nowhere else was this dichotomy more evident than in television programming.

Television played a vital role in the way we saw the world and the events that were changing it. First and foremost, people were watching prime-time news programs more than ever. We saw the massacre of students in Beijing's Tiananmen Square and the murder of fourteen young women at L'École Polytechnique in Montreal. We watched as Nelson Mandela was finally freed, and as Margaret Thatcher finally resigned. When the news wasn't on television, informing us that the U.S. was bombing Iraq, we turned to fictional programs.

Most people tend to remember the late 1980s and early 1990s as a wasteland of disposable music, television and movies because they forget that many products of the time were more than just entertaining distractions — many products, in fact, encouraged consumers to think about the issues and problems facing society. Television in both Canada and the U.S. was shaped by the events of the time in which it was produced, and its programming reflected how society was dealing with the current climate of discord. Of the Canadian shows that embraced the new decade, none was as encompassing as the *Degrassi* series.

The first show in the series, *The Kids of Degrassi Street*, ran from 1979 to 1985. In its reincarnation in 1987, it became *Degrassi Junior High* (*DJH*), which was neither a sequel to *The Kids of Degrassi Street* nor a new series, since many of the same actors played different characters. During its run, *DJH* won critical and popular success. It was nominated for and won multiple Geminis and continually received high ratings. *DJH* incorporated much of what the 1980s were about. It was praised for its unabashedly progressive look at the world of teenagers growing up in a tumultuous time. In 1989, the characters left junior high, bringing *DJH* to a close, and soon *Degrassi High* followed, continuing the story of regular high-school students and how they dealt with everything from problems with family and friends to more difficult issues involving drugs and sex. In many countries, these subjects as well as other taboo subjects still have not been addressed on television programs geared for teenagers.

With the beginning of a new decade, the U.S. tried to create a happier, glossier atmosphere in their television programming. Shows that portrayed teenagers in impossible or unlikely situations such as *Doogie Howser, M.D.* and *The Fresh Prince of Bell Air* swept the ratings, and television executives scrambled to produce more shows that would appeal to the teenage set. While *Degrassi High* was premiering in Canada, two new favourites in the U.S. emerged: *Saved by the Bell* and *Beverly Hills 90210*. American teenagers finally had television programs that were supposed to reflect the trials and tribulations of "normal" high-school students.

Like the *Degrassi* shows, *Saved by the Bell* (*SBTB*) was a mature reincarnation of its younger version, which originally aired under the name *Good Morning Ms. Bliss* and featured the antics of a middle-school crowd. When the show began to focus on high school, some of the characters remained, many disappeared and a few new cast members were brought in. Also like the *Degrassi* shows, *SBTB* was predominantly set within a school, with teachers and principals appearing as regular characters.

Beverly Hills 90210 was created by famed producer Aaron Spelling. When coming up with the idea for *90210*, Spelling turned to his previous hit shows for inspiration. He wanted a "Dallas" for teens. With this in mind, he created a plot and assembled an ensemble cast that revolved around a set of twins (Brandon and Brenda Walsh) who had just moved from Minnesota to Beverly Hills for their first year of high school. Although the twins were the focal point at the beginning of the series, in later years the plot lines shifted focus from character to character, and eventually, as in *Degrassi*, there were no main characters. Through to its finale in 2000, the ensemble cast saw a few actors come and go, including Brenda (played by Shannon Doherty), but most of the original cast remained.

Set in high school, revolving around the lives of teenagers, appealing to a younger crowd, one can inevitably draw correlations when comparing *Degrassi*, *SBTB* and *90210*. However, aside from the premise of teenagers going to school and interacting with friends and family, there are really very few similarities between the Canadian depiction of life as a teenager and the American hits aimed at the same demographic. In the following sections, I illustrate the different ways *Degrassi High*, *Saved by the Bell* and *Beverly Hills 90210* characterized the transition of adolescence. Specifically, the years in which all three shows overlapped, 1989 to 1991, will be examined, although *90210* ran an additional nine years after the finale of *Degrassi High*.

While they all tried to address the concerns and interests of teenagers, only *Degrassi High* successfully represented the reality of the 1990s. Its candid portrayal of teenagers was criticized by some, praised by others and raised questions for many about the role and effects of the media in the lives of teens. Opponents of realistic teen programming argued that by exposing teenagers to risky behaviours, such as drug use and sexual activity, viewers would be encouraged to emulate those behaviours; if television did not directly address such issues, the argument went, the viewers would not engage in those behaviours. Proponents of realistic teen shows such as *Degrassi High* argued that honest depictions of teenagers, negative behaviour and all, would teach young viewers important life lessons. With stories focusing honestly on issues that teenagers might be experiencing themselves, television could act as a means through which viewers learned about the realities rather than the myths of drugs, sex and money.

DRUGS AND ALCOHOL: FEELING "STRESSED OUT"

Taboo plot lines in youth programming often involve drugs and alcohol. While *Degrassi High, Saved by the Bell* and *90210* all dealt with the issue in some capacity, each employed different techniques for working alcohol- and drug-related narratives into the show. Whether it was a one-show plot or an ongoing storyline, each show varied in the manner, and realism, in which it addressed the subject of adolescent drug use.

For the show's enthusiasts, the most coveted *SBTB* moment is the now infamous "Jessie's Song." In this episode, Jessi Spano (Elizabeth Berkley), Bayside High's top student and ardent feminist is overwhelmed by her academic and extracurricular activities. Balancing final exams and a video shoot proves to be too much for Jessie and she starts to take caffeine pills to keep up the energy her gruelling schedule requires. During a study session, her friend, A.C. Slater (Mario Lopez), finds out that Jessie has been taking pills to stay awake and tries to warn her about their habit-forming potential. Though Jessica reassures A.C. that they are safe and non-addictive, he later finds the pills in Jessie's book bag, leading him to suspect that she is abusing them. Upon confrontation, Jessie becomes angry and frustrated, telling him to mind his own business and refusing to hand over the pills. When A.C. tries to inform Jessie's good friend Zack (Mark-Paul Gosselaar) that she may be on drugs, Zack cannot believe it. He is sure that a person as smart as Jessie would never use drugs.

Eventually, Jessie's friends start to realize that her behaviour is odd. One night, Zack goes over to her house to remind her that she needs to perform live for a record executive; as Jessie begins to panic, she begins searching for her pills. When Zack sees that she is in fact taking caffeine pills, he knocks them out of her hand and stops her. To prove to him that she is fine and can perform, she starts to sing and dance but is near to collapsing. Zack grabs her shoulders to hold her up. "I'm so excited … I'm so excited … I'm so … so … scared, Zack." Upon realizing that she does have a drug problem, Zack calms Jessie down and tells her to get some rest. Jessie goes to bed, learns that she cannot take on too many activities at once and knows that she will not abuse caffeine pills again. Later that same evening, Zack apologizes to A.C. for not listening to him, Jessie apologizes to A.C. for not heeding his warnings and tells him that she and her mother are going to see a doctor the next day for counselling on how to effectively deal with her stress. Note that Jessie did not use drugs for pleasure, experimentation, rebellion or even relaxation. Her motivation was purely academic; and, ultimately, it was a learning experience.

Michelle (Maureen McKay) from *DH* succumbed to caffeine pill dependency as well. Much like Jessie, she had too many things to do. She was studying for final exams, which was very important because of the low marks she had recently been receiving, and working part-time in a dough-nut shop so that she could support living on her own after moving out of her father's house. The stress of living on her own had become apparent earlier in the season as she struggled to work, make time for her boyfriend, compromise with her father and study. For several episodes we see Michelle trying to maintain a stable life, but her job becomes more and more de-manding and her school and relationships consequently suffer.

As Michelle becomes more dependent on stimulants to keep up with the pace of her schedule, her work is detrimentally affected by her addiction. Although she is staying awake all night studying, the quality of her work declines and she reaches a point where she can no longer function. After snapping at her boyfriend, who tried several times to intervene, and hav-ing a mild anxiety attack, she collapses. Eventually, she speaks to a school nurse who describes to her the effects of stimulants, and she admits to her boyfriend that he was right in his protest.

Both *SBTB* and *DH* used the premise of an overachiever who, trying to function under time constraints and the stress of too many responsi-bilities, cannot achieve her usual level of accomplishment in school and in her personal relationships. By organizing these plot lines around positive, successful characters, both shows were able to demonstrate that teenagers can become addicted to drugs under certain circumstances. Jessie and Michelle were not deviant characters who usually caused trouble; they were well-adjusted characters who mistakenly thought that using caffeine pills would enhance their academic performance. Both shows illustrated that addiction to these sorts of drugs does not lead to success. On *SBTB*, however, the pressure Jessie was under is not a common situation for the average teenager. Few students have to prepare for MTV video shoots while trying to become class valedictorian. On *DH,* on the other hand, Michelle was in a predicament that many teenagers find themselves in: balancing work with school. Although Michelle's situation of living on her own was not typical, many teenagers might identify with the stress that comes from fighting with parents or working part-time.

Although on both shows stress was the factor that motivated the characters to use stimulants, the process of becoming overwhelmed, turning to drugs and then overcoming the abuse was depicted in very different ways. In a single episode Jessie had exams, formed a band, landed a recording contract, became addicted to caffeine pills and kicked the habit after a brief intervention. Michelle's downfall occurred over several episodes that chronicled the accumulation of her stress and how it affected her life on several levels. Although she was able to overcome her addiction, she ultimately lost her boyfriend as a result of her hectic schedule. Michelle was transformed throughout the season — she still had to cope with stress and responsibility, but learned to do so in a more balanced way.

A plot line that involves a student turning to stimulants in an attempt to do better in school is a relatively safe way to broach the subject of teens and drugs. It is shocking enough for parents and networks to see teenagers abusing legal over-the-counter drugs, and these stories are clearly a way of demonstrating how abuse of even the "safest" drug can be damaging. On *SBTB*, "Jessie's Song" was the only episode in which a character experimented with drugs of any sort. Drugs were never central to an *SBTB* plot line that showed several characters using them for pleasure.

90210, however, did introduce the use of alcohol in several plot lines, the first of which was related to Kelly's mother, a former fashion model (played by Ann Gillespie) who had "fallen off the wagon." In another episode, at a party attended by "deviant" Beverly Hills teens, Brandon's (Jason Priestley) drink is spiked and Kelly (Jennie Garth) gets drunk and has sex with her former boyfriend Steve (Ian Ziering). Later on, Brandon drinks at yet another party, kisses a friend, is arrested for drunk driving and attends an Alcoholics Anonymous meeting. In these episodes, Brandon, a lead character representing a supposed normal Midwestern American background, is depicted as having no agency in his original consumption of alcohol whereas Kelly, a native of Beverly Hills with an abnormally sordid and glamorous background, is depicted as actively drinking and subsequently having a meaningless sexual encounter. In later years, the characters on *90210* experiment more heavily with drugs and alcohol, and Brandon ends up a "temporary alcoholic," behaviour originating from his first spiked drink.

90210 had a lot of plots that revolved around the differences between the transplanted Walshes and the local teenagers; the latter being represented as wealthy, deviant and exotic — someone to whom the viewers were not supposed to relate. Creating a dichotomy between the "regular" and the "atypical" characters, the writers were able to address touchy subjects from a safe distance. The viewers felt detached from the Beverly Hills teenagers, making storylines about drugs and alcohol acceptable precisely because they were not supposed to reflect the behaviour of the average American teen. If a plot ever showed Kelly's drink being spiked, or Brenda drinking and having sex freely, the show would have been much more controversial than it already was, because Brenda would have to be subtyped as an atypical "average" teenager and Kelly as an atypical "exotic" teenager. By maintaining stereotypical beliefs of wholesome Midwesterners and unruly, sophisticated urban teenagers, the storyline remained safe, and sex and alcohol were distanced from the majority of teens.

Fans who are familiar with *DH* know that the use of drugs has been a theme throughout the series. On both *DJH* and *DH* many of the characters freely explored drugs at one point or another. Although *DJH* showed an extreme case of the consequences of drug use when Shane (Bill Parrott) took acid, jumped off a bridge and became mentally impaired from the injury, the norm for the *Degrassi* series was to portray different types of students trying various drugs for different reasons with many different results.

One particular example is presented in the *DH* episode "The All Nighter." The plot revolves around a sweet-sixteen slumber party where Kathleen (Rebecca Haines), one of the more prudent and moralistic characters, brings a joint as a surprise. The characters at the slumber party are a clique of good students who do not usually get into trouble. They are average, curious young girls. During a game of truth or dare, Kathleen asks Maya (Kyra Levy), "Have you ever tried drugs … would you like to?" and then admits that she "smoked up lots of times when [she] was going out with [her ex-boyfriend] Scott." Four of the five girls eventually try the marijuana, three of them smoking it until they are high. Kathleen ends up paranoid and withdrawn; Melanie and Diana (played by Sara Ballingall and Chrissa Erodotou) become giddy.

While there are no extreme outcomes resulting from their experimentation, there is a fallout between best friends Kathleen and Melanie after Melanie confesses, in another game of truth or dare, that she read Kathleen's diary and then proceeds to tell the group how Kathleen was anorexic, abused by her boyfriend and has an alcoholic mother. Despite a following apology, the friendship never regains its former closeness. Unlike *SBTB*, *DH* showed regular teens using drugs for regular reasons. Characters did not have to be under tremendous stress to experiment with drugs, and while the characters in "The All Nighter" expressed remorse for having experimented with drugs, none of them required a drastic intervention like the method used on *SBTB*.

In the early 1990s, when the most frequently used drug in Canada and the U.S. by both teenagers and adults was marijuana, *DH* gave a realistic profile of the typical user.[1] Considering that in 1989, 63.2 percent of American students reported that marijuana in addition to cocaine, crack and uppers or downers were easily available to them at school and that approximately 50 percent had tried marijuana, American television did not accurately depict how the average teen experimented with drugs.[2]

SEX: "A NEW START" OR JUST "DREAM ON"

One topic in youth programming that may be even more taboo than drugs is sex. Although the "boy meets girl" relationship is an integral part of almost every teenage-driven storyline, very few mainstream programs have realistically addressed the issue.

While *Beverly Hills 90210* did have plot lines that revolved around teenagers losing their virginity to their "first loves," the series depicted sex in either a romanticized or a demonized manner. In an episode aptly titled "The First Time," Brandon's girlfriend (Paula Irvine) from Minnesota comes to visit him in Beverly Hills. One night, she sneaks into his bedroom and they consummate their long-term relationship. During her visit, Brandon's girlfriend becomes enamored of the glitz of Beverly Hills and ends up hitting on one of his friends. Eventually, Brandon learns that his girlfriend had not even been a virgin. The lesson suggested by this episode is that girls who aren't virgins are likely to cheat on their boyfriends and are not trustworthy.

Conversely, later in the season we are shown that when girls lose their virginity to boys who have already had sex, it can be a trusting, learning experience. This comes through in the episode "Spring Dance," in which Brenda and Dylan (Luke Perry) have sex for the first time, after dating for a year. For Brenda, it was her first time, but not for Dylan. Being a "bad boy," he was not a virgin, and this prompted him to make sure the evening was a romantic, sensitive affair. In the next episode, Brenda learns that her family may be moving away from Beverly Hills and that she may be pregnant. As a result, she decides to break up with Dylan, despite his attempts to keep the relationship together. After an inconclusive home pregnancy test, Brenda gets her period and realizes that not only is she not pregnant but she is not quite ready for the responsibilities that come with having sex. In this storyline, Brenda represented a safe middle ground of female sexuality as compared with the Beverly Hills teens who were extreme examples of sexual activity: either being very sexually active like Kelly or remaining a virgin for many years like Donna. The male characters of *90210* had more freedom and agency in their sexuality and were not defined by their level of experience.

AIDS was another sex-related topic addressed by *90210*. While none of the permanent characters contracted AIDS or any other sexually transmitted disease during the show's run, one of them did flirt with a speaker from a sex education workshop who later revealed that she was HIV positive and another had a friendship with an AIDS-infected gay man (see chapter 10 in this volume). The sex ed scene may have brought attention to the fact that people other than gay men could contract AIDS, and after hearing the sex education talk, Brenda temporarily slowed down her physical relationship with Dylan. But other than that, there seemed to be no effect on any of the main characters. The most risqué sexual behaviour *Saved by the Bell* ever represented was the occasional close-lipped kiss between characters who had been a couple for quite some time.

Degrassi Junior High had already blazed a path in youth programming by depicting teen pregnancy, sexual confusion and homosexuality in such episodes as "It's Late," "Rumor Has It" and "He Ain't Heavy." *Degrassi High* took its depiction of sex a step further, giving its characters real agency over their own sexuality. The *Degrassi* series' depiction of sex provided an accurate portrait of the confusion, excitement and pain that can result from teenage sexual activity. Not all the characters experienced negative consequence as a result of their sexuality, nor did they make life-altering decisions because of their sexual activity. However, all the characters dealt with the very realistic scenarios that can accompany sex.

The first two episodes of *Degrassi High*, "A New Start," revolve around one girl's decision to have an abortion and her twin sister's and schoolmates' reactions. Despite being pleaded with not to abort her fetus and feeling confused, Erica (Angela Deiseach) decides for herself that an abortion is the best thing for her. The episodes end with Erica and her sister Heather (Maureen Deiseach) entering an abortion clinic where protestors yell and hold out figures of fetuses to them. When this scene aired in the United States, it was edited so that the protestors were not shown with their signs and fetus figures. Rather than show the more graphic protest scenes, the U.S. version cut away to the girls' faces as they entered the clinic. PBS, the station that aired *DH* in the U.S., might have found the original ending to be too aggressive, frightening or disturbing. The ending that did air did not adequately show what Erica and Heather had to face as they approached and entered the clinic.

The topic of Erica's abortion was a recurring theme over many subsequent episodes. First, word spread that Erica had been pregnant, then an altercation took place with another student who was fiercely anti-abortion. The topic resurfaced again much later on when Erica began to date again. When Erica became involved with a new boyfriend, her sister Heather was haunted by the memories of the abortion and worried that Erica would get pregnant again. She became overprotective and somewhat hostile at the prospect of her sister having an intimate relationship. The abortion was never forgotten and continued to affect both their lives throughout the series.

Another consequence of sexual activity that *DH* depicted was the contraction of sexually transmitted diseases. In "Bad Blood," the school bully, Dwayne (Darrin Brown), discovers that he is HIV positive. This was a forceful storyline because it not only straightforwardly addressed the culture of

AIDS in the late 1980s and early 1990s but it also dispelled the stereotypes about who could be infected with AIDS. Dwayne, a white heterosexual male, contracted the disease through intercourse with a white heterosexual female. After being erroneously identified as "the gay cancer" in the 1980s, AIDS was still thought to be predominantly a problem for gays, minorities and drug abusers. "Bad Blood," however, showed that anyone could be affected. Episodes Part One and Two mixed storylines of Dwayne's HIV experience with the school's sex education month and the introduction of condom machines in its restrooms. This enabled many characters and teachers to discuss their beliefs about and the stereotypes surrounding sex and sexually transmitted diseases. The HIV plot line developed at a time when the median age of people being infected with HIV/AIDS dropped from approximately thirty-two in 1982–83 to twenty-three in 1986–90.[3] Furthermore, the average age of transmission for other sexually transmitted diseases also dropped in the late 1980s and early 1990s. Of all Canadian women, teenage girls aged fifteen to nineteen have the highest reported rates for gonorrhea and chlamydia.[4]

The students have mixed reactions to the introduction of condom machines and the role of sex education in general, which is a debate that still persists in the school system today. The character Lucy (Anais Granofsky) interviews various students about their feelings towards the new condom machines:

Clutch (Steve Bedernjak): "There's no way I'd use condoms, I mean, suppose you're getting all hot and heavy with this chick, there's no way I'd say, 'Excuse me while I slip into some latex.' There's no way."

Spike, a teenage mother (Amanda Stepto): "I think some kids are going to have sex whether their parents like it or not so we should at least try to protect them against pregnancy, I can tell you about that, and disease."

Kathleen (Rebecca Haines): "Condom machines should not be in school bathrooms. That condones sex. It's like saying, 'Here! We know you're doing it.' It makes it easier. If the machines weren't here I know a lot of people who would think twice about having sex."

Melanie (Sara Ballingall): "The fact is a lot of people aren't going to use them. I can't see myself walking in to a bathroom and buying them. It's embarrassing. I don't want all of my friends to know [if] I'm having sex."

At the doctor's office, Dwayne explains his own reasoning for not having used a condom for protection during sex. He says that his girl-friend was taking birth control pills; that the sex was unplanned; that he did not have a condom and did not want to ask her for one. Eventually Dwayne has to admit that he is HIV positive: "I didn't do anything wrong. I was just careless that's all. And now I'm going to die."

Other *Degrassi* episodes address misconceptions about safe sex as well. In the *DJH* episode "It's Late," Spike believed that she did not have to use protection because she thought she could not get pregnant the first time she had sex, and when Heather asked her sister Erica about whether she used condoms, Erica responded that she did, "most of the time." Both Spike and Erica became pregnant when they did not practise safe sex. Other episodes showed characters learning how to use condoms through sex education courses, talking with friends or by asking a boyfriend if he had condoms — important steps in teaching teenage girls responsibility and agency over their own sexual activity.

Although the topics of AIDS and abortion were forceful approaches to addressing sex, *Degrassi* also used less dramatic storylines to illustrate what modern teenagers were dealing with on a daily basis. In *DJH*'s "Dream On," Arthur K (Duncan Waugh), who had a problem with erotic dreams on *DJH* in "Great Expectations," once again experiences sexual frustration that culminates in a series of dreams about the popular girl, Caitlin (Stacie Mistysyn), on whom he develops a crush. Similarly, other characters em-bodied the frustration and confusion that accompany sexual development, as in "Just Friends," when a female character is left feeling embarrassed after having flirted with a male friend only to be rejected.

Degrassi's representation of teenage sexuality ranged from the extreme to the mundane, just like real life. More teenagers were having sex in 1990 than in previous years, and it was a peak time for teenage pregnancy in the United States.[5] Although there has been a 17 percent drop in teenage pregnancy in the U.S., the rate of teen pregnancy in the mid-1990s was more than double that of Canada's.[6] *Degrassi* and *Beverely Hills 90210* both portrayed teens having sex, but only the *Degrassi* series reflected statistics that were current with the time.

MONEY: "EVERYBODY WANTS SOMETHING"

One facet of teenage life that has been addressed on *Degrassi*, *SBTB* and *90210* is money: how to get it, how to spend it and what to do if you do not have it. Some episodes of these shows took a direct approach to addressing social class, and two of the shows wove the concept of class and money throughout the series, using subtle, consistent themes to approach the topic. The most overt display of class differences was illustrated on *90210*, whose entire premise was based on the interaction between the middle class and the upper class.

90210 used economic status as a revolving plot line, juxtaposing the normalcy of the middle-class Walshes with the decadence of their Beverly Hills neighbours to create ongoing themes of difference. In the third episode of the series, Brenda goes shopping with her new friends and is embarrassed by the fact that she cannot afford all the same clothes her classmates can. In the same episode, Brandon becomes a waiter at an upscale restaurant, only to quit after being treated poorly and realizing that his minority co-workers were being paid less than minimum wage. After quitting the upscale restaurant, Brandon gets new job at a local diner, owned by a tough-talking but caring blue-collar man. At the end of the episode, the Walshes end up hiring a maid. This episode introduced us to the income divide between the Walshes and their neighbours, but it also showed us that the Walshes were upwardly mobile yet sill hard working and grounded.

Despite this slight change in status, we still see subtle signs of class difference between the Walshes and their peers. Brandon struggles to maintain his car, and Brandon and Brenda continue to be awestruck by their wealthy friends' glamorous families and lives. In other episodes, Brandon again champions the working class by helping both a fellow student and the maid's niece maintain their illegal status as West Beverly High School students when really they come from other school districts. One core character depicted as working or lower middle class was Andrea (Gabrielle Carteris) who stood apart from the Walshes and the Beverly Hills elite. The *90210* portrayal of low-income characters was as reductive as the portrayal of middle- and upper-class characters: the rich were troubled, the poor were noble and the middle-class Walshes were observers of these two different types of lifestyles.

SBTB, for the most part, made its characters as homogenous as possible.

The lack of demarcations between the characters reflected the common belief of American exceptionalism[7] — that is, that in America there is no detrimental effect of social class. While *90210* used this construct to illustrate that anyone can succeed regardless of their class, *SBTB* used it to illustrate that in America there is no such thing as social class. In the single episode of *SBTB* that focused on money, "The Prom," one character's father was laid off from his job at the defence department right before the big night. After daydreaming about the dress she was going to wear, the character Kelly (Tiffani-Amber Thiessen) is interrupted by her father (John Mansfied) with the bad news.

Kelly: "Is something wrong?"

Father: "I'm afraid so ... world peace broke out."

Kelly: "But that's good, isn't it?"

Father: "For the world yes, but not when you work for a defence plant. I lost my job today."

After learning of her father's employment situation and wanting to contribute to the family funds, Kelly gives back the money her father gave her the previous week for her prom expenses. Embarrassed by her father's lack of employment and her own lack of a dress, Kelly cancels her prom plans, leading her boyfriend Zack to think there is something wrong with their relationship. Eventually, Zack discovers the real reason she can't go to the prom and surprises her with a nighttime picnic outside the dance. Kelly's socio-economic status and her father's employment situation are never mentioned again.

On *Degrassi*, the characters were not economically polarized as they were on *90210* nor were they completely homogenous as on *SBTB*. Money and the need for it, however, were constant themes throughout the show. While some characters like Lucy had wealthier parents, others had parents who worked average blue-collar jobs. The most overt reference to social class occurred on *Degrassi Junior High* when Arthur's mother won the lottery. While the characters are originally overjoyed at the news, it eventually becomes a hardship for Arthur, who temporarily loses his best friend Yick (Siluk Saysanasay), a very poor refugee. The two reconcile, but the subject of Arthur's new wealth continues to surface all the way into *Degrassi High*, where many students try to take advantage of his money.

More common fiscal situations appeared throughout the *DH* series, one of which was Joey's constant need for money — for a car, a demo tape or a trip to a strip club. The extremity of his desperation is shown in the episode "Bad Blood," which has him walking through the cafeteria naked in order to raise money to buy a car. After only saving $75 from his summer job, Joey has to come up with the rest of the $3,000 for a used car. First he turns to his parents for a loan. They inform him that they do not have enough money at the moment but may be able to help him in the upcoming months. Since he has to make a down payment within the day, he decides to take bets as to whether or not he'll go through with the "naked stunt." By doing it, he raises $314, which might be considered a small amount on *90210*, but is worth the humiliation on *DH*.

DH's Michelle, who struggled with stimulants to maintain her hectic work and school schedule, continuously worried about her financial situation. She rented a cramped apartment with loud roommates because it was the cheapest she could find, and worked overtime in order to pay her bills. In addition to the stimulant addiction, she strained herself academically and emotionally trying to earn enough money to care for herself. Eventually she opts to move back in with father rather than continue to jeopardize her grades, but she still works part-time in order to pay rent to her father and have some financial freedom.

Michelle's character is a very honest portrayal of the delicate balance between work and school with which many teenagers struggle. On *90210* and *SBTB*, some characters held down after-school jobs, but it was out of interest instead of necessity. On *90210*, Brandon's decision to work at the Peach Pit Diner after his falling out at the upscale restaurant was not a decision based on financial obligations. If he were working in order to pay rent and bills, he may have decided to remain at the fancier restaurant where he was sure to get better tips instead of quitting to protest unequal wages and seeking out another job.

As on *90210*, Kelly on *SBTB* worked after school at a local teen hangout, not out of necessity (despite the brief scare of her father's unemployment) but out of desire. Although she appears to work at a diner almost every day, she never complains about the hours and money and she never refers to the stress of her job and school responsibilities. *SBTB* provides a picture of teenage employment as one that allows plenty of free time, is not tiring, doesn't directly relate to money and is never stressful. Consequently, the message is conveyed that money and work are effortless and are not necessarily synonymous. On *SBTB*, it appears that money is always present and work is something one only does if one feels like it.

Serious Treatment of Serious Issues

Saved by the Bell, Beverly Hills 90210 and *Degrassi High* each addressed drugs, sex and money in its own way. Despite the statistics that show how prevalent drugs and sex were among teenagers in Canada and the United States during the 1989–91 period, only *DH* represented the reality of the times.

Representations of drug use on *DH* varied greatly, from casual smoking and drinking to experimentation with marijuana and stimulants. On *90210* and *SBTB* the characters used drugs and alcohol either accidentally or to improve their academics. Only the deviant atypical characters on *90210* used alcohol deliberately, and even they didn't use marijuana. The one character on *SBTB* to use drugs only did so under unrealistic amounts of stress and was able to quit within the same episode. While *DH* also used the plot line of an overachieving student to demonstrate the effect of stimulants, the scenario was much more realistic and more fully developed over several episodes. On *SBTB*, Jessie stops abusing stimulants after one friend intervenes, but on *DH*, Michelle did not stop using stimulants until she fainted, regardless of her boyfriend's pleas. Considering that approximately 50 percent of American teenagers have reported trying marijuana at least once,[8] the fact none of the characters on *SBTB* or *90210* experimented with it in any episode is highly implausible.

Sex on American programming was represented almost as unrealistically as drug use. If characters did have sex, it was either because, like Kelly of *90210*, they were "different" from regular teenagers or, like Brenda and Brandon, they wanted to lose their virginity. Male teenagers such as Brandon and Dylan on *90210* had more leeway with their sexual activity, which is why they were not labelled based on how many women they had had sex with, nor was their level of sexual activity the definitive trait of their characters. Female characters such as Donna and Brenda remained virgins or lost their virginity to their more experienced boyfriends. On the few occasions where characters did have sex, there were positive outcomes if it took place in the context of the romantic consummation of a long-term relationship. The negative outcomes of sex were no more than embarrassment in Kelly's case. Although there were, and still are, more teen pregnancies in the U.S. than in Canada,[9] television programming in the U.S. did not show anything more severe than Brenda's pregnancy scare.

Teenage pregnancy had already been addressed on *DJH*, and two episodes that focused on a teenager having an abortion started off the *DH* series. The show did not begin with the character already having had the abortion, but rather took the viewers through every step, from Erica learning that she was pregnant, to deciding what to do and dealing with the objections of family, friends and anti-abortion protestors. The character who had the abortion wasn't a rebellious or unusual teenager but quite normal and religious. *DH* showed a realistic situation that many average teenagers find themselves in and developed the story throughout the series, rather than in one episode, to more effectively convey the emotional impact of abortion.

Sexually transmitted diseases were only brought up in the form of HIV and AIDS on *90210* and *DH*. *Degrassi High*, however, took greater steps in advocating safe sex in general and, though *90210* did make a statement that anyone can be infected with AIDS, the show still did not demonstrate this possibility in any of its core characters. *DH* put a main character with HIV in the classroom to demonstrate that anyone could contract AIDS, including a teenager who was sexually careless. *SBTB* did not address the topic of sexually transmitted diseases at all.

DH was also much more realistic and varied than *90210* and *SBTB* in its depiction of social-class differences and in the overall economic diversity of its cast. On *SBTB* money was never an issue, and on *90210* money and social-class differences were used as pivots around which the show revolved. In these two shows the concept of social class was either ambiguous or polarized, but only in a positive direction: that is, it was never suggested that class struggles are a dominating facet of American society. Characters were either upwardly mobile, like the Walshes on *90210*, or uniformly middle class as on *SBTB*. *DH* had characters who would be found in any typical public school. Students ranged from upper to working class, and most of the students worried about money at some point. Many of the characters were constantly trying to borrow money from parents, and in the episode "Bad Blood," Joey explicitly laments that his parents don't have enough money to give him a small loan. The need for money is one facet of teenage life many viewers can relate to, yet in *SBTB* and *90210* it is overlooked. While sex and drugs in youth programming are often taboo, social class is simply ignored.

DH was more diverse and realistic than *SBTB* and *90210* in every aspect of teenage life. The characters on *SBTB* were homogenous and *90210* based all of its diversity on the Midwestern versus Beverly Hills premise. Critics of realistic programming like *DH* argued that by exposing teenagers to sex and drugs on television the show encouraged the same behaviour in viewers. What the critics may not have taken into account was that risky behaviour was on the rise in the 1980s and 1990s and there was very little difference in behaviour between American and Canadian teenagers, despite which programs were popular.

Degrassi High candidly and pragmatically provided insight to the average life of teenagers. The show portrayed friendships, love, problems and anger while also offering advice and lessons. Through the diversity of the cast and plots, any type of teenager could find a character to whom they could relate; not in a distanced or idealized manner, but realistically and truthfully. *Degrassi High* reflected the regular trials and tribulations of teens, and whether it was socially acceptable or not, a lot of those problems revolved around drugs, sex and money — facets of teenage life that other programs chose to misrepresent, simplify or disregard.

NOTES

1. "Statistical Summaries." *Prevention Source BC.* Retrieved March 10, 2003, from www.preventionsource.bc.ca/statsheets/prevalence.htm.

2. K.A. Chandler, C.D. Chapman, M.R. Rand and B.M. Taylor, *Students' Reports of School Crime: 1989 and 1995,* NCES 98-241 / NCJ-169607 (Washington, DC: U.S. Departments of Education and Justice, 1998). Available from www.ojp.usdoj. gov/bjs/pub/pdf/srsc.pdf.

3. "HIV/AIDS Epi Update." *Health Canada.* Retrieved January 26, 2003, from www. hc-sc.gc. ca/hppb/hiv_aids/can_strat/strat_admin/backgrounder.htm.

4. "Youth and HIV/AIDS." *Wellington, Dufferin, Guelph Health Unit.* Retrieved April 30, 2003, from www.wdghu.org/topics/sexualhealth/hiv_youth.htm.

5. "Teen Pregnancy in Canada and the Provinces, 1974-1998." *B.C. Teachers Federation.* Retrieved March 10, 2003, from www.bctf.ca/ResearchReports/99sd01/report.html.

6. "Teen Pregnancy and Birth Data." *National Campaign to Prevent Teen Pregnancy.* Retrieved April 30, 2003, from www.teenpregnancy.org/resources/data/national.asp.

7. Louis Hartz, *The Liberal Tradition in America* (New York: Harcourt Brace Jovanovitch, 1955).

8. Chandler et al., *Students' Reports of School Crime.*

9. "Teen Pregnancy and Birth Data," as per note 6.

PART III

WEB SITES, FAN CLUBS

& REMINISCENCES

CHAPTER 13

DEGRASSI.CA:
BUILDING A FAN COMMUNITY ONLINE

Mark Aaron Polger

ONE OF MY FIRST EXPERIENCES of going online in the early 1990s was to search for information on *Degrassi*. Unfortunately, there were only a few episode guides and a few Web pages here and there. The show had ended in 1992, and I had wondered if there were any newsgroups on the Internet devoted to the show. I was also curious to see if it was shown in reruns in other countries. I remember finding three Web sites about *Degrassi* and feeling a sense of nostalgia. It was nice to see other fans devoting their time and energy to a television show that meant a great deal to them. Over the previous ten years, I had collected newspaper and magazine articles, episode guides sold by WGBH Boston and news clippings; I felt a strong need to contribute to the online fan community but did not know how to create a Web site.

In the fall of 1995, I decided to learn how. I took out books on HTML and over the next few months, using a variety of online tutorials, I learned basic HTML. I started with a one-page Web site all about myself. It was called "Dr. Doolittle's Rainbow's Homepage." That nickname was created because of my love for animals and tie-dye patterns. I downloaded free HTML editors like Coffee Cup, Hippie and HotDog. I practised creating other Web pages and I learned how to upload them to the small space on Concordia University's Alcor server. Although the "Doolittle" site started out as a brief bio with a list of a few links to my favourite sites, it grew into many pages. By the next year, I gave my site the name "Mosaic" to describe the medley of links to various sites.

Eventually, I got bored with my own Web site and decided to start developing a site for one of my four favourite television programs: *Degrassi, Thirtysomething, The Wonder Years* and *Sisters*. Since I had collected so much information about *Degrassi* over the years, and had written a research paper on it in grade nine, I decided it would be a *Degrassi* Web site and began to develop it in the summer of 1997. Over the years "Mosaic" was moved to its present location at www.degrassi.ca/mark/ and I have been updating it ever since. In 2001, when I moved to Toronto and ventured off into other Web projects, two of my friends and I started the site www.torontobrunch.com, a searchable database of restaurant reviews in the Greater Toronto Area.

This chapter discusses how I developed the *Degrassi* site from scratch and how it grew to be one of the largest and most comprehensive of all *Degrassi* fan sites. It also discusses how I initiated the first-ever Degrassi electronic mailing list and co-organized the first-ever *Degrassi* convention in Toronto.

GOING ONLINE

I first went online in the summer of 1994 while attending Marianopolis CEGEP (a post-secondary college) in Montreal and working at the circulation desk of the Georges P. Vanier Library at Concordia University. I checked out material, checked in material, served library patrons and did some shelving in the stacks. During our Saturday shift, the security guard, Jeff, sat and talked to us about a new phenomenon called the Internet. He claimed that the Internet was a network of computers sharing information, which was mostly used by universities across the United States and Canada. He also mentioned that it was used by the U.S. military.

I expressed no interest since I was not in university yet and I was not in the military. How could the Internet benefit me? Why would I want to check it out? He told us we could access the Internet on our "dummy terminals"[1] that contained the circulation software and the library catalogue. He also showed us LYNX, a text browser for the Web. He told us that the World Wide Web was like one big library catalogue that could search through many topics quickly. For fun, I searched for the song lyrics of an old Annie Lennox album. I was so excited when I found what I was looking for. Jeff talked about downloading and uploading and I was ignorant to this new jargon. I began taking out books about the Internet, big thick, guides from the *For Dummies* series. Their covers were always illustrated by a spinning globe with consumer goods attached to it, like books, clothing and other goods. I was also introduced to a system called Pine, a textual e-mail editing program.

In addition to being introduced to the Internet, I was also introduced to newsgroups, often refered to as USENET. These were modelled after online bulletin board systems (BBS) developed in the 1980s, which allowed people to enter subject-specific online forums where they could post messages to one another on a particular topic. I hadn't known that electronic mail went back to the mid-1970s and the Internet back to the late 1960s, and that the Web had been created in the late 1980s. My Internet searches for *Degrassi* lead me to a newsgroup called alt.tv.degrassi, which does not exist anymore. (The current *Degrassi* newsgroup is at rec.arts.tv.) The first newsgroup was created and initiated by a Concordia student I used to serve in the library. Her name is Jennifer Hollett, and she is now a popular personality with MuchMusic in Toronto. Below are her two postings to the *Degrassi* newsgroup. The second one announces the successful creation of the newsgroup alt.tv.degrassi. (Please note that Jennifer Hollett's e-mail address is no longer valid.)

From:oneofthose(j_holle@alcor.concordia.ca)
Subject: PROPOSAL alt.tv.degrassi
Newsgroups:alt.config
Date: 1996/05/16

alt.tv.degrassi   gee, i gotta go to school

The newsgroup alt.tv.degrassi will provide the opportunity for discussion, analysis, and reflection on the Canadian Degrassi series millions around the world have come to know and love. Discussion and postings can pertain to: *The Kids of Degrassi Street, Degrassi Junior High, Degrassi High, School's Out and Degrassi Talks.*

Related WWW sites:
http://www.fl.net.au/~parasail/degrassi.htm
http://www.tcc.co.uk/inside/highlights/degrassi.html
http://gaus.technion.ac.il/~nashtir/degrassi.html
http://www.libertyst.com

and an FAQ is already in progress.

I welcome all comments and suggestions.
Jennifer Hollett
j_holle@alcor.concordia.ca

   ★

From j_holle@alcor.concordia.ca Mon Jul 15 23:08:53 1996
Date: Fri, 12 Jul 1996 10:58:51 -0400 (EDT)
From: one of those <j_holle@alcor.concordia.ca>
Subject: alt.tv.degrassi now exists

Good news *Degrassi* Fans. My *Degrassi* newsgroup proposal has now gone through, and is in full effect. It can be reached at alt.tv.degrassi.

The charter: The newsgroup alt.tv.degrassi will provide the opportunity for discussion, analysis, and reflection on the Canadian *Degrassi* series millions around the world have come to know and love. Discussion and postings can pertain to *The Kids of Degrassi Street, Degrassi Junior High, Degrassi High, School's Out* and *Degrassi Talks*. Not all sites will carry this at first ... but here is some friendly advice from Anne Bennet of Concordia University's Computer Services. "You'll find that a lot of sites ignore alt hierarchy control messages, or implement them only by request of a local user. You might ask the Web sites you mention to put up a note that the group now exists, and say that users should request it from their local newsadmin." So if your school or server doesn't carry it, e-mail them and request it. Pass this info on to *Degrassi* Fan Alumni everywhere.

Playing With Time,
Jenn

THE DEGRASSI WEB SITE AND MAILING LIST

After looking through the newsgroups, I decided to check out *Degrassi* on the World Wide Web. In 1995, I found very little material. At the time there was only one *Degrassi* site, David Nashtir's from Israel. Oren Shay

(Israel) and Kim Gilmour (Australia) developed their sites in early 1996, but Nashtir's site was the most extensive. He received much help from fans around the world. He had sections for photos, video captures, sounds, an episode guide and interviews. Kim Gilmour was interviewed in 1999 about the history of her Web site. She claims to have started it in 1995 as a one-pager and quickly added more images and other information.

I interviewed Oren Shay on October 27, 1999, and he explained how he and his friend Guy Meiroz developed the *Degrassi* Fan Club site, a collection of character profiles, *Degrassi* images and wallpaper, screensavers and fan contributions.[2] In an interview with Sharon Mulholland, she explained that she created her site in the fall of 1996. Mulholland, a student at the time in York University's student residence, wanted to document all the *Degrassi* stories, sightings and updates that she was finding out about the former *Degrassi* cast members. It seemed like a fun idea for *Degrassi* fans to trade this type of information. At the time, she claimed all of this information was posted in her dorm room (on the door) but when she kept getting more information, she decided to put up a Web site. When I interviewed her, Mulholland claimed that she updated her site three to four times a year and that hers was the oldest Web site.[3] Angela Ferguson, from Australia, recalls that she put up her first *Degrassi* site in 1994 or 1995, at the end of high school or start of university.[4]

A.J. Taylor recalls putting up his Web site in February 1997. "I uploaded the *Degrassi* page ... and received many e-mails from people who 'remembered that show' and found my site funny, on the other hand I also got e-mail from people who couldn't take a joke and said I was a bad seed. Both sides of the e-mails are great however."[5] A.J.'s site was seen as a bad seed because his character profiles were slightly mean, sarcastic and sometimes cruel. Some people were offended when they read his politically incorrect comments.

In July 1997, the first phase of my *Degrassi* site was posted on the server of my ISP (Internet service provider), a teeny little place called aardvark. au. Soon after I discovered Alphalink, which is where the current pages reside. Posting the page was not a big decision. I enjoyed learning HTML (we didn't have WYSIWYG HTML apps back then, it was all in text), and I enjoyed the research. My *Degrassi* site went through two evolutions: the first site was a single long page, with very few graphics. It was basically a cast list and a patchy episode guide, with a preamble around what I thought of the show. The second site branched into multiple pages, there were more graphics and some comments on the *Degrassi* movie *School's Out*.

Here is the e-mail I sent out in late 1997 announcing my *Degrassi* mailing list, Web ring and my upcoming Web site (note that these e-mail addresses are no longer valid):

From: Mark Aaron Polger (ma_polg@alcor.concordia.ca)
Subject: Degrassi Mailing List, everyone is invited, SUBSCRIBE!!
Newsgroups: alt.tv.degrassi
Date: 1997/12/24

Hello Degrassi Fans,

My name is Mark Polger and I am a fellow member of the *Degrassi* Fan Club. I would like to take this opportunity to invite all members to a new *Degrassi* mailing list. The list will be all about the *Degrassi* television series. The *Degrassi* mailing list will come out in digest format once per week, with postings about the series, the fan club members and about trading *Degrassi* articles.

If you want to subscribe, please send an e-mail with the message "subscribe" in it to Degrassi_Digest@yahoo.com. There is no deadline, and the more the merrier. If the digest gets very busy, I will have to send out a digest twice a week, instead of once a week.

Any questions or comments about the *Degrassi* mailing list can be sent to me at ma_polg@alcor.concordia.ca.

Postings to the list are sent to Degrassi_Digest@yahoo.com. Any questions about the list or anything you want to know can go to my school address.

Thank you for taking the time in reading this e-mail.

Hope to hear from you soon,
Mark Polger
ma_polg@alcor.concordia.ca
Degrassi_Digest@yahoo.com
http://alcor.concordia.ca/~ma_polg

★

From: Mark Aaron Polger (ma_polg@alcor.concordia.ca)
Subject: Interested in joining a Degrassi Web ring?
Newsgroups: alt.tv.degrassi
Date: 1997/12/24

Hello Everyone!
I am in the process of making a *Degrassi* Web site, and so I thought it would be appropriate if all *Degrassi* Web sites united. I have created a *Degrassi* Web ring, and any *Degrassi* related Web sites are welcomed to join.

If you are interested in joining the *Degrassi* Web ring please let me know by e-mailing me with your name, URL and e-mail address. I will send you the html coding to put on your page to link us together.

Thank you,
Mark Polger
ma_polg@alcor.concordia.ca
Degrassi_Digest@yahoo.com

I contacted Oren Shay and Guy Meiroz of the *Degrassi* Fan Club in Israel and they sent me a list of their members' e-mail addresses. Shay and Meiroz were supposed to develop a mailing list but the project never materialized. I took this opportunity to create a digest format mailing list that could be distributed via electronic mail. I called it the *Degrassi* Digest and the first issue was sent on December 12, 1997. Over the years, the number of subscribers grew from 2,000 to 3,000, but currently there are fewer than 1,500. *Degrassi* Digest turned seven years old in December 2004 and continues to be a monthly compilation of postings made by subscribers that are sent to my e-mail addresses.

As I mention above, I started work on my *Degrassi* Web site in July 1997. By then I was in university and this was a school project for a computer course. I went to the professor and decided to work on it before the fall term started. I learned Microsoft Front Page, a Web page editor, because I needed to use it at my place of work (Canadian Jewish Congress National Archives). We were also encouraged to learn HTML code from scratch.

I wanted to transfer all of the information I had collected over the years into this project. As I mentioned earlier, since I was a teenager, I had been collecting magazine and newspaper articles, episode guides and news clippings. I had also done extensive library research to collect news articles to familiarize myself with the background and technical aspects of the show, its producers, the production company and the history of the show, all of which I wanted to share online.

My first version of the site was called "The Unofficial *Degrassi* Web Site," and was launched in January 1998. The following month I acquired the domain www.degrassi.org and in 2000 I acquired www.degrassi.ca.[6] The Web site began as a one-pager, containing an introduction, an episode guide to all seasons of *The Kids of Degrassi Street, Degrassi Junior High* and *Degrassi High.* I had scanned some photos and kept an archive page of all the *Degrassi* Digests. I also collected electronic news clippings, which I scanned and organized by date so that they were readily available for users to read and download.

In April 1998, Natalie Earl, a *Degrassi* fan from California, contacted me. She expressed an interest in helping me with my Web site and had initiated *Degrassi* World Fan Fiction, a fan fiction series that would accompany the Web site. From April 1998 to April 2000, Earl wrote most of the stories. As of October 2003, there were sixty-one "episodes" of *Degrassi* Fan Fiction. When Earl began to pursue other interests in late 2000, other writers began to contribute pieces.

There were various stories in the *Degrassi* Fan Fiction series. Some revolved around background characters, while other stories took place in the future. Some focused on *Degrassi* couples, while others continued storylines that began on *The Kids of Degrassi Street.* One set of stories was called "Degrassi: The Next Generation," which revolved around the character of Emma Nelson who attended Degrassi Junior High. Emma is the daughter of Spike, one of the characters from the original series. As well, there was a character named Paige, named after one of the *Degrassi* Web site owners with the same name. It is interesting to note that the new *Degrassi* television series, *Degrassi: The Next Generation,* focuses on Emma. Some *Degrassi* fans were angered and shocked to learn that their stories and characters were allegedly "lifted" from the Fan Fiction archive and made into episodes for the new show. To this day, Epitome Pictures has never acknowledged or given credit to *Degrassi* fans for their contribution to promoting a *Degrassi* community online and they have never given credit to any of the Fan Fiction authors who developed characters and stories similar to those of the new *Degrassi* series.

CREATING A SENSE OF COMMUNITY ONLINE

I wanted to create a sense of community in an online environment. The literature on community gives several definitions of the term. Some argue that community is restricted to people who live in a common physical location who share common beliefs, goals and values. The concept of the online or virtual community centres around people who share common interests and ideologies, values, goals and similar likes and dislikes, regardless of their physical location. A virtual community can be a bulletin board service that caters to *Star Trek* fans or stay-at-home mothers who share information about their caregiving techniques for their children, or a cancer support group in the form of a mailing list, newsgroup or Web site.

In his book *The Virtual Community: Homesteading on the Electronic Frontier*, Howard Rheingold chronicles his experiences in the mid-1980s with the WELL — the Whole Earth 'Lectronic Link (www.well.com). The WELL was one of the first online message boards on the Web where users could interact with one another in an online environment. Rheingold explains that to connect to his online community, he would plug his telephone into his computer and instantly be connected to thousands of people. He argues that independent communities took shape as people kept bumping into each other on the BBS (bulletin board systems, now referred to as USENET or newsgroups), and that community has nothing to do with physical vicinity or geographical location. He thinks that the sense of a virtual community has to do with common interests. Rheingold states that the development of virtual communities is "in part a response to the hunger for community that has followed the disintegration of traditional communities around the world."[7]

These virtual communities are based in chat rooms and conferencing systems. Rheingold goes on to say that members of virtual communities join together to do everything that others do in the physical world. The obvious difference is that members of online communities interact exclusively via text on computer screens. He describes it is as going into the same pub or coffee shop with the same group of people each time. He actually gets to meet his virtual friends in real life (i.e., offline) and attends weddings, parties and funerals. The virtual community, for Rheingold, has become an extension of his offline life.

Robin Hamman, a scholar in the field of cyber communities, has written a great deal about the virtual community and online relationships. He has teamed up with Rheingold to debate virtual communities on Electric Minds (www.minds.com), a Web site founded by Rheingold. In his article, "Introduction to Virtual Communities Research and Cybersociology Magazine" (which appeared in the first issue of *CyberSociology*, an online magazine dedicated to virtual communication on the Internet), Hamman illustrates that there are ninety-four sociological definitions of the term "community," which include the following elements: a group of people, sharing a social interaction, sharing common ties between themselves and other members of the group, and sharing a physical or virtual space for a specific time period.[8]

Based on Hamman's analysis, I have made the following observations about the *Degrassi* community:

- Members come from all walks of life, all socio-economic groups, all races and ethnicities

- Members are between the ages of thirteen and thirty

- Members have connected with the show because of high-school trauma— bullying, peer pressure, feeling oppressed, being left out, feeling alienated

- Members identify with one or more characters of the show

In his book, *The Great Good Place,* Ray Oldenburg illustrates how the demise of community can be blamed on the loss of what he refers to as the "great good place," which is the third place that is important to us in our everyday lives after home and work. In this third place, we meet members of our community on neutral ground, leaving possible divisions such as class or industrial rank at the door in the spirit of inclusion rather than exclusion. Oldenburg describes these third places — coffee shops, bookstores, bars, hair salons — as "the core settings of informal public life" that are necessary for a community to survive. These are places where members of a community interact with others and come to know the ties that they have in common.[9]

I would argue that for teenagers the "great good place" could be television, going out with friends to the movies, playing video games or, within the last seven to ten years, going online and interacting with others. Virtual communities allow users (teenagers and adults) to enter a new realm, escape their own realities and chat with someone from across the world. Over the last seven years more kids have been going online at a younger age. With the advent of online communities like degrassi.ca, mailing lists, chatrooms and message boards, there is more opportunity to develop online relationships and community.

TAKING COMMUNITY OFFLINE: HOSTING THE FIRST DEGRASSI CONVENTION

In early 1999, Natalie Earl and I decided to host the first-ever *Degrassi* convention in Toronto, Ontario. Living only five hours away in Montreal, I thought it would be an excellent idea, and Natalie and her husband Scott decided to make the trip from California. I did not have that much money, as I was an undergraduate student still living at home with my parents, so Natalie and Scott funded the convention. We promoted the convention through my Web site www.degrassi.ca, through word of mouth and by sending out periodic announcements in the *Degrassi* Digest. Natalie and I e-mailed some of the cast via electronic mail. Natalie contacted Linda Schuyler of Epitome Pictures and asked if she could send out official invitations to all of the *Degrassi* cast and crew. Natalie also asked Linda for financial help and for the loan of some memorabilia like *Degrassi* posters. (To this day, we do not know if those invitations were ever sent out. In a June 2000 conversation with Ms. Schuyler, she mentioned that she was not comfortable promoting the convention to the cast because two of the actresses from *Degrassi* had been stalked for several years and she didn't want to further endanger them.) We set up a Web page where people could register online to get a sense of how many people we could expect. I gave a deadline of one week before the convention but I kept checking my e-mail to see if anybody else registered.

Although we had invited all of the cast members, only seven came to the convention, along with forty fans from the Toronto area. It was held at the location where *Degrassi High* was filmed for two years, the Bell Centre for Creative Communications, which is part of the Centennial College campus at Carlaw and Mortimer Streets and is now called the Centre for Creative Communications.

From left to right: Michelle Goodeve (Ms. Avery), Cathy Keenan (Liz) and Anna Keenan (Rainbow), August 21, 1999.

From left to right: Michelle Goodeve (Ms. Avery), Darrin Brown (Dwayne) and Cathy Keenan (Liz), August 21, 1999.

From left to right: Michelle Goodeve (Ms. Avery), Daniel Woods (Mr. Raditch) and Roger Montgomery (Mr. Garcia) talking about their experiences playing teachers on the show, August 21, 1999.

From left to right on bottom row: Byrd Dickens (Scott), Darrin Brown (Dwayne), Cathy Keenan (Liz) and Michelle Goodeve (Ms. Avery), August 21, 1999.

The convention was held on Saturday, August 21, 1999, from 6:00 p.m. to midnight. I arrived in Toronto at 5:00 a.m. Saturday, had breakfast at a coffee shop near the bus station and checked my e-mail for last minute convention registrations. I met Natalie and her husband Scott at 10:00 a.m., and we got to work: we bought party supplies (helium balloons, chips, soda, cookies) and hired a security guard for most of the evening. We were given a PA system and we decorated the front area of the Centre with balloons, streamers, the framed posters of *Degrassi* shows that Kit Hood had lent us from his personal collection and other paraphernalia. When done, the entranceway resembled the set of "One Last Dance," the final episode of *Degrassi High*.

People started arriving at 6:00 p.m. and we greeted them at the front door. The surprise of the evening was an appearance by Corey and Laurie Mistysyn, mother and brother of Stacie Mistysyn (who played Caitlin). Another surprise was the appearance of Chris Nuttall-Smith, a reporter from the *Toronto Star* who arrived with a photographer. He interviewed several people, asked them where they were from and why they loved *Degrassi*. It was exciting to have a journalist and photographer stop by and they told us we might get front page news in the Monday issue. The cast in attendance were Cathy Keenan (Liz, Spike's best friend), Anna Keenan (an extra named Rainbow), Byrd Dickens (Scott, Kathleen's abusive boyfriend), Darrin Brown (Dwayne), Michelle Goodeve (Ms. Avery), Roger Montgomery (Mr. Garcia) and Dan Woods (Mr. Raditch). A highlight of the evening came when Darrin took everyone on a tour of the building and explained where everything took place. The building had been renovated in 1993, but most of the interior still looked the same. The exterior also still looked the same: the famous ramp had not changed and the outdoor courtyard (known as the quad on *Degrassi High*) remained intact.

This was an important event for Natalie and me because we wanted to meet many of the fans that we interacted with online and we wanted to share our experiences about how important *Degrassi* was to us when we were teenagers. This convention was a way of connecting, of being nostalgic and of meeting our fellow fans. Throughout the evening I had this permanent "high" feeling. I could not believe Natalie and I had pulled this off. Having the cast there was a way for fans to thank them for their work and having the fans there allowed other fans to connect and form new friendships. Natalie Earl recounted her experiences on her Web site "*Degrassi* Legacy":

That night, August 21, 1999, *Degrassi High* came back to life. Weaving through the room in a dreamy daze of pastel balloons and crepe paper streamers, fans finally interfaced with some of their favorite *Degrassi* faces. Michelle "Ms. Avery" Goodeve, escorted by her partner Glenn Norman, arrived in her satin blue *Degrassi Junior High* jacket and looked as young and beautiful as she did on the series. We were charmed by the appearance of Darrin "Dwayne" Brown. We rubbed elbows with Dan "Mr. Raditch" Woods who was accompanied by his wife Megan and two children. Roger "Mr. Garcia" Montgomery was escorted by his wife Lisa. Byrd "Scott the Bully" Dickens was escorted by his girlfriend Heather. A nice surprise was the appearance of Laurie and Corey Mistysyn (Stacie Mistysyn's mother and brother). Cathy "Liz" Keenan arrived with her sister Anna "Rainbow" Keenan and their mother. Darrin Brown became our impromptu tour guide, pointing out the condom machine battle, the principal's office and the resource center (the glorified euphemism for library). Everybody made a big deal about climbing the famous ramp where so many significant scenes happened and seeing "Liz," "Dwayne" and "Scott" together at arm's distance. Dan Woods delighted us with some obscure *Degrassi* trivia and some funny Mr. Raditch impersonations. His cute kids amused us by popping balloons and skipping about gleefully from their sugar highs. Glenn brought a rare *Degrassi* bloopers tape (ooooh, the grungy little *Degrassi* secrets revealed) and the pilot movie of *Flights With Mom*, which co-stars Stacie Mistysyn (as Dana) and Michelle Goodeve (as Kate) as a mother-daughter flight adventure team.[10]

That Monday (August 23), I was pleasantly surprised to find an article about the conference featured on the bottom half of the *Toronto Star*'s front page. Natalie and I were happy that we had such a successful evening. Of course we would have liked to have more cast and crew come but it was not widely advertised and there was not enough promotion. Nonetheless, we were very happy with the turnout. I was very nervous about meeting Natalie and Scott for the first time. I must admit it was awkward since we'd only corresponded via e-mail and phone and suddenly we were thrown together for an entire day and evening. Over the course of the day we did become more comfortable with each other. I would definitely organize another *Degrassi* convention if I had the time, extra money and the support of other *Degrassi* fans.

★

At the time of this writing, *Degrassi: The Next Generation* just ended its fourth season (February 2005) and a new generation of fans has emerged, with many old fans tuning into the show. Many original *Degrassi* fans have e-mailed me several times asking me to organize another *Degrassi* convention, but it isn't possible. I work full time and have little time to devote to the mailing list let alone the planning of a convention, although I do update my Web site several times per week by adding new content, mostly news items to the news database. Along with the new generation of fans, there are now close to fifty Web sites devoted to the *Degrassi: The Next Generation*. Some are very comprehensive, while others are merely photo galleries. The new generation of fans are more Web savvy and more comfortable with technology, thus their sites appear more professional. As of July 2003, Sharon Mulholland's site and mine were the longest-running Web sites devoted to the original series.[11] The original *Degrassi* will always be a memory in the minds of the original fans, but it is clear that the new series has a life of its own.

NOTES

All photos by Mark Aaron Polger.

* I would like to acknowledge the following people who are pioneers in their contributions to the development of an online *Degrassi* community: David Nashtir from Israel, Sharon Mulholland from Toronto, Angela Ferguson from Australia, Kim Gilmour from Australia, Oren Shay and Guy Meiroz from Israel, A.J. Taylor from Canada, and Jennifer Hollett from Canada. I would lastly like to thank Natalie Earl from California who co-organized the *Degrassi* convention with me in 1999. Lastly I would like to thank my family, friends and colleagues for listening to me talk about *Degrassi* all these years.

1. A dummy terminal is a workstation in a networked environment. Generally these terminals will have a monitor, network card, keyboard and mouse and are used in a corporate environment where there are several hundred computers to help save costs.

2. Oren Shay, interview with Mark Aaron Polger, October 27, 1999. Available at www. degrassi.ca/Interviews/.

3. Sharon Mulholland, interview with Mark Aaron Polger, n.d. Available at www. degrassi.ca/Interviews/.

4. Angela Ferguson, interview with Mark Aaron Polger, n.d. Available at www.degrassi. ca/Interviews/.

5. A.J. Taylor, interview with Mark Aaron Polger, n.d. Available at www.degrassi. ca/Interviews/.

6. In February 2000, I was contacted by Epitome Pictures about a future meeting to discuss the development of an official *Degrassi* Web site. I was excited as I thought I would be involved in the development of the site. Playing With Time, the production company responsible for *Degrassi*, was renamed Epitome Pictures in late 1992–early 1993 when Linda Schuyler parted with life partner and co-owner Kit Hood. In June 2000, I went to Epitome Pictures to meet Linda Schuyler and Stephen Stohn at which time I was asked to give my domain names www.degrassi. ca and www.degrassi.org (and others) to Epitome Pictures. The company wanted to use them for the official *Degrassi* Web site that would accompany the new program in development, *Degrassi: The Next Generation.* I refused. Following several months of discussion, I was served with a draft statement of claim in December 2000, which claimed that I was using my Web site in bad faith, that I had sold goods and services and that I was confusing the public with my Web site. I felt harassed, so I contacted the local, provincial and federal media, faxing them a press release (that can be found at www.degrassi.ca/index2.html). After much support from *Degrassi* fans online, Epitome Pictures/Playing With Time withdrew their allegations and registered their own domain as www.degrassi.tv. For additional information about this legal altercation, please see www.degrassi.ca/index 2.html.

7. Howard Rheingold, *The Virtual Community: Homesteading on the Electronic Frontier* (New York: Harper Perennial, 1993), 418.

8. Robin Hamman, "Introduction to Virtual Communities Researchand Cybersociology Magazine," *CyberSociology Magazine*, April 15, 2002. Available at www.socio.demon.co.uk/magazine/2/is2intro.html.

9. Ray Oldenburg, *The Great Good Place: Cafes, Coffee Shops, Bookstores, Bars, Hair Salons, and Other Hangouts at the Heart of a Community* (New York: Marlowe 1999), 72.

10. Natalie Earl, "My Degrassi Pilgrimage," *Degrassi Legacy*. Retrieved October 2003 from http://www.degrassi.ca/dl/convention/journey.htm. "*Degrassi* Legacy" was online from 1998 to 2000 and is permanently archived at http://dl.degrassi.ca.

11. In May 2005, Sharon Mulholland's site was taken down. It had not been updated since July 2003.

THE QUEEN'S UNIVERSITY DEGRASSI CLUB

Mark Janson

The Queen's University Degrassi Club (QUDC) celebrated its one-year anniversary in September of 2003. The club was started by three former Degrassi fans in hopes of sharing their love of this classic Canadian melodrama with others. The curious buzz that continually surrounded the QUDC throughout its first year of existence showed that the idea of Degrassi continues to resonate powerfully with the university community. Degrassi lovers have grown up but their sentimentality for the show seems to go beyond the episodes themselves to a point where the idea of Degrassi is valued in peculiar ways. To commemorate its first anniversary, outgoing QUDC president Mark Janson looks back on the first year of the club's existence ...

THE IDEA FOR THE QUDC came from the experiences of a bunch of shy frosh in Brockington House during the first few weeks of term in the fall of 1999. The mandatory "getting to know each other" games during frosh week and the first few keg parties had only glazed over the social awkwardness of first year. Deep down we all knew the bitter truth — that we were surrounded by new faces, each with a past completely disconnected from our own. For most of us on "Brock 2," this was our first time in such an environment, so we simply fell back on the power of numbers and travelled as a complete forty-five-person social group between the cafeteria, the bars and our residence. Logistically speaking, factions had to be made.

One afternoon during a channel-surfing procrastination session, a small group of us stumbled upon an episode of *Degrassi Junior High*. We were really excited to see the show again and watched the episode intently. Shared memories of a childhood television show may seem like shaky ground for a relationship, but for those lacking any other grounds, it was embraced. While we didn't know each other very well, we all knew the gossip about Joey Jeremiah, Ms. Avery and Claude, so watching the show and remembering all of its quirks helped to melt the ice between us. We laughed at the 1980s lingo, tried to remember the plots and constantly made jokes about Wheels's mullet and tight jeans. "*Degrassi* Hour" quickly became a part of our weekdays. Each week we posted a summary of upcoming episodes in the hallway so that our floormates could plan which classes to skip in case a big episode was coming up. Word of Brock 2's *Degrassi* Hour spread and we even recruited a few people from other residences, but our core group of about eight dedicated *Degrassi* fans remained. The highlight of our year was the trip to Toronto to attend the *Degrassi* reunion sponsored by *Jonovision*, an after-school teen talk show on CBC, hosted by Jonathan Torrens (which ran from1996 to 2001). Disregarding the fact that we all had exams the next morning, we borrowed a car and made the trek down to the CBC studios for the show, which was incredible. We were treated to behind the scenes information, met *Degrassi* cast members and witnessed the birth of the idea for *Degrassi: The Next Generation* (in the form of a letter from cult film director Kevin Smith, pleading for a continuation of the series).

When we returned to Queen's for our second year, we realized that the halcyon days of CBC's 4 to 5 p.m. airings of *Degrassi* were gone, so we decided to put more effort into school than into *Degrassi*. Two years later, we found ourselves in our last semesters of Queen's hungry for more *Degrassi*. With lighter course loads and a growing boredom with campus life, we decided it was time to resurrect the old *Degrassi* Hour, but this time we wanted to make it more than just a casual get together for our friends by forming an official Queen's University club. Days after this decision, Showcase began airing the show on Saturday mornings. It was like a sign from Kit Hood himself ...

After getting in touch with our student government about applying for official club status (their first reply: "an interesting idea"), we realized that becoming a club involved quite a lot of red tape. To become an official club at Queen's, we had to fill out a few applications, create a constitution ("We the *Degrassi* fans of Queen's University ..."), set up a Web site (www.myams. org/degrassi), fill out room allocation forms, establish an executive and so on. It seemed a bit funny to be going through all these bureaucratic formalities for a little club that did nothing more than watch 1980s television, but there was no way to sidestep university policy. Nevertheless, it was not long before the Queen's University *Degrassi* Club was recognized as an official club by the student government at Queen's University at Kingston.

We first grasped the response our club was going to have at Clubs Night — an annual showcase of all campus clubs where thousands of students stroll by display stands deciding which extracurricular activities they would like to join. Somehow we had been placed among prestigious clubs like UNICEF, Amnesty International and the Model UN. Despite feeling somewhat out of place, our booth held its own. We had worked hard on our classic three-panel "science fair style" presentation board, plus we had a TV showing episodes of *Degrassi* and we gave away free *Degrassi* stickers. Most people who passed by the booth would glance at us, do a double take, then laugh and move on. But of the thousands that passed us by, hundreds stopped and checked out the QUDC. It quickly became clear that we were among the most popular clubs there. As our list of potential members grew, so did the bitterness of the Astronomy Club beside us. Maybe this had something to do with the fact that we had six females signing up for every one male we recruited. By the end of the night, we had gathered a list of over 250 names and e-mail addresses of people who wanted to be kept up to date on QUDC activities.

Neilson and Jake of the QUDC "executive" work the booth at Clubs Night.

The QUDC Presentation Board

After the Clubs Night success we wanted to keep the momentum going, so we made some posters advertising our club and posted them all over campus and student neighbourhoods. Late one night, we put up hundreds of posters featuring headshots of Joey, Snake and Wheels — the quintessential *Degrassi* characters. These posters received a good response and the QUDC got e-mails from a number of people who enjoyed seeing The Zit Remedy's faces taped to telephone polls on the way to their 8:30 a.m. classes.

THE QUDC "EXECUTIVE" BRINGS THE ZIT REMEDY FOR
A SURPRISE VISIT TO THE QUEEN'S CAMPUS.

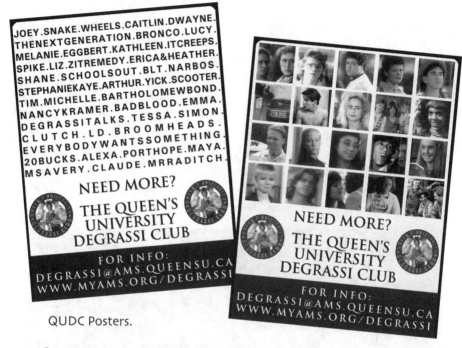

QUDC Posters.

Our growing presence around Queen's led to a few campus newspaper stories about the QUDC, which intensified interest in our club. *The Queen's Journal* said that we had "been creating a buzz on campus," called us a "Queen's sensation" and lauded our "unprecedented success."[1] Another campus paper, *Diatribe*, said the QUDC had created "the biggest buzz at Clubs Night."[2] It seemed that everybody was curious. People wanting to know more about the QUDC frequently stopped us on the street to chat. Somehow our Web site had gone global and soon our weekly e-mail updates were heading to *Degrassi* fans on four different continents who wanted to be kept up to date on the club's activities.

All of the commotion had given us high hopes for the first QUDC meeting. We booked a 350-seat lecture hall and printed off hundreds of our *Degrassi* surveys, to be used for the *Degrassi* Family Feud game later in the semester. Given the great response we'd had so far, we were surprised that only thirty people made it out to the meeting. Nevertheless, it was still a great time and it was a blast to watch the show with a group of people. After the first meeting, we relocated the QUDC meetings to a pub on campus where we met weekly for the rest of the year. After five or six of these weekly meetings, the faces of the QUDC members had become quite familiar and our group of loyal *Degrassi* fans gradually got to know one another. From MAs to PHDs to people who didn't even go to Queen's, it seemed that everyone enjoyed the meetings. Every week we watched two episodes (chronologically starting with the *DJH* episode #1, "Kiss Me, Steph"), talked about the shows and tried to stump each other with *Degrassi* trivia. We mixed up the meetings with other events too: *Degrassi* trivia championships, a "dress as a *Degrassi* character" theme party, guest speakers (Mark Aaron Polger of www.degrassi.ca and former *DJH* director and Queen's film professor Clarke Mackey), two eight-hour-long *Degrassi* marathons, *Degrassi* Family Feud, screenings of the *Jonovision* reunion, behind the scenes *Degrassi* tapes, the CBC documentary and the "*Degrassi* Raps" video.

CLARKE MACKEY TALKS TO THE QUDC ABOUT HIS DEGRASSI EXPERIENCES.

Throughout the year, we developed some QUDC merchandise, which always disappeared very fast. First there were the few hundred stickers we made for Clubs Night. We saw them on binders around campus and we heard reports from residence that frosh-room doors and telephones were covered with an assortment of our bright pink stickers, which read I Partied At Lucy's; I Am Wheels's Biological Father; or I ♥ [Insert *Degrassi* Character Here]. Midway through the year we branched out into QUDC clothing and kitchenware. Whether it was the "Zit Remedy Road Crew" QUDC hooded sweatshirt or the "Everybody Wants Something" QUDC coffee mug, our merchandise was always in hot demand. We intended to sell our stuff to only club members to help pay off our various costs, but news of this "hot" *Degrassi* merchandise spread fast. People who weren't even members of the club frequently spent forty dollars on a QUDC sweatshirt. Once a week a strange face came knocking at our door, looking to buy a QUDC mug. Eventually one of our sweatshirts sold on eBay for eighty dollars.

QUDC SWEATSHIRT PROTOTYPE #7 — CHOSEN BY A MAJORITY OF MEMBERS

Springtime brought the annual campus-wide flood of graduating high-school students touring potential universities with their parents. One day we got a call from the Queen's student government asking if they could use our club as part of their recruitment campaign. To our surprise, they had chosen the QUDC to help sell the image of the school on these tours. They borrowed our presentation board and some of our posters to use as part of their pitch to prospective students about the extracurricular activities Queen's had to offer. Kingston's cultural life has a difficult time comparing itself to that of Montreal or Toronto, thus it seemed that the student government wanted to use our club to help avoid the stigma of a cultural wasteland by showing that Queen's students did indeed have the opportunity to engage in some "alternative" culture. We found it kind of funny that traditional old Queen's, with all of its Ivy League aspirations, was using our little club as a selling point to prospective students.

Eventually classes came to an end for the year and final exams started. By this time, only the hard-core *Degrassi* fans were still coming out to QUDC events. We had a good turnout for our final screening of the year (the *Degrassi* TV movie, *School's Out*), but we could only muster eight QUDC members for the field trip to Toronto to tour the various *Degrassi* location sites and to meet up with Dan Woods (Mr. Raditch himself) for some drinks. As the shool year came to a close, things wound down quietly for the QUDC. We made a vague plan of how to keep the club going for the next year and then all headed into our final exams.

QUDC MEMBERS WITH DAN WOODS (MR. RADITCH) DURING A SNOWY YEAR-END FIELD TRIP TO TORONTO.

The first year of the QUDC was full of many bizarre and wonderful surprises that changed the way I look at *Degrassi*. I knew the show had a powerful cultural appeal, but I never dreamed it would affect so many people in so many different ways. Why did hundreds of people continue to want weekly e-mail updates of a club they were not even a part of? Why was our club featured in so much campus media, over all of the other clubs on campus? Why were people buying merchandise of a club they did not even belong to? Why was the QUDC suddenly worthy of being a poster club for Queen's? How had twenty people meeting weekly in a bar to watch an old TV show created such a fuss?

The answers to these questions probably lie somewhere between serious ideas like Canadian national identity and inferiority complexes combined with the frivolity of our sentimentality for the hideousness of growing up in the 1980s — ideas that are discussed in a more scholarly fashion elsewhere in this volume. What continues to shock me is that the incredible stir our club created far outweighed anything that we actually did. Our club created this buzz not because we did anything truly remarkable, but because the idea of *Degrassi* resonates so powerfully in the minds of our generation. This resonation ultimately found many different ends for the QUDC. Not only were we a hot topic of conversation but we also became a marketable force, promoting both retail products and an institution of higher learning. It seemed that although many people had no real connection to our club, they were quite happy simply knowing that our club existed. As the QUDC continues on this year, we will see if the students of Queen's are still so interested in our club, or if this kind of sentimentality only comes in small doses.

NOTES

All photos by Mark Janson.

1. Carolyn Coles, "Zit Remedy Playing This Monday," *The Queen's Journal*, 27 September 2002, 12; Kate Hopwood, "A Real Club with Real Clout: A Queen's Sensation: The One and Only Degrassi Club Is Here," *The Queen's Journal*, 19 September 2002.

2. Greg Hughes, "Everybody Wants Something," *Diatribe*, 26 September 2002.

CHAPTER 15

I Wasn't Born in the South, but I Got Here as Quickly as I Could

Sean Bilichka

Or so says the needlepoint in my kitchen. My mom received this gift after our third week in the great state of North Carolina. Our neighbour discovered she lived next to a genuine family of carpetbaggers and decided that this handmade object represented the Southern hospitality that is usually associated with the natives below the Mason-Dixon Line. As for me, I was not so readily impressed with my new home.

I was a precocious eleven year old, already missing my friends at my private school in Connecticut. Even worse, I had to go to a public school, midway through the term. Yes, I was entering into middle school and I had no friends.

In homeroom the next day, I sat in the back, in the corner, and stared at my West Woods Christian Academy folder, waiting for the first person to make fun of me. My mom had dropped me off for school far too early, and I sat there by myself with the teacher who, I'm pretty sure, never even noticed me. After about ten minutes, kids started filing in. No one sat at the desks. Instead, they grabbed beanbag chairs from a closet and began to set them up around the TV. At exactly 8:30, my homeroom teacher put down her book, walked over to the TV and turned it on.

"Wake up in the morning, feeling shy and lonely. Gee, I gotta go to school ..." I'm guessing that like me you can finish the rest of that song word for word, even if you can't get that last "Junior Hiiiigh" note. If ever my feelings have been more encapsulated in one song, it was at that moment in my life. I was shy and lonely. From my perch in the back of the room, I tried to catch up with the episode. It was the famous (or perhaps infamous) first performance of Joey Jeremiah and The Zit Remedy at the school dance. From the comments of the kids in the class, I could tell I had a lot to catch up on.

The semester went on, and despite my fears, I eventually did make a few friends. The morning ritual of beanbags and *Degrassi* lasted until I left middle school. Looking back, these daily viewings were when I first began to socialize with my new classmates. Yeah, sometimes it was hard to get past the Canadian accents, but then again, my New England accent didn't have the drawl of the eastern North Carolinian students in my classes either.

I think one key issue with my viewing of *Degrassi* is that we never watched the program in any particular order; I still don't understand why. Not just out of order in one season, but we would watch a video from season one then another from season three. I have always imagined some librarian just grabbing a video out of a stack and throwing it in the master VCR that sent the show to the televisions throughout the school. For me, on a Monday, Shane would jump off a bridge, but by Wednesday, he's eating dinner with Spike and his parents. I think this allowed me to focus more on a particular character in each episode and not be concerned with the overarching plot. I would never really focus on linking together all the events and occurrences or keep up with the minutia of the show. Each show had a lesson and executed it through a particular member of the cast. But beyond that, the disjointed nature of my viewing forced me to simply take each episode for what it was worth, because I often found if I got too wrapped up in thinking about what might happen to a certain cast member in the future, it would often happen that I did not see that episode for a week or two. Particularly problematic were the two-part episodes. Once I realized I was unable to watch the show with any kind of continuity, I just learned to like episodes for what they gave me.

The familiar pattern of watching the show every morning, with people who I was now getting used to, had a familiarizing effect on me. After a few weeks, I could talk about what I thought of Lucy's shoplifting habit at lunch, just like everyone else. I originally had very little in common with those around me, but *Degrassi Junior High* helped me to acclimatize socially and gave me a way to start up conversations with those around me; it helped me adapt to my new home in North Carolina, probably more than any needlepoint could. Between *Degrassi Junior High* and universal health care, I've got to think that the Great White North is doing something right.

TRUE TO MY SCHOOL:
AN AMERICAN'S LOVE AFFAIR WITH *DEGRASSI*

Brian C. Jones

"FOR THE LOVE OF GOD, WHERE THE HELL IS DAISY STREET?"

I must have asked that question sixty-eight times as I weaved through the seemingly aimless set of roads in the Etobicoke area of Toronto during the summer of 1999. Daisy Street was on my map, it really was. But for some reason, I kept running into Lake Ontario. It finally dawned on me, Daisy was on the *other* side of Lakeshore Drive. At that moment I realized that my lifelong dream of becoming an Etobicoke tour guide would never come true.

With the problem solved, I made the turn onto Daisy Street and my treasure was found. Standing before me on that beautiful summer afternoon was Vincent Massey School. To most, this was just a little school tucked away in the charming suburbs of Canada's largest city. To me, though, it was so much more. It was a place that had been such a big part of my adolescence and adulthood. It was the setting for a cast of characters that would teach, inspire and endear. This wasn't just a school, this was Degrassi Junior High.

★

Most people don't understand my genuine love and slightly unbalanced obsession with the Canadian melodrama set in the fictional community known as Degrassi. And I suppose I understand their lack of understanding.

Degrassi didn't get as much press, play or hype in the United States as other shows in the teenage genre like *Saved by the Bell* or *Beverly Hills 90210.* Few Americans have ever heard of the show at all and even fewer could tell you anything about Joey, Snake or Wheels.

Degrassi was a wonderful little gem that a small group of people in the United States — including me — had the honour of enjoying. *Degrassi* was a niche, a specialty store, a boutique and a trailblazer. It appealed to me in ways that other shows couldn't or didn't.

For me, that appeal has endured for almost twenty years. I can watch the same fifty-or-so episodes over and over again. They still entertain and they still make me laugh despite the fact that I know every turn that is coming and every twist in the plot. Like every other person I have spoken with about the show, I have often wondered why. What is it about *Degrassi* that has prompted such adulation and loyalty? This chapter seeks to answer — once and for all — that question. I don't know if I can do that completely, but there are a couple of things I do know.

I know I love *Degrassi's* clever writing and the sarcastic banter. I know I admire the courage it took the show's creators to tackle very difficult, complex and often controversial issues. I know I love the characters who feel so real that they very well might have lived next door to me when I was growing up. I love the honesty. Nothing is glossed over. Nothing is solved in one thirty-minute episode. As they do in real life, problems depicted on *Degrassi* persist and evolve, and then change and resolve. Most of all, I love the fact that this show was able to teach and entertain me as a teenager and then once again as an adult.

★

I watched my first episode of *Degrassi Junior High* in 1987, when I was thirteen. Growing up in Rhode Island, I was fortunate in that WGBH Boston (a public television affiliate) helped bring the Canadian series to the United States. While I don't remember the exact episode that first caught my eye, I do remember that it featured a gorgeous young lady named Stephanie Kaye. To say I was in love would be an understatement.

From that first encounter, I was hooked. I remember making sure that my schedule was clear every Friday night because of my date with Stephanie, er, *Degrassi.* Looking back, that was sort of stupid — I was thirteen. What plans would have really gotten in the way? From time to time, my parents would take my brothers and me out to dinner and I would need to make sure that our family's VCR was set to tape the night's episode. On more than one occasion, my older brother would feign kindness in helping program the machine, only to purposely set the channel to the evening news. He always was a jerk.

I eventually did get to see all of the episodes from that first junior high season of *Degrassi* and I quite literally loved every minute. I loved how real the characters were — they might have lived on my street. I loved the diversity, complexity and realism of the storylines. And man, did I love the fact that the show had no commercials. God I hated commercials as a kid. Actually, still do. And did I mention that I loved Stephanie Kaye?

As the years went on, I stuck with the *Degrassi* kids as we both moved from junior high into high school. It was strange, though, because the show seemed to be my own private special thing. No one else at school ever mentioned it and so I just assumed that no one else knew anything about it. And that was just fine with me. Like most things, I figured that less people meant less of a chance of a good thing being spoiled.

Degrassi became my secret addiction and, like most addictions, I wasn't quick to admit I had a problem. Looking back, I most certainly did. I ordered the teacher's guides and the cast newspapers and tried to get my hands on anything *Degrassi*. I memorized the actors' names, their hobbies and their favourite foods. It was a little scary at times. When you can answer the question "Name Nicole Stoffman's favorite snack" in a nanosecond with "Pizza," you know you have some problems.

The first and really only bit of *Degrassi*-related buzz at my high school occurred in my junior year when the famous season premiere "Erica is going to have an abortion" aired. There were stories in my local papers as well as in the big boys like *The New York Times*. People were talking about my little show and it was strange. I didn't particularly like it. It's sort of like when people suddenly discover a vacation getaway that they have known about and loved for a while. You get that scowl on your face and that feeling of "Go find your own cool thing. Leave mine alone."

The buzz soon died down, though, both at my school and in my life. As so often happens, priorities and interests change. For me, *Degrassi* was no different. I spent my senior year of high school and my first year of college focused on other things. As a result, I never got to see many of the final episodes and knew nothing of the now infamous *School's Out*. Instead, *Degrassi* became a memory that I would look back on from time to time with fondness.

Yet I never lost interest. In fact, on more than one occasion I looked into the possibility of purchasing the entire series on video. At the time, the price of the videos was right around three thousand dollars. They might as well have cost a million because I had about four cents to my name as a poor, broke college student. I would have to get my *Degrassi* fix somewhere else and somewhere cheaper. In the fall of 1996, I finally found that place.

It was in that year that the Internet had really established itself as the place to find information. And while surfing the Web on a particularly slow day at work, I decided to run a search on my old friend, *Degrassi*. I was amazed at how much information I found. Fan sites in the hundreds. Episode guides and cast interviews. Candid production photos. I must have spent the next five hours looking through it all. It was as if I had stumbled upon a huge trunk of lost family photos and mementos.

Through my research, I made two important discoveries. The first was that *Degrassi* was filmed in Toronto. I had no idea. In fact, because the show was distributed through WGBH, I assumed that it was produced in Boston. The other thing I found — which was far more important — was the strong *Degrassi* fan base. Amidst the endless posts, I found e-mail addresses of people who had something I wanted: copies of all the *Degrassi* episodes. And not for three thousand dollars.

Some of these folks had no desire to help me out. Others wanted hundreds of dollars. *Hey pal, Voula would be ashamed and also, that's illegal.* But one guy agreed to help me out. He only wanted one thing in return — a Degrassi street sign. At first, I really didn't know how I was going to fulfill my end of the bargain. Short of heading to Toronto and ripping one down from a lamppost, there were few options. So I went to a graphic design shop and had one created American style; it was Kelly green with white writing and cost me a mere fifteen bucks.

Fifteen bucks for ten tapes of every episode. Without question, those were the best fifteen dollars I ever spent. We made the trade and when my videos came (after what seemed to be an eternity), I started watching. All the memories of the show I loved so much came flooding back. And with them, the memories of what was going on in my life at the time. I had a wonderful time getting reacquainted with Spike and Dwayne and Yick Yu.

And I finally got to see all the shows I had missed when they originally aired.

I also got to see the *Degrassi* finale, *School's Out*, for the first time and to say I was affected would be an understatement. And not in a good way. It was so raw and so damn depressing. I was pretty shocked the writers chose to end such a genuinely upbeat and inspiring series in this way. Because I wouldn't have believed you if you had told me that Wheels was going to end up a drunk-driving killer (including a baby?!?), Lucy was going to end up blind and almost dead, Joey was going to employ a Kennedy-esque love of philandering only to leave one girl broken-hearted and the other pregnant, and Snake was going to betray years of friendship by selling out his best friend.

The movie left me disappointed and confused. But hey, even the best pitchers have a bad game once in a while. It's too bad though that *School's Out* was *Degrassi's* last chapter (until recently with the advent of *Degrassi: The Next Generation)* and the one that served as the final answer to any lingering questions. I can think of no better movie that would benefit from an alternate ending as a DVD feature. Thank goodness *TNG* helped provide that different ending for me.

Despite the experience, I must have watched my video tapes six hundred times during those first few months of having them. Every time I did, I found new and interesting things I hadn't seen or heard before. I picked up jokes and references the crews and writers put in and figured out the context that made them so funny. I listened closely to the often hilarious announcements that would play faintly in the background on the school's PA system — announcements like "The final changes to the altered exam schedule have been changed." I loved the witty dialogue that was missing from so many other television shows, including those geared towards adults.

After wearing the heads out of two VCRs watching my videos, I decided to develop different ways to fulfill my interest in *Degrassi*. And so I thought it would be a great idea to plan a trip to see all the places on my tapes in person. It was time to go north. I had never been to Canada and to be honest, really had no idea where the hell Toronto was. But thanks to the Internet once again, I was able to "Magellan" out a plan.

Also around that time, I had read an interview with Mr. Raditch himself, actor Dan Woods. At the end of the interview, Woods's e-mail address was listed. Not fearing much of anything, yet not expecting anything either, I sent off a quick note to him asking what *Degrassi* landmarks I should hit. To my amazement, Woods sent back an e-mail outlining every place I needed to go and even offered to show me around in person.

I was shocked and amazed at his gesture of kindness. Unfortunately, bad weather forced me to postpone my trip and thus miss out on my guided tour. But to this day, I can't adequately express how impressed I was with Dan Woods's generosity. I'm not sure Mr. Raditch would have been as nice.

Six months later I finally did make it to Toronto and to all the sites from *Degrassi* lore. Degrassi Junior High. Degrassi High. The school from *The Kids of Degrassi Street*. The Degrassi Grocery (warning if you go, the owner isn't particularly kind to Degrassi gawkers). The hospital where L.D.'s dad dealt with angina. The clinic where Spike found out she was pregnant. The store where Joey got Clutch to buy him beer (I always laugh at the name — "The Beer Store"). And on and on. What a wonderful trip on a beautiful weekend.

For me, seeing things in person has always carried a special impact, much more so than seeing them on television or reading about them in books. Being able to stand in the spaces, breath in the air and look around at the same places people of interest to me have is the best way to learn, experience and enjoy life. This journey was no exception. I returned home to America and immediately started to identify other sites to visit on my next trip to my neighbour to the north.

That visit came two years later. A little more familiar with Toronto's layout, I moved around the city with greater ease and being a creature of habit, I revisited many of the sites I had visited before. This time though, one of my stops was exciting in a whole new way. This was due to the fact that it was November, Centennial College was in session, and its doors were open. I would actually get to walk the halls of Degrassi High. Yes, I fully acknowledge that I am a dork. Despite more than ten years having passed since the show was filmed there, the school looked remarkably similar to how it was seen on television. The old school ramps, the lunchroom, the courtyard, the stairs, everything. I walked around the school as if I were a student — up one hallway and down another. I can't even imagine what the real students must have thought of my creeping around. Then again, I didn't really care. This was an exciting moment for me.

With that experience under my belt, I felt that I had done a pretty good job pretending to be a site scout for Playing With Time circa 1990. Like most addicts, though, I still wanted more. So I decided to take off (just like Wheels) to the Ontarian coastal town of Port Hope.

The thing that was so silly about that idea was that I based my entire trip on the theory that the things and places I saw on television that were supposedly in the town of Port Hope were actually there. To my great surprise and excitement, they were. The drive to Port Hope also held another surprise. By chance, I pulled down the same dirt road that the travelling salesman did when he tried to molest the wayward Wheels. (For the record, that episode is the greatest reason why I have never attempted to hitchhike in my life.)

The discovery came as I tried to get a better view of one of the most beautiful sunsets I had ever seen. Wanting to see it from the shores of Lake Ontario, I pulled off the highway and made my way down a dirt road towards the great lake. About a half mile down, I said to myself, This looks really familiar. My suspicions were confirmed when I came to a turn in the road with a bridge up above. This was it. This was where poor Wheels learned why walking always beats hitching a ride, no matter how many miles you need to go. A picture I took and compared with the video of "Taking Off, Part One" when I got home confirmed my thoughts about the spot. The *Degrassi* gods certainly were smiling down on me that day. That or I was just damn lucky.

Later that night I got lucky again. After making it to Port Hope, I began searching for the hotel Wheels's father Mike was staying at while playing with his band. Port Hope ain't all that big so I didn't think it was going to be that hard a location to find, but the darkness wasn't helping. On my last pass around town, the hotel caught the corner of my eye. Again, it didn't look any different at all from how it appeared on the show. I walked in the front door and saw the famous (well to me at least) staircase Wheels walked up to his father's room. I actually contemplated walking up too, but the hotel manager came down and asked if I wanted a room. Realizing that a response of "No, I just really want to walk up your stairs" might get me arrested or shot, I feigned interest by asking the rate and quickly exited. As I pulled away, I got a glimpse of Mem'ries Lounge too. With that, I left Port Hope a very happy camper.

I am currently trying to come up with new *Degrassi* landmarks to visit while on future trips to Toronto. It's a great town and a great way to continue being a *Degrassi* fan. And man, there are a lot of fans out there throughout the world. Fans like me that can watch the same episodes a hundred times. Fans making pilgrimages to Toronto and Port Hope. Fans anxiously waiting for a new chapter in a beloved story.

So when the announcement came that Linda Schuyler and Epitome Pictures were going to produce that new chapter in the form of *Degrassi: The Next Generation*, I was excited, but cautiously excited. I sort of had that feeling that comes when you hear that a sequel to an old movie you love is coming out. You are pumped up, but a little nervous at the same time. It could be great or it could totally suck. Now that I have watched many of the episodes, I have mixed feelings. The writing is good and the storylines are timely, but the show just doesn't grab me the way the original did. It seems too polished, too professional and too MTV. It reminds me of *90210* or *Saved by the Bell*. All of the actors are great looking and smart and well spoken. That isn't to say the cast of the original series didn't have these qualities, but rather it just doesn't seem as real. I feel like I am watching a television show. And that's fine, but it just strikes me as so un-*Degrassi*. So I am not the biggest fan. Then again, everything has to change with the times (including me), so maybe my criticism isn't completely fair.

After all I didn't think there was anything wrong with *90210* or *Saved by the Bell*. In fact, I loved those shows almost as much as I loved *Degrassi*. But they were different. Different in tone. Different in seriousness. Different in writing. Different in really everything. For those reasons, it's often hard to compare them with *Degrassi* and proclaim one better or worse. *Saved by the Bell* was a sitcom set in a high school and *90210* was a soap opera set in a high school. *Degrassi* sort of fell somewhere in the middle and yet occupied a completely different and unique category at the same time. So when I watched any of these shows (or watch them today), I went into each with different expectations and came out with different reactions. In the end, comparing them is really a problem of apples and oranges.

And that's what I think it all comes down to — *Degrassi* was one of a kind. To this day, there really hasn't been a television show that has had a remotely similar impact. Considering the amount of TV I watch, that's quite a statement. And despite the thousands of channels I could stop on these days, most of the time I prefer to pop in a *Degrassi* tape simply because I know it will be good. I know it will make me laugh. And think. And laugh some more. So that's the best I think I can come up with and the best way I think I can boil it all down. That's why I love *Degrassi*.

★

Not too long ago, I bought a *Degrassi Junior High* wristwatch from the show's resident superstar, Pat Mastroianni. The fact that the watch is a wonderful and authentic piece of *Degrassi* history makes it a valuable and treasured memento. The fact that I got it from Joey Jeremiah himself makes it just plain cool. But the watch also reminded me of something — *Degrassi* is timeless. Its lessons are as relevant today as they were almost twenty years ago. The show can educate and entertain today as much as it did then. Its quality in writing means that it still has the power to move people, as it moved me twenty years ago, and still moves me today.

It moves me so much that I can't wait for my kids to watch *Degrassi*, and learn from *Degrassi* and be inspired by *Degrassi*. I can't wait to give my children my collection of tapes. Then again who am I kidding, I will probably make them get a set of their own.

AFTERWORD

Linda Schuyler

I'M SITTING IN THE LA AIRPORT with my husband and partner Stephen Stohn, preparing to fly home to Toronto. *Degrassi: The Next Generation* has just won the Television Critics Award. Simultaneously, two of the cast of *Degrassi* are en route to Atlanta for a much anticipated mall appearance. The *Degrassi Generations* book, celebrating twenty-five years of *Degrassi,* is on a boat being shipped from Singapore. In Australia, France, Israel and almost forty other countries around the world young people are watching repeats of *Degrassi: TNG* Season Four. Meanwhile, back in Toronto, the cast and crew are hard at work on this hot and humid summer day, shooting scenes from *Degrassi: TNG* Season Five, and elsewhere in Toronto, Sumach Press is preparing its print run for this most excellent collection of essays complied by Michele Byers.

Not a bad reach for a little show that began production twenty-five years ago with a few dollars, tons of enthusiasm and a commitment to tell honest stories from a young person's perspective.

So how did this former junior-high teacher end up in the LA airport with a TCA award?

I'm honestly not sure!

I have not spent the last twenty-five years consecutively producing *Degrassi.* In fact, if anyone would have told me in 1991, when we wrapped on the movie-of-the-week *School's Out,* that I would return to *Degrassi* production ten years later in 2001, I never would have believed them. This is not because I was tired of storytelling for young people, or because the money dried up, it was simply because it felt, as the classic cast graduated, that the end of an era had been reached.

During the 1990s, I continued to work as an independent producer and as an active member of the professional community. And, on and off over that period, Yan Moore and I often I talked about developing a new series for teens. It was only when Yan said "If Spike's baby were real, she would now be the right age to attend Junior High" that we realized the time could be right for a *Degrassi* resurgence.

In 2001, the first episodes of *Degrassi: The Next Generation* went to air, this time on CTV. And, I have to admit, I was scared. I was afraid that fans of the classic show would dismiss the new slicker version of *Degrassi*, performed by professional actors with agents and dressing rooms, as a pale imitation of its former self.

And, I was nervous that the new generation of viewers, who are far more technologically and media savvy than their older counterparts, would find the direct and classic storytelling, told exclusively from the youth perspective, too tame. What a relief, a huge relief, when *Degrassi: The Next Generation* was embraced by audiences and critics alike.

There is much that is different between *Degrassi Classic* and *Degrassi: The Next Generation*. Many of these differences have been eloquently discussed in these excellent essays. However, there are a few basic fundamentals that cross over both series, allowing them to share a title.

• *Degrassi* is fearless in its storytelling. If young people are discussing an issue in the schoolyard, at the mall or on the Net, then it is a subject matter fit for *Degrassi*. This can mean issues of their sexuality, teen suicide, pregnancy, drug use, racism, cutting, oral sex and domestic violence. The list is endless.

• Tough teenage issues are balanced with lighter storytelling and liberal doses of humour. Adolescents are funny and have endless stories of bad hair days, embarrassing parents, lost homework and even malfunctioning penis pumps. *Degrassi* embraces these moments.

- Although many scripts are issue driven, they are also equally character driven. And, the main character for a story must come from the *Degrassi* ensemble cast. We do not fly a guest star in to be a pregnant teen for an episode then lose her the following week. When a *Degrassi* character faces an issue, she or he lives with the consequences.

- All *Degrassi* actors are cast age appropriately (within a year or two). Although this sounds like a small detail, its impact on the reality of the show is vitally important. It would be easy to cast twenty-four and twenty-five year olds to play teenagers, and they may well look the part, but they bring with them eight or nine years of life experience that our young cast does not possess.

- Our *Degrassi* screenwriters must not only be good writers (actually they are some of the best in the country) but also be good listeners and be very patient. Every *Degrassi* script is workshopped with the cast and writers before it is published. This allows our young actors an opportunity to have an honest and open dialogue with the writers about each script.

- At all times we aim to keep a youth-centric environment. As much as is possible, in an adult-dominated environment, we try to make cast members feel relaxed and free to offer their opinions.

- *Degrassi* is also unabashedly Canadian. It is liberal, multicultural and proud of its roots in east-end Toronto.

However important these principles might be, are they enough to allow a series to endure on and off for twenty-five years? I highly doubt it.

As with all successes, timing and good fortune play a hugely important role. *Degrassi Classic* came of age at a time when there was no material on television, north or south of the border, which used drama to directly speak to adolescents. Timing was right.

By the time *Degrassi: TNG* came along, the marketplace was very different. A multitude of programs existed for young viewers and, in fact, entire channels were dedicated to them. But, interestingly, nowhere in this vast landscape did there appear to be shows that spoke directly to young teens as *Degrassi* did. Once again, timing seemed to be right.

Degrassi has enjoyed much good fortune. We have worked with the best public broadcaster (CBC) and the finest private broadcaster (CTV) this country has to offer. We have had the good fortune to be the recipients of government funding at the federal level (Telefilm Canada, Canadian Television Fund, the Government of Canada); at the provincial level (Ontario Media Development Corporation, the Government of Ontario); from private sources (Shaw Rocket Fund, Dr. Geoffrey R. Conway Fund, Independent Production Fund, Mountain Cable Program, Ontario Arts Council, Cogeco Program Development Fund, Bell Broadcast and New Media Fund, Snap Media), and from a legion of private investors to whom we are most grateful. We have had the good fortune to be represented by Alliance Atlantis, Isme Bennie International, McNabb and Connolly, Magic Lantern and to collaborate with international partners such as The N, the United States Corporation for Public Broadcasting and WGBH Boston.

And for me, good fortune has also meant the opportunity to work with great people. Kit Hood and I shared a vision for the *Classic* series and this has been carried on by Stephen and myself. We've also had the pleasure to work with amazing writers, who have been many, including as top contributors Yan Moore, Susin Nielsen, Aaron Martin, James Hurst and Shelley Scarrow.

Many great Canadian talents have worked in front and behind the scenes at *Degrassi*. But my single best fortune is to have had twenty-five years to work with a large group of talented, open, honest, funny, endearing Canadian teenagers who have allowed two generations of international audiences the privilege of watching them grow up on television.

And, after all the success, and opportunities to work with great people, there is one intangible that I have received from *Degrassi* that defies words. I can only describe it as a tremendous calm that comes over me when I read letters and testimonials from our young audience who talk about the way that *Degrassi* has affected their lives, and in some cases influenced life decisions. No awards, reviews or financial benefits can match the feelings of these moments. Because, at the end of the day, a former teacher still needs her classroom, and I will be forever grateful for the opportunity I have had to reach my expanded class.

Thank you Michele for this wonderful collective work and for asking me to write the afterword. I'm flattered and overwhelmed by the words of you and your colleagues, and I also appreciate having had my hand gently slapped a couple of times!

I trust that as your readers digest these essays and thoughts on *Degrassi* that they might well be able to shed a better light on this little Canadian success story than I have been able to do. So, for the time being, I will settle down for my flight, enjoy the *Degrassi* successes and only hope that I have another twenty-five years of such rewarding work. Perhaps by then, I'll have figured out how to get it more right!

Linda Schuyler
AIR CANADA LOUNGE
LOS ANGELES INTERNATIONAL AIRPORT
July 24, 2005

Cast List

Degrassi Classic and *Degrassi: The Next Generation*

This list was compiled with help from www.degrassi.ca; the character's name is followed by the actor's name.

Degrassi Classic

Michelle Accethe (Maureen McKay)
Melanie Brodie (Sara Ballingall)
Tessa Campinelli (Kristen Bourne)
Luke Cassellis (Andy Chambers)
Cindy (Marsha Ferguson)
Bronco Davis (L. Dean Ifill)
Lorraine "L.D." Delacorte (Amanda Cook)
Simon Dexter (Michael Carry)
Diana Economopoulos (Chrissa Erodotou)
Erica Farell (Angela Deiseach)
Heather Farrell (Maureen Deiseach)
Lucy Fernandez (Anais Granofsky)
Maya Goldberg (Kyra Levy)
Voula Grivogiannis (Niki Kemeny)
Amy Holmes (Jacy Hunter)
Allison Hunter (Sara Holmes)
Stephanie Kaye (Nicole Stoffman)
Authur Kobalowsky (Duncan Waugh)
Joey Jeremiah (Pat Mastroianni)
Nancy Kramer (Arlene Lott)
Shane McKay (Bill Parrott)
Kathleen Mead (Rebecca Haines)
Rick Munro (Craig Driscoll)
Dwayne Myers (Darrin Brown)
Christine "Spike" Nelson (Amanda Stepto)
Alexa Pappadopoulos (Irene Courakos)
Patrick (Vincent Walsh)
Tim O'Connor (Keith White)

Liz O'Rourke (Cathy Keenan)
Trudi Owens (Tammy Campbell)
Mr. Daniel Raditch (Dan Woods)
Susie Rivera (Sarah Charlesworth)
Joanne Rutherford (Krista Houston)
Caitlin Ryan (Stacie Mistysyn)
Archie "Snake" Simpson (Stefan Brogren)
Claude Tanner (David Armin-Parcells)
Bryant "BLT" Thomas (Dayo Ade)
Derek "Wheels" Wheeler (Neil Hope)
Alex Yankou (John Ioannou)
Yick Yu (Siluck Saysanasay)

Degrassi: The Next Generation

Liberty Van Zandt (Sarah Barrable-Tishauer)
Dylan Michalchuk (John Bregar)
Archie "Snake" Simpson (Stefan Brogren)
Alex (Deanna Casaluce)
Sean Cameron (Daniel Clark)
Paige Michalchuk (Lauren Collins)
J.T. Yorke (Ryan Cooley)
Rick (Ephraim Ellis)

Craig Manning (Jake Epstein)
Ellie Nash (Stacey Farber)
Toby Isaacs (Jake Goldsbie)
Jimmy Brooks (Aubre Graham)
Gavin "Spinner" Mason (Shane Kippel)
Kendra Mason (Katie Lai)
Hazel Aden (Andrea Lewis)
Jay (Mik Lobel)
Joey Jeremiah (Pat Mastroianni)
Ashley Kerwin (Melissa McIntyre)
Cailtin Ryan (Stacie Mistysyn)
Chris (Daniel Morrison)
Marco Del Rossi (Adamo Ruggiero)

Terri MacGregor (Christina Schmidt)
Manuella "Manny" Santos (Cassie Steele)
Angela Jeremiah (Alex Steele)
Christine "Spike" Nelson (Amanda Stepto)

Principal Raditch (Dan Woods)

Partial Episode Guide*

DEGRASSI JUNIOR HIGH

Note: All episodes originally aired on CBC.

AIR DATE	TITLE	WRITER	DIRECTOR
SEASON 1			
01/18/1987	Kiss Me Steph	Yan Moore	Kit Hood
01/25/1987	The Big Dance	Avrum Jacobson	Kit Hood
02/08/1987	The Cover Up	John Oughton, Yan Moore	Kit Hood
02/22/1987	Rumour Has It	Yan Moore	Kit Hood
03/01/1987	The Best Laid Plans	Yan Moore	Kit Hood
03/15/1987	What a Night	Yan Moore	Kit Hood
03/22/1987	Smokescreen	Kathryn Ellis	John Bertram
03/29/1987	It's Late	Yan Moore	Kit Hood
04/12/1987	Revolution	Yan Moore	Kit Hood
SEASON 2			
01/04/1988	Eggbert	Yan Moore	Kit Hood
01/18/1988	Great Expectations	Yan Moore	Kit Hood
03/07/1988	Censored	Kathryn Ellis	Mike Douglas
03/28/1988	Pass Tense	Yan Moore	Kit Hood
SEASON 3			
11/07/1988	Can't Live With'Em (1)	Yan Moore	Kit Hood
11/15/1988	Can't Live With 'Em (2)	Yan Moore	Kit Hood
12/13/1988	He Ain't Heavy	Yan Moore	Kit Hood
12/20/1988	The Whole Truth	Susin Nielsen	Eleanor Lindo
01/03/1989	Food for Thought	Susin Nielsen	Eleanor Lindo
01/17/1989	Taking Off (1)	Yan Moore	Kit Hood
01/24/1989	Taking Off (2)	Yan Moore	Kit Hood
02/14/1989	Pa-arty!	Yan Moore	Kit Hood
02/21/1989	Bye Bye Junior High	Yan Moore	Kit Hood

Degrassi High

Note: All episodes originally aired on CBC.

Air Date	Title	Writer	Director
Season 1			
11/06/1989	A New Start (1)	Yan Moore	Kit Hood
11/13/1989	A New Start (2)	Yan Moore	Kit Hood
11/20/1989	Breaking up is Hard to Do	Susin Nielsen	Kit Hood
11/27/1989	Dream On	Yan Moore	John Bertram
12/04/1989	Everybody Wants Something	Yan Moore	Kit Hood
12/18/1989	Just Friends	Kathryn Ellis	Kit Hood
01/02/1990	Sixteen (1)	Yan Moore	Kit Hood
01/09/1990	Sixteen (2)	Yan Moore	Kit Hood
01/16/1990	All in a Good Cause	Susin Nielsen	Eleanor Lindo
01/23/1990	Natural Attraction	Yan Moore	Kit Hood
02/06/1990	It Creeps	Yan Moore	Kit Hood
Season 2			
11/05/1990	Bad Blood (1)	Yan Moore	Kit Hood
11/12/1990	Bad Blood (2)	Yan Moore	Kit Hood
11/26/1990	A Tangled Web	Yan Moore	Kit Hood
12/03/1990	Body Politics	Susin Nielsen	Philip Earnshaw
12/17/1990	The All-Nighter	Kathryn Ellis	Eleanor Lindo
12/24/1990	Home Sweet Home	Susin Nielsen	Kit Hood
01/07/1991	Showtime (1)	Yan Moore	Kit Hood
01/14/1991	Showtime (2)	Yan Moore	Kit Hood
01/28/1991	One Last Dance	Yan Moore	Kit Hood

01/22/1992 *School's Out*
A film by Linda Schuyler and Kit Hood; screenplay by Yan Moore

DEGRASSI: THE NEXT GENERATION

Note: All episodes originally aired on CTV.

AIR DATE	TITLE	STORY BY	DIRECTOR
SEASON 1			
10/14/2001	Mother and Child Reunion	Y. Moore, A. Martin	Bruce MacDonald
11/11/2001	Eye of the Beholder	Y. Moore, T. Cameron	Eleanor Lindo
11/18/2001	Parents' Day	Y. Moore, A. Martin	Eleanor Lindo
11/25/2001	The Mating Game	Y. Moore, T. Cameron	Anthony Browne
12/02/2001	Basketball Diaries	Y. Moore, A. Martin	Jim Allodi
12/16/2001	Coming of Age	Susin Nielson	Bruce MacDonald
01/06/2002	Rumours and Reputations	A. Martin, Y. Moore	Paul Fox
02/17/2002	Cabaret	A. Martin, J. Hurst	Laurie Lynd
03/03/2002	Jagged Little Pill	A. Martin, J. Hurst	Bruce MacDonald
SEASON 2			
10/13/2002	Karma Chameleon	A. Martin, S. Scarrow	Stefan Scaini
10/20/2002	Weird Science	J. Hurst, S. Scarrow	Bruce MacDonald
11/03/2002	Shout (1)	A. Martin, C. Cornell	Phil Earnshaw
11/10/2002	Shout (2)	A. Martin, C. Cornell	Phil Earnshaw
11/17/2002	Mirror in the Bathroom	J. Hurst, C. Ross Dunn	Paul Fox
12/01/2002	Take My Breath Away	A. Martin, Yan Moore	Stefan Scaini
01/03/2003	Hot for Teacher	J. Singer, C. Ross Dunn	Phil Earnshaw
01/05/2003	White Wedding	A. Moore, T. Cameron	Bruce MacDonald
01/08/2003	Careless Whisper	A. Martin. C. Cornell	Laurie Lynd
01/12/2003	Message in a Bottle	James Hurst	Bruce MacDonald
01/15/2003	Dressed in Black	A. Martin, S. Jara	Gavin Smith
02/02/2003	Fight for Your Right	A. Martin, S. Jara	Chris Deacon
02/09/2003	How Soon is Now	J. Hurst, C, Cornell	Eleanor Lindo
SEASON 3			
10/01/2003	U Got the Look	J. Sinyor, B. Yorke	Stefan Scaini
12/10/2003	This Charming Man	A. Martin, N. Demerse	Stefan Scaini
01/26/2004	Accidents Will Happen (1)	N. Demerse, J. Hurst	Eleanor Lindo
02/09/2004	Accidents Will Happen (2)	N. Demerse, J. Hurst	Eleanor Lindo
03/15/2004	It's Raining Men	A. Martin, J. Hurst	Andrew Potter

* For a complete episode guide, see Kathryn Ellis, *Degrassi: Generations* with an introduction by Kevin Smith (Toronto: Fenn Publishing/Madison Press, 2005)

Degrassi on the WWW

www.degrassi.tv

The official Web site of *Degrassi: The Next Generation*. Find schedules and related events, and register to be part of the online Degrassi Community School.

www.epitomepictures.com

The official site of *Degrassi*'s production company.

www.degrassi.ca

The oldest unofficial site for all things *Degrassi*. This site is extensive and is a good place to go to find information. For one thing, it has a huge archive of press clippings about all the series.

www.patmeup.com

The official site of Pat Mastroianni.

http://en/wikipedia.org/wiki/Degrassi:_The_Next_Generation

The free encyclopedia reference for *Degrassi*.

http://www.museum.tv/archives/etc/D/htmlD/degrassi/degrassi.htm

The Museum of Broadcast Communications entry for *Degrassi*.

http://clubs.myams.org/degrassi/news.html

The Queen's University *Degrassi* Club site. The club is no longer operating, but the site is still up!

http://www.jumptheshark.com/d/degrassijuniorhigh.htm

Jumptheshark.com: "It's a moment. A defining moment when you know that your favorite television program has reached its peak. That instant that you know from now on … It's all downhill. Some call it the climax. We call it *jumping the shark*." Find out if (and when) *Degrassi* fans think the show jumped.

http://degrassi.meetup.com

Find a *Degrassi* meet-up group in your area: there are currently 124 groups worldwide!

http://www.tvtome.com

The ultimate site for all things TV. Check out the pages for each of the *Degrassi* series.

http://ecards.sympatico.ca/Degrassi

Send a friend a *Degrassi* card!

www.chuma.org/degrassi

Play the *Degrassi* drinking game!

www.degrassi-boards.com

Chat with others about *Degrassi*.

You can link up to *Degrassi* through the Web sites of its networks — CTV.ca, the-n.com, abc.net.au; and you can order *Degrassi* products from amazon.com. There are also dozens of other *Degrassi* fan and fan fiction sites on the WWW not listed here. Go wild!

Contributors

SEAN BILICHKA is a student at Western Carolina University, majoring in English literature and creative writing. He writes poetry and fiction, and is currently at work on his first novel.

MICHELE BYERS is Associate Professor at Saint Mary's University in Halifax. She wrote her doctoral dissertation on *Buffy the Vampire Slayer* (University of Toronto, 2000) and has published articles in *Signs, Higher Education Perspectives, Studies in Popular Culture and Culture, Theory and Critique,* as well as many chapters in published anthologies. She has written about such TV series as *Buffy, Beverly Hills 90210, Roseanne, ER, Party of Five, My So-Called Life, Sex and the City, The O.C., Curb Your Enthusiasm, Arrested Development, Ready or Not, renegadepress. com, Drop the Beat* and *Moccasin Flats.* She is co-editor of (with David Lavery) "'Dear Angela': Remembering My So-Called Life" and (with Val Johnson) "The 'CSI Effect': Television, Crime and Critical Theory." She is currently finishing a work long in progress on images of the "other" on *Buffy the Vampire Slayer.*

REBECCA J. HAINES is currently a PhD (ABD) candidate at the Department of Public Health Sciences, Faculty of Medicine, University of Toronto. For the past five years she has worked in child and adolescent mental health research at the Hospital for Sick Children. Her current research interests include racial identity and youth/popular cultures, the social construction of substance use problems and young women's health and tobacco use.

KYLO-PATRICK R. HART is chair of the Department of Communication Studies at Plymouth State University, New Hampshire, where he teaches courses in film studies, television studies and popular culture. He is author of the book *The AIDS Movie: Representing a Pandemic in Film and Television,* as well as numerous research essays that have appeared in academic journals (including *Journal of Film and Video, The Journal of Men's Studies* and *Popular Culture Review)* and media anthologies (including *Television: Critical Concepts in Media and Cultural Studies* and *Gender, Race, and Class in Media: A Text-Reader).*

MARK JANSON has studied history at Queen's and Dalhousie Universities. He currently resides in Brockville, Ontario.

BRIAN C. JONES is an American originally from the suburbs of Rhode Island who attended college in Virginia and then relocated to Washington, DC. He has worked on Capitol Hill for members of both the House of Representatives and the Senate, and served as writer and researcher in President George W. Bush's speechwriting office at the White House. He currently is a lawyer living in Washington, DC, who stills loves watching his *Degrassi* videos whenever he can.

SHERRI JEAN KATZ is a student in the media ecology program at New York University. She has her BA in public relations and political science from the Newhouse School of Public Communication at Syracuse University. She has worked on marketing and advertising for Broadway and Off Broadway shows and North American touring shows, including *Joe's Café, Forever Tango, Tap Dogs* and *The Sound of Music.* She managed advertising and marketing for the North American tour of *Fame: The Musical,* which premiered in Toronto and ran for three years.

JENNIFER MACLENNAN is currently Professor and D.K. Seaman Chair in Technical and Professional Communication in the College of Engineering at the University of Saskatchewan. Her primary research interest is the rhetoric of cultural identity formation, and in particular expressions of Canadian identity (as demonstrated in her chapter for this volume), but she has also written extensively about rhetorical theory, professional-organizational communication, interpersonal communication, public speaking and teaching as rhetorical praxis. The author of five texts on communication, she holds a PhD in rhetoric from the University of Washington, as well as degrees in English language and literature from McMaster and St. Francis Xavier Universities. For the past dozen years she has been very active in curricular and programme development, and — though the U of S has no formal graduate program in rhetoric — she is currently supervising six graduate students through the university's Interdisciplinary Graduate Studies Option.

MARY JANE MILLER became Professor of Dramatic Arts Emerita at Brock University in 2004. She has written *Turn up the Contrast: CBC Television Drama since 1952* (University of British Columbia Press and CBC, 1987) and *Rewind and Search: Conversations with Makers and Decision Makers of CBC Television Drama* (McGill-Queen's University Press, 1996) as well as publishing articles on Canadian television drama and earlier Canadian dramatic literature. She is completing a book *Outside Looking In* for McGill-Queen's University Press about the representation of First Nations people in series television.

RYAN ROBERT MITCHELL started junior high the same year that *Degrassi Junior High* premiered. He is a graduate student in sociology at Queen's University. His interests vary from Japanese pro-wrestling and ultimate fighting leagues to obscure French social and aesthetic theory.

Ravindra N. Mohabeer is a PhD candidate in the Joint Graduate Programme in Communication and Culture at York University. His research focuses on media studies and media education with special attention to girls and media, children's culture and youth culture, consumer society, and ecological theories of communication. He is particularly interested in the relationship between media, identity and power, and the cultural production of media by youth about youth.

Tom Panarese has been a *Degrassi* fan since his junior high days in Sayville, New York. He has been featured as an online writer in *Snowball, Headlight Journal, One Magazine, Success e-zine* and *Bad Movie Night.* He is the author of the audio book *Surviving Unemployment* and the novel *Sayville.* He lives with his fiancée, Amanda, in Arlington, Virginia.

Mark Aaron Polger hails from Montreal, Quebec, where he completed his BA in sociology at Concordia University. He grew up watching the *Degrassi* television series and has always appreciated its honesty and realism. He completed his MA in sociology at the University of Waterloo and his master's in library information science at the University of Western Ontario. He lives in Toronto and works as a psychology and sociology librarian at the University of Waterloo, and is a part-time instructor in the Faculty of Continuing Education at Seneca College. He still updates his *Degrassi* Web site after all these years. Visit him at www.degrassi. ca.

Bettina Spencer is a doctoral student of social psychology at the Graduate Faculty of Political and Social Science of the New School University in New York City. She received her master's degree in psychology, and her previous work includes research on the role of the media in implicit gender stereotyping. She is currently working on a study of how social class shapes the educational system.

Michael Strangelove is a pioneer in Internet-facilitated marketing, Internet consumer behaviour and electronic publishing. He is lecturer in the Department of Communication at the University of Ottawa and has recently published *The Empire of Mind: Digital Piracy and the Anti-Capitalist Movement* (University of Toronto Press, 2005).

Laura Tropp is an Assistant Professor at Marymount Manhattan College. She teaches classes on communication and the future; media history; youth, culture and the media; and political communication. Her research interests include studies on digital television, representations of motherhood in the media, and voter mobilization efforts using the media. She is on the board of the New York State Communication Association and the Media Ecology Association, and has presented papers at several communication conferences.

Selected Bibliography

Anderson, Benedict. *Imagined Communities*. London: Verso, 1991.

Ang, Ien. *Desperately Seeking the Audience*. New York: Routledge, 1992.

Aristotle. *The Rhetoric and Poetics*. Trans. W. Rhys Roberts. Ed. Friedrich Solmsen. New York: The Modern Library, 1954.

Bannerji, Himani. *The Dark Side of Nation: Essays on Multiculturalism, Nationalism and Gender*. Toronto: Canadian Scholar's Press, 1994.

Baumgardner, Jennifer, and Amy Richards. *Manifesta: Young Women, Feminism, and the Future*. New York: Farrar, Strauss and Giroux, 2000.

Bell, David V.J. "The Sociocultural Milieu of Canadian Politics: Political Culture in Canada." In Michael S. Whittington and Glen Williams, eds., *Canadian Politics in the Eighties*. Toronto: ITP Nelson, 1993.

Bernstein, Jonathan. *Pretty in Pink: The Golden Age of Teenage Movie*. New York: St Martin's Griffin, 1997.

Berton, Pierre. *Hollywood's Canada: The Americanization of Our National Image*. Toronto: McClelland and Stewart, 1975.

—. *Why We Act Like Canadians*. 2d ed. Toronto: McClelland and Stewart, 1987.

Bodroughkozy, Aniko. *Groove Tube: Sixties Television and the Youth Rebellion*. Durham, NC: Duke University Press, 2001.

—. "As Canadian as Possible ...: Anglo-Canadian Popular Culture and the American Other." In Henry Jenkins, Tara McPherson, and Jane Shattuc, eds., *Hop on Pop: The Politics and Pleasures of Popular Culture* (Durham, NC: Duke University Press, 2003).

Boorstin, Daniel. *The Image: A Guide to Pseudo-Events in America*. New York: Vintage Books, 1992.

Brooker, Will. "Living on *Dawson's Creek*: Teen Viewers, Cultural Convergence and Television Overflow." *International Journal of Cultural Studies* 4 (2001): 456-472.

Byers, Michele. "Race In/Out of the Classroom: *Degrassi (Junior High)* as Multicultural Context." In Charmaine Nelson and Camille Nelson, eds., *Racism Eh? A Critical Inter-Disciplinary Anthology of Race in the Canadian Context*. Concord, ON: Captus Press, 2004.

Cadwell, Steve. "Twice Removed: The Stigma Suffered by Gay Men with AIDS." *Smith College Studies in Social* Work 61, no. 3 (1991): 236–246.

Capsuto, Steven. *Alternate Channels: The Uncensored Story of Gay and Lesbian Images on Radio and Television.* New York: Ballantine Books, 2000.

Coombe, Rosemary J., and Andrew Herman. "Culture Wars on the Net: Trademarks, Consumer Politics, and Corporate Accountability on the World Wide Web." *The South Atlantic Quarterly* 100, no. 4 (Winter 2001): 919-947.

—. *The Cultural Life of Intellectual Properties: Authorship, Appropriation and the Law.* Durham, NC: Duke University Press, 1998.

Corbin, Carol, and Judith A. Rolls. *The Centre of the World at the Edge of a Continent.* Sydney, Australia: UCCB Press, 1996.

Corner, John. "Performing the Real." *Television & New Media* 3, no. 2 (August 2002): 255–269.

Crimp, Douglas, ed. *AIDS: Cultural Analysis, Cultural Activism.* Cambridge, MA: The MIT Press, 1988.

Croteau, James, and Susanne Morgan. "Combating Homophobia in AIDS Education."*Journal of Counseling & Development* 68, no. 5 (1989): 86–91.

Davis, Glyn, and Kay Dickinson. *Teen TV: Genre, Consumption and Identity.* London: The British Film Institute, 2004.

Deming, Robert H. "*Kate & Allie*: 'New Women' and the Audience's Television Archives." In Lynn Spigel and Denise Mann, eds., *Private Screenings: Television and the Female Consumer.* Minneapolis: University of Minnesota Press, 1992.

Eisenstein, Elizabeth L. *The Printing Press as an Agent of Change: Communications and Cultural Transformations in Early Modern Europe,* Volumes I and II. Cambridge, UK: Cambridge University Press, 1979.

Elwood, William N., ed., *Power in the Blood: A Handbook on AIDS, Politics, and Communication.* Mahwah, NJ: Lawrence Erlbaum Associates, 1999.

Fairclough, Norman. *Language and Power.* New York: Longman, 1989.

Feig, Paul. *Kick Me: Adventures in Adolescence.* Three Rivers Press: New York, 2003.

Fiske, John. *Understanding Popular Culture.* London: Methuen, 1989.

Fuchs, Cynthia. "Too Much of Something is Bad Enough: Success and Excess in *SpiceWorld*." In Frances Gateward and Murray Pomerance, eds., *Sugar, Spice, and Everything Nice: Cinemas of Girlhood.* Detroit, MI: Wayne State University Press, 2002.

Galbraith, John Kenneth. *The New Industrial State.* Boston: Houghton Mifflin, 1967.

___. *Economics and the Public Purpose.* Scarborough, ON: The New American Library of Canada, 1975.

Gray, Herman. *Watching Race*. Minneapolis: University of Minnesota Press, 1995.

Griffin, Gabriele. *Representations of HIV and AIDS: Visibility Blue/s*. New York: Manchester University Press, 2000.

Goffman, Erving. *The Presentation of Self in Everyday Life*. New York: Doubleday,1959.

Gross, Larry. "What is Wrong With This Picture? Lesbian Women and Gay Men on Television." In R. Jeffrey Ringer, ed., *Queer Words, Queer Images: Communication and the Construction of Homosexuality*. New York: New York University Press, 1994.

Ha, Louisa. "Enhanced Television Strategy Models: A Study of TV Web Sites." *InternetResearch* 12, no. 3 (2002): 235–247.

Haines, Rebecca J. "'Break North': Rap Music and Hip-Hop Culture in Canada." In H. Troper and M. Weinfeld, eds., *Ethnicity and Public Policy in Canada*. Toronto: University of Toronto Press, 1999.

Hart, Kylo-Patrick R. "Retrograde Representation." *The Journal of Men's Studies* 7, no. 2 (1999): 201–213.

—. *The AIDS Movie: Representing a Pandemic in Film and Television*. New York: The Haworth Press, 2000.

Hebdige, Dick. *Subculture: The Meaning of Style*. London: Routledge, 1979.

Herek, Gregory. "The Social Context of Hate Crimes: Notes on Cultural Heterosexism." In Gregory Herek and Kevin Berrill, eds., *Hate Crimes: Confronting Violence Against Lesbians and Gay Men*. Newbury Park, CA: Sage Publications, 1992.

Hewitt, Roger. *White Talk-Black Talk: Inter-racial Friendship and Communication Amongst Adolescents*. Cambridge, UK: Cambridge University Press, 1986.

Higson, Andrew. "The Limiting Imagination of National Cinema." In Mette Hjort and Scott Mackenzie, eds., *Cinema & Nation*. New York: Routledge, 2000.

Hill, Matt. *Fan Cultures*. London: Routledge, 2002.

Innis, Harold. *The Bias of Communication*. Toronto: University of Toronto Press, 1995.

Jenkins, Henry. "Empowering Children in the Digital Age: Towards a Radical Media Pedagogy." *Radical Teacher* 50 (1997): 30–35.

—. "Interactive Audiences?" In Dan Harries, ed., *The New Media Book*. London: The British Film Institute, 2002.

Jones, Simon. *Black Culture, White Youth*. London: Macmillan Press, 1988.

Kaveney, Roz, ed. *Reading The Vampire Slayer*. New York: Tauris Parke Paperbacks, 2002.

Knelman, Martin. *Home Movies: Tales from the Canadian Film World*. Toronto: Key Porter Books, 1987.

Leonard, Marion. "'Rebel Girl, You Are the Queen of My World' Feminism, Subculture' and Grrrl Power." In Sheila Whiteley, ed., *Sexing the Groove: Popular Music and Gender*. New York: Routledge, 1997.

MacLennan, Jennifer, and John Moffatt. "An Island View of the World: Canadian Community as Insularity in the Popular Writing of Stompin' Tom Connors." In Conny Steenman-Mar, ed., *The Rhetoric of Canadian Writing*. Amsterdam: Rodopi Press, 2002.

___. "Reclaiming 'Authenticity': *Cape Breton's Magazine* and the Commodification of Insularity." In Sherry Devereaux Ferguson and Leslie Regan Shade, eds., *Civic Discourse and Cultural Politics in Canada: A Cacophony of Voices*. Westport, CT: Greenwood Press, 2002.

McChesney, Robert W. *Rich Media, Poor Democracy: Communication Politics in Dubious Times*. New York: The New Press, 2000.

McLuhan, Marshall. *Understanding Media: The Extensions of Man*. Cambridge, MA: The MIT Press, 1995.

McKinley, E. Graham. *Beverly Hills, 90210: Television, Gender, and Identity*. Philadelphia: University of Pennsylvania Press, 1997.

McQuillen, Jeffrey S. "The Influence of Technology on the Initiation of Interpersonal Relationships." *Education* 123, no. 3 (2003): 616–623.

Meyrowitz, Joshua. *No Sense of Place: The Impact of Electronic Media on Social Behavior*. New York: Oxford University Press, 1986.

Moseley, Rachel. "The Teen Series." In Glen Creeber, ed., *The Television Genre Book*. London: The British Film Institute, 2001.

Murray, Susan. "Saving Our So-Called Lives: Girl Fandom, Adolescent Subjectivity and My So-Called Life." In Marsha Kinder, ed., *Kids' Media Culture*. Durham, NC: Duke University Press, 1999.

Netzhammer, Emile, and Scott Shamp. "Guilt by Association: Homosexuality and AIDS on Prime-Time Television." In R. Jeffrey Ringer, ed., *Queer Words, Queer Images: Communication and the Construction of Homosexuality*. New York: New York University Press, 1994.

Nicks, Joan. "*Straight Up* and Youth Television: Navigating Dreams without Nationhood." In Joan Nicks and Jeanette Sloniowski, eds., *Slippery Pastimes: Reading the Popular in Canadian Culture*. Waterloo, ON: Wilfrid Laurier University Press, 2002.

Ong, Walter. *Orality & Literacy: The Technologizing of the Word*. New York: Routledge, 1982.

Perelman, Chaim H., and L. Olbrechts-Tyteca. *The New Rhetoric: A Treatise on Argumentation*. Trans. John Wilkinson and Purcell Weaver. Notre Dame: University of Notre Dame Press, 1971.

Perloff, Richard. *Persuading People to Have Safer Sex: Applications of Social Science to the AIDS Crisis*. Mahwah, NJ: Lawrence Erlbaum Associates, 2001.

Postman, Neil. *Amusing Ourselves to Death*. New York: Penguin Books, 1986.

____. *Technopoly: The Surrender of Culture to Technology*. New York: Vintage Books, 1993.

Rosenberg, Jessica, and Gitana Garofalo. "Riot Grrrl: Revolutions from Within." *Signs: Journal of Women in Culture and Society* 23, no. 3 (1998): 809–841.

Sawicki, Jana. *Disciplining Foucault: Feminism, Power, and the Body*. New York: Routledge, 1991.

Schiller, Herbert I. *Culture Inc: The Culture Takeover of Public Expression*. Oxford: Oxford University Press, 1989.

Simonetti, Marie-Claire. "Teenage Truths and Tribulations Across Cultures: *Degrassi Junior High* and *Beverly Hills 90210*." *Journal of Popular Film and Television* (Spring 1994): 38-42.

Slade, Christina. *The Real Thing: Doing Philosophy with Media*. New York: Peter Lang, 2002.

Strangelove, Michael. *The Empire of Mind: Digital Piracy and the Anti-Capitalist Movement*. Toronto: University of Toronto Press, 2005.

Wagman, Ira. "Wheat, Barley, Hops, Citizenship: Molson's "I Am [Canadian]" Campaign and the Defense of Canadian National Identity Through Advertising." *The Velvet Light Trap* (Fall 2002): 77–89.

Waiters, Elizabeth D. "*90210* in Black & White and Color: Inter-Ethnic friendship on Prime Time Television." In Murray Pomerance and John Sakeris, eds., *Pictures of a Generation on Hold: Selected Papers*. Toronto: Media Studies Working Group, 1996.

Wasko, Janet. *Understanding Disney: The Manufacture of Fantasy*. Cambridge, UK: Polity Press, 2001.

Weissman, Rachel X. "The Kids are All Right—They're Just a Little Converged." *American Demographics* 20, no. 12 (1998): 30–32.

Wilcox, Rhonda V., and David Lavery, eds. *Fighting the Forces: What's at Stake in Buffy The Vampire Slayer*. New York: Rowman and Littlefield, 2002.

OTHER TITLES FROM THE WOMEN'S ISSUES PUBLISHING PROGRAM

Feminism, Law, Inclusion: Intersectionality in Action
Edited by Gayle MacDonald, Rachel L. Osborne and Charles C. Smith

Troubling Women's Studies: Pasts, Presents and Possibilities
Ann Braithwaite, Susan Heald, Susanne Luhmann and Sharon Rosenberg

Doing IT: Women Working in Information Technology
Krista Scott-Dixon

Inside Corporate U: Women in the Academy Speak Out
Edited by Marilee Reimer

Out of the Ivory Tower: Feminist Research for Social Change
Edited by Andrea Martinez and Meryn Stuart

Strong Women Stories: Native Vision and Community Survival
Edited by Kim Anderson and Bonita Lawrence

Back to the Drawing Board: African-Canadian Feminisms
Edited by Njoki Nathane Wane, Katerina Deliovsky and Erica Lawson

Cashing In On Pay Equity? Supermarket Restructuring and Gender Equality
Jan Kainer

Double Jeopardy: Motherwork and the Law
Lorna A. Turnbull

Turbo Chicks: Talking Young Feminisms
Edited by Allyson Mitchell, Lisa Bryn Rundle and Lara Karaian
WINNER OF THE 2002 INDEPENDENT PUBLISHERS AWARD

Women in the Office: Transitions in a Global Economy
Ann Eyerman

Women's Bodies/Women's Lives: Women, Health and Well-Being
Edited by Baukje Miedema, Janet Stoppard and Vivienne Anderson

A Recognition of Being: Reconstructing Native Womanhood
Kim Anderson

Women's Changing Landscapes: Life Stories from Three Generations
Edited by Greta Hofmann Nemiroff

Women Working the NAFTA Food Chain: Women, Food and Globalization
Edited by Deborah Barndt, WINNER OF THE 2000 INDEPENDENT PUBLISHERS AWARD

Cracking the Gender Code: Who Rules the Wired World?
Melanie Stewart Millar, WINNER OF THE 1999 INDEPENDENT PUBLISHERS AWARD

Redefining Motherhood: Changing Identities and Patterns
Edited by Sharon Abbey and Andrea O'Reilly

Fault Lines: Incest, Sexuality and Catholic Family Culture
Tish Langlois